Dialectics for the New Century

Dialectics for the New Century

Edited by

Bertell Ollman and Tony Smith

First published 2008 by
PALGRAVE MACMILLAN
Houndmills, Basingstoke, Hampshire RG21 6XS and
175 Fifth Avenue, New York, N.Y. 10010
Companies and representatives throughout the world

PALGRAVE MACMILLAN is the global academic imprint of the Palgrave Macmillan division of St. Martin's Press, LLC and of Palgrave Macmillan Ltd. Macmillan® is a registered trademark in the United States, United Kingdom and other countries. Palgrave is a registered trademark in the European Union and other countries.

ISBN-13: 978–0–230–53531–2 hardback

A catalogue record for this book is available from the British Library.

Library of Congress Cataloging-in-Publication Data
Dialectics for the new century / edited by Bertell Ollman
    and Tony Smith.
      p. cm.
    Includes bibliographical references and index.
    ISBN 0–230–53531–3 (hardback : alk. paper)
    1. Dialectic. 2. Dialectical materialism.   3. Philosophy,
    Marxist. I. Ollman, Bertell. II. Smith, Tony, 1951–
    B809.8.D483 2007
    146'.32—dc22   2007051219

10   9   8   7   6   5   4   3   2   1
17   16   15   14   13   12   11   10   09   08

Transferred to Digital Printing in 2010.

Contents

List of Contributors

Christopher J. Arthur, Department of Philosophy (Emeritus), University of Sussex, England

John Bellamy Foster, Department of Sociology, University of Oregon, US

Ira Gollobin, lawyer and independent scholar, US

Nancy Hartsock, Department of Political Science, University of Washington, US

David Harvey, Department of Anthropology, City University of New York, US

Fredric Jameson, The Literature Program, Duke University, US

Joel Kovel, Division of Social Studies, Bard College, US

Richard Levins, School of Public Health, Harvard University, US

Bill Livant, Department of Psychology, University of Regina, Canada

Michael Löwy, National Center for Scientific Research, Paris, France

István Mészáros, Department of Philosophy (Emeritus), University of Sussex, England

Savas Michael-Matsas, University of Athens, Greece

Bertell Ollman, Department of Politics, New York University, US

Thomas T. Sekine, School of Commerce, Aichi-Gakuin University, Japan

Lucien Sève, independent scholar, France

Tony Smith, Department of Philosophy and Religious Studies, Iowa State University, US

1
Introduction

Bertell Ollman and Tony Smith

> If one were to attempt to define in a single word the focus, so to speak, of the whole [Marx/Engels] correspondence, the central point at which the whole body of ideas expressed and discussed converges – that word would be *dialectics*. The application of materialist dialectics to the reshaping of all political economy from its foundations up, its application to history, natural science, philosophy and to the policy and tactics of the working class – that was what interested Marx and Engels most of all, that was where they contributed what was most essential and new, and that was what constituted the masterly advance they made in the history of revolutionary thought.
>
> (Lenin, 1973, 554)

With such excellent press – for similar comments can be found in the works of Trotsky, Lukács, Gramsci, Luxemburg, Mao, and Sartre – one might have thought that, at least among Marxists, dialectics would be well understood by now and dialectical studies the norm rather than the exception. As we all know, this is not the case.

In an 1858 letter to Engels, Marx said that if time permits he would like to write something to clarify his rational reconstruction of Hegel's dialectical method (Marx and Engels, 102). With the urgent demands of his life as a revolutionary and his work on political economy spreading far beyond its initial confines, Marx never found the time to return to dialectics. It was left for his followers to construct this dialectic from his widely dispersed remarks on this subject and from the use to which he put dialectics in his theories. Without Marx's guidance, however, the chief result has been a century and more of bitter disputes that has left some Marxist scholars – Althusserians a generation ago, those who call themselves 'Analytical Marxists' more recently – urging that we abandon dialectics altogether. But no idea can be grasped apart from its form, and the form of all of Marx's theories is dialectical. Hence, so long as Marxism helps us understand the world, we will need to study dialectics in order to improve our understanding of Marxism.

The present volume is not intended as an 'Introduction to Dialectics,' nor as a systematic restatement of what it is or of how to use it, nor as a survey of the main debates going on in this field, though something of each will be found in the following pages. It would be an exaggeration, too, to claim that the collection offers an adequate overview of the current state of dialectical thought, though several varieties of Marxist dialectics are represented here.

Instead, we have simply tried to showcase some of the more important Marxist thinkers now working on dialectics. It is not surprising, there-fore, that – taken as a whole – what they have written also constitutes an unusual 'Introduction to Dialectics,' an uneven but still systematic restatement of what it is and of how to use it, a survey of the main debates in the field, and – through its variety – as good a picture of the current state of the art of dialectics as one is likely to find.

Is a brief definition of 'dialectics' possible? In the history of Western thought the term has meant quite different things in different contexts.[1] Dialectics in the Western tradition is customarily said to begin with Heraclitus. He insisted that the cosmos was in endless flux, in contrast to those for whom 'true' reality was immutable. For Socrates, dialectic had less to do with the dynamism of the cosmos than with the dynamism of intellectual discussion when pushed forward by challenges to the underlying assumptions of interlocutors. Aristotle then systematized Socratic dialectic, treating it as a form of argument that fell some-where between rhetoric and logic. While dialectical speech, like rhetoric, aimed at persuasion, Aristotle believed its efforts to overcome disagree-ments through rational discussion made it more like logic. Unlike logical argumentation, however, dialectical speech does not derive necessary consequences from universally accepted premises. Instead, by revealing the contradictions in particular arguments, it forces their modification or even abandonment, and moves the contending parties closer to a rational consensus. This notion of dialectics continued to hold sway in Western philosophy throughout the medieval and early modern periods.

A major shift occurred with Kant. For him, 'dialectics' does not refer to a process by which discussions can advance toward rational agree-ment, but to the frustrating and inclusive results that arise whenever reason transgresses its proper limits by attempting to investigate the ultimate nature of things. In Kant's philosophy, dialectics becomes an endless series of debates in which each side reveals the contradictions of the other without being able to resolve its own. Following Kant, Hegel concedes that as long as contending positions are taken as complete and independent in themselves, the opposition between them is irresolvable. But why, Hegel asks, must we take the opposed positions as complete and independent? Why choose, for example, between 'freedom' and 'necessity'? Another, far better option is available: to recognize that the apparently opposed positions only offer one-sided accounts of a complex reality. 'Truth is the whole,' he famously claims, and to be adequately comprehended we must find a place in our thinking for all these partial and one-sided truths. The key to Hegel's notion of dialectic is the movement to a positive result in which previously antagonistic positions are reconciled within a higher-order framework (Pinkard, 1987). His *Science of Logic* is an unprecedented and unrepeatable attempt to show that all the fundamental categories of Western philosophy can be fit together in one coherent whole – once, that is, the contradictions which arise when they are taken as independent standpoints are rigorously confronted and resolved. In *The Philosophy of Right* Hegel attempted to show that neither a one-sided emphasis on the autonomous subjectivity of individual agents, nor a one-sided emphasis on the priority of the community over the individual, can adequately comprehend the reconciliation of both 'principles' found in the social and political institutions of modern society.

Marx himself testified to the importance of Hegelian dialectics in his own intellectual development, although it remains a matter of dispute what he took over from Hegel more or less intact, what he modified, and what he rejected. There is no dispute that Marx unequivocally rejected Hegel's claim that the antagonisms of the modern order are adequately overcome in the modern state. Marxian dialectics is thus critical where Hegel's is affirmative. Marx's dialectics is also largely developed from the standpoint of engaged practical agency, rather than from the sort of detached intellectual contemplation that characterized dialectical thinking in the West from the Greeks through Hegel.

While extremely compressed and oversimplified, this sketch of the history of the term 'dialectics' in the West should be enough to warn readers not to expect a consensus on what it is. Introductions, however, are allowed to simplify if that helps to prepare new audiences for the complexities of the upcoming text, so – with apologies to those of our contributors who will disagree – here is dialectics, the potted version.

Dialectics is a way of thinking and a set of related categories that captures, neither misses nor distorts, the real changes and interaction that go on in the world or any part of it. It is also, therefore, a characterization of the world, including society, in so far as it possesses these qualities. It also offers a method for investigating a reality so conceived, and of presenting our findings to others, most of whom do not think dialectically. Taking capitalism as our main subject of study, dialectics can't be said to explain capitalism. Rather, it helps us see and investigate the capitalist relations and processes, of which we ourselves are part, as they have unfolded, are now unfolding, and have yet to unfold. Using dialectics – and with a lot of hard empirical research – we can develop a theory that can explain capitalism in its becoming. Marxism is such a theory.

Having risked this brief definition of 'dialectics,' we hasten to add that practically every aspect of it is contested. That emerges clearly from a glance at the major debates in the field: Is Marx's dialectic a reflection of what the world really is (is it an ontology?), or is it a way of learning about the world (is it an epistemology?), or is it both? Does it apply to all of nature, including society, or only to society? Is it limited to organic interaction within the capitalist mode of production, or does it deal with historical change as well? Is it primarily a method of exposition, and that chiefly for Marx's major work, *Capital*, or does it also involve a method of inquiry? And, of course, which one or couple of categories associated with dialectics – contradiction, internal relations, totality, identity/difference, quantity/quality, negation of the negation, etc. – is central to Marx's account? Finally, how does Marx's dialectic differ, if at all, from the view of dialectics presented in far more detail in the writings of Engels? While our volume is not organized around these debates, all of them receive some attention in the pages that follow.

A proviso and a challenge: There are serious limits to how dialectical our thinking can become in capitalist society. With its frequent upheavals of all kinds, no society requires dialectics as much, but it is also true that with its reified social forms and constantly expanding consciousness industry no society makes it so difficult for its inhabitants to think dialectically. Without these hindrances, dialectics would probably come easily to people. It is with this in mind that some have envisioned dialectics as the common sense of communism, when all such hindrances have been removed. The question we face, however, is, Can we help people think *more* dialectically *today?* We can only try but try we must, since grasping more of the relevant connections and of the larger (and longer) picture – given the relation between dialectics and becoming class conscious – is a necessary prerequisite for bringing any communist future into existence.

This volume is organized to allow relatively easy entry and exit. Bertell Ollman's essay presents the problems, both epistemological and political, for which dialectics serves as some kind of solution. His chief concern here is with how dialectics helps us understand and investigate potentiality, especially as it applies to the socialist and communist future that Marx sees 'concealed' inside the capitalist present.

Richard Levins contrasts dialectics with systems theory, whose notions of mutual dependence and totality have often been confused with their 'equivalents' in dialectical thinking. For him, systems theory represents a positive though still necessarily limited attempt by a reductionist scientific establishment to come to grips with the problems posed by complexity and change.

While many 'Western Marxists' explicitly rejected the notion of a 'dialectics of nature' as 'Engelsian,' John Bellamy Foster argues that ecological Marxism, which stresses the internal relations between society and nature within a single totality, is much closer to Marx's own dialectical ontology. It is also best suited for comprehending our society's worsening alienation from nature and offers the only adequate framework for addressing the current ecological crisis.

Lucien Sève discusses the logical problems linear (non-dialectical) thinkers have in conceiving the process of emergence, a process of crucial concern in both the natural and social sciences. For him, only dialectics enables us to grasp emergence as a process that intertwines parts of what existed beforehand with the genuinely new qualities that come into existence during change.

David Harvey examines absolute, relative, and relational definitions of 'space' and 'time,' as well as the experience of 'spacetime.' The importance of keeping space and time in dialectical tension with each other is illustrated through analyses of complex phenomena ranging from 'Ground Zero' in Manhattan to the Marxian theories of value and class consciousness.

Fredric Jameson conceives of the dialectic as a way of thinking for the future that is but imperfectly realized in the present. Marx, Hegel, Derrida, Barthes, and Brecht are the main figures interrogated in his search for a contradiction-centered dialectic that is historically situated and completely open-ended.

István Mészáros' article reclaims the base/superstructure metaphor, which is usually associated with positivistic versions of Marxism, for a dialectical analysis in which the notion of totality plays the central role.

After identifying the main structural constraints on thinking that come from the base, he examines the changes that would be necessary for the emergence of a totalizing consciousness adequate to the task of political transformation.

Michael Löwy discusses how Trotsky's, Lenin's, and Lukács' dialectical comprehension of the unity of opposites and the category of totality helped them to avoid economic determinism and to understand history as a contradictory and open-ended (rather than predetermined) process. Understanding the need for a dialectical synthesis between the specificity of particular social formations and the universality of world capitalism also protected them from all the temptations of nationalism.

Savas Michael-Matsas insists that dialectical method remains what Marx originally asserted it to be: a scandal and an abomination to the ruling class and ruling ideology. Appealing to Walter Benjamin's notion of a 'Now' that breaks with linear time, he develops a dialectic of negativity of globalized capitalism, revealing the latter's contradictions and transient nature.

Tony Smith argues for a dialectical connection between the (1) social-state, (2) neoliberal, (3) catalytic-state, and (4) democratic-cosmopolitan models of globalization, with each addressing the 'immanent contradictions' of the previous model. He concludes that the irresolvable contradictions and social antagonisms of the capitalist global order can only be overcome by a socialist form of globalization.

Tom Sekine presents dialectics as the logic of capital (and *Capital*), a logic we can learn by listening carefully to capital as it 'tells' us its story. We can 'hear' it, because it is a story we ourselves have created by carrying out our social roles in the capitalist mode of production.

Christopher J. Arthur agrees with Sekine that Marx's dialectic is systematic and not historical. For Arthur, Marx's dialectic, like Hegel's, expresses the logical connections among concepts whose meanings reflect the equally interdependent conditions of the whole to which they refer (capital for Marx, thought for Hegel).

Nancy Hartsock wants to construct a dialectical method that would be of special interest to feminists. In pursuit of this aim, she devotes most of her attention to the dialectical theory of truth, the place of subjectivity and agency in history, and the relation between knowledge and power, particularly in the capitalist era.

Joel Kovel's article insists that the dialectic is not just a method for seeking the truth, but also a form of praxis. Starting with its history, he claims that dialectics arises in societies undergoing struggle, using the logic (whether formalized or not) of the struggle to help bring about needed change.

Ira Gollobin concludes our volume by making explicit the connection between dialectics and wisdom that others may have been hinted at but no one has developed. From the intellectual gropings of primitive man to the creation of Marxism, Gollobin argues, the development of dialectical thought is coextensive with the growth of wisdom.

Bill Livant's four short pieces, which are distributed throughout the book, show how one of our most creative Marxist teachers introduces his neophyte students to the 'mysteries' of identity/difference, contradiction, essence/appearance, and dialectical motion.

Finally, the editors would like to thank David Laibman, the tireless editor of *Science and Society*, for his support in this project, which grew out of a special issue of the journal (Volume 62, Number 3, 1998) for which we were guest editors.

Note

1. Much work remains to be done to trace the many and varied contributions to dialectical theorizing found outside the Western philosophical tradition.

References

Lenin, V. I. 1973. *Collected Works,* Vol. XIX. Moscow: Foreign Languages Publishing House.

Marx, Karl and Friedrich Engels. 1941. *Selected Correspondence,* trans. D. Torr. London: Lawrence and Wishart.

Pinkard, Terry. 1987. *Hegel's Dialectic: The Explanation of Possibility.* Philadelphia: Temple University Press.

2
Why Dialectics? Why Now?

Bertell Ollman

I

> The law locks up the man or woman
> Who steals a goose from off the common,
> But leaves the greater the greater villain loose
> Who steals the common from the goose.

Anonymous, 15th century, English

The common, of course, was the land owned by everyone in the village. By the late middle ages, feudal lords were claiming this land as their own private property. In universities today, we can discern two opposing kinds of scholarship: that which studies the people who steal a goose from off the common ('Goose From Off the Common Studies', or G.F.C. for short) and that which studies those who steal the common from the goose ('Common From the Goose Studies', or C.F.G. for short). If the 'mainstream' in practically every discipline consists almost entirely of the former, Marxism is our leading example of the latter.

But someone steal a goose from off the common is a relatively simple matter – you only have to be there, to open your eyes, and to look – seeing someone steal the common from the goose is not, neither then nor now (Russia today is a possible exception). Here, the theft is accomplished only gradually; the person acting is often an agent for someone else; force is used, but so are laws and ideology. In short, to recognize a case of C.F.G., one has to grasp the bigger picture and the longer time that it takes for it to come together. It's not easy, but there is nothing that we study that is more important. Hence – and no matter what happened in the Soviet Union and in China – Marxism will continue to be relevant until we reclaim the common from those who stole it from us and who go on helping themselves to it with impunity right up to this moment.

Just how difficult it is to grasp the bigger picture was recently brought home to us when a group of astronomers announced that they had discovered what they called 'The Great Attractor'. This is a huge structure composed of many galaxies that is exerting a strong attraction on our galaxy and therefore on our solar system and on the planet on which we live. When questioned as to why something so big was not discovered earlier, one of the astronomers replied that its very size was responsible for the delay. These scientists had focused so intently on its parts that they couldn't see what they were parts of.

Capitalism is a huge structure very similar to the Great Attractor. It, too, has a major effect on everything going on inside it, but it is so big and so omnipresent that few see it. In capitalism, the system consists of a complex set of relations among all people, their activities (particularly material production), and products. But this interaction is also evolving, so the system includes the development of this interaction over time, stretching back to its origins and forward to whatever it is becoming. The problem people have in seeing capitalism, then – and recognizing instances of C.F.G. Studies when they occur – comes from the difficulty of grasping such a complex set of relations that are also developing in this way and on this scale.

No one will deny, of course, that everything in society is related in some way and that the whole of this is changing, again in some way and at some pace. Yet, most people try to make sense of what is going on by viewing one part of society at a time, isolating and separating it from the rest, and treating it as static. The connections among such parts, like their real history and potential for further development, are considered external to what each one really is, and therefore not essential to a full or even adequate understanding of any of them. As a result, looking for these connections and their history becomes much more difficult than it has to be. They are left for last or left out completely, and important aspects of them are missed, distorted, or trivialized. It's what might be called the Humpty Dumpty problem. After the fall, it was not only extremely hard to put the pieces of poor Humpty together again, but even to see where they fit. This is what happens whenever the pieces of our everyday experience are taken as existing separate from their spatial and historical contexts, whenever the part is given an ontological status independent of the whole.

II

The alternative, the dialectical alternative, is to start by taking the whole as given, so that the interconnections and changes that make up the whole are viewed as inseparable from what anything is, internal to its being, and therefore essential to a full understanding of it. In the history of ideas, this has been called the 'philosophy of internal relations'.[1] No new facts have been introduced. We have just recognized the complex relations and changes that everyone admits to being in the world in a way that highlights rather than dismisses or minimizes them in investigating any problem. The world of independent and essentially dead 'things' has been replaced in our thinking by a world of processes in relations of mutual dependence. This is the first step in thinking dialectically. But we still don't know anything specific about these relations.

In order to draw closer to the subject of study, the next step is to abstract out the patterns in which most change and interaction occur. A lot of the specialized vocabulary associated with dialectics – 'contradiction', 'quantity–quality change', 'interpenetration of polar opposites', 'negation of the negation', and so on – is concerned with this task. Reflecting actual patterns in the way things change and interact, these categories also serve as ways of organizing for purposes of thought and inquiry whatever it is they embrace. With their help, we can study the particular conditions, events, and problems that concern us in a way that never loses sight of how the whole is present in the part, how it helps to structure the part, supplying it with a location, a sense, and a direction. Later, what is learned about the part(s) is used to deepen our understanding of the whole, how it functions, how it has developed, and where it is tending. Both analysis and synthesis display this dialectical relation.

What's called 'dialectical method' can be broken down into six successive moments. There is an ontological one having to do with what the world really is (an infinite number of mutually dependent processes that coalesce to form a structured whole or totality). There is the epistemological moment that deals with how to organize our thinking in order to understand such a world (as indicated, this involves opting for a philosophy of internal relations and abstracting out the main patterns in which change and interaction occur). There is the moment of inquiry (where, based on an assumption of internal relations among all parts, one uses the categories that convey these patterns as aids to investigation). There is the moment of intellectual reconstruction or self-clarification (where one puts together the results of such research for oneself). This is followed by the moment of exposition (where, using a strategy that takes account of how others think as well as what they know, one tries to explain this dialectical grasp of the 'facts' to a particular audience). And, finally, there is the moment of praxis (where, based on whatever clarification has been reached, one consciously acts in the world, changing it and testing it and deepening one's understanding of it all at the same time). These six moments are not traversed once and for all, but again and again, as every attempt to understand and expound dialectical truths and to act upon them improves one's ability to organize one's thinking dialectically and to inquire further and deeper into the mutually dependent processes to which we also belong. In writing about dialectics, therefore, one must be very careful not to single out any one moment – as so many thinkers do – at the expense of the others. Only in their internal relations do these six moments constitute a workable and immensely valuable dialectical method.[2]

So – Why dialectics? Because that's the only sensible way to study a world composed of mutually dependent processes in constant evolution, and also to interpret Marx, who is our leading investigator into this world. Dialectics is necessary just to see capitalism, given its vastness and complexity, and Marxism to help us understand it, to instruct us in how to do 'Common From the Goose Studies', and to help us develop a political strategy to reclaim the common. Capitalism is completely and always dialectical, so that Marxism will always be necessary to make sense of it and dialectics to make correct sense of Marxism.

III

Why now? The current stage of capitalism is characterized by far greater complexity and much faster change and interaction than existed earlier. But if society has never been so imbued with dialectics, the efforts to keep us from grasping what is taking place have never been so systematic or so effective – all of which makes a dialectical understanding more indispensable now than ever before.

Socialism's sudden loss of credibility as a viable alternative to capitalism, however, a loss largely due to the collapse of the Soviet Union, has given Marxists still another important reason to devote more attention to dialectics. For many socialists, even some who had always been critical of the Soviet Union, have reacted to this recent turn of history by questioning whether any form of socialism is possible. Perhaps unsurprisingly, one result has been a kind of 'future shyness' that has afflicted the writings of many on the Left today. What does a critical analysis of capitalism without any accompanying conception of socialism look like? It describes how capitalism works, shows who gets 'screwed' and by how much, offers a moral condemnation of same, prescribes – *faute de mieux* – reformist solutions, and – because these no longer work – lapses into emotional despair and cynicism. Sound familiar?

Marx would not have been pleased, for, despite the absence of any single work on socialism/communism, there are no writings of his, no matter how small, where we are not given some indication of what such a future would be like. If Hegel's Owl of Minerva comes out and also goes back in at dusk, Marx's Owl stays around to herald the new dawn. This imaginative reconstruction of the future has been sharply attacked not only by his opponents but also by many of Marx's followers, such as Eduard Bernstein (1961, 204–5, 209–11) and, more recently, Erik Wright (1995), who view it as a lapse into utopianism that contaminates his otherwise scientific enterprise. But do all discussions of the future have to be 'utopian'? With Rosa Luxemburg (1966, 40) and others, I do not think it is utopian to believe that a qualitatively better society is possible or to hope that it comes about. What is utopian is to construct this society out of such hopes; to believe, in other words, that such a society is possible without any other reason or evidence but that you desire it.

As opposed to this utopian approach, Marx insisted that communism lies 'concealed' inside capitalism, and that he is able to uncover it by means of his analysis (1973, 159). And elsewhere, he says, 'we wish to find the new world through the critique of the old' (1967, 212). Rather than a moral condemnation, Marx's 'critique of the old' shows that capitalism is having increasing difficulty in reproducing the conditions necessary for its own existence, that it is becoming impossible, while at the same time – and through the same developments – creating the conditions for the new society that will follow. The new world exists within the old in the form of a vast and untapped potential. Marx analyses capitalism in a way that makes this unfolding potential for turning into its opposite (communism) stand out. As part of this, he is not averse to describing, if only in a general way, what the realization of this potential would look like.[3]

The central place of potential in dialectical thinking has been noted by a variety of thinkers. C. L. R. James (1992, 129) referred to the internal relation between actuality and potentiality as 'the entire secret' of Hegel's dialectics (meaning Marx's as well). Marcuse claimed to find an indissoluble bond between the present and the future in the very meanings of the concepts with which Marx analyses the present (1964,

295–6). Maximilien Rubel made a similar point when he suggested, half seriously, that Marx invented a new grammatical form, the 'anticipative-indicative', where every effort to point at something in front of him foreshadows something else that is not yet here (1987, 25). But this still doesn't explain how Marx does it. Where exactly is the future concealed in the present? And how does Marx's dialectical method help him to uncover it?

In brief, most of the evidence for the possibility of socialism/communism surrounds us on all sides, and can be seen by everyone. It lies in conditions that don't seem to have anything particularly socialist about them, such as our developed industries, enormous material wealth, high levels of science, occupational skills, organizational structures, education, and culture; and also in conditions that already have a socialist edge to them, such as workers and consumers cooperatives, public education, municipal hospitals, political democracy, and – in our day – nationalized enterprises. Evidence for socialism can also be found in some of capitalism's most distinctive problems, such as unemployment and worsening inequality. For Marx and his followers, it is clear that it is the capitalist context in which all these conditions are embedded that keeps them from fulfilling their potential and contributing to a truly human existence. Abstracting from this context, Marxists have no difficulty in looking at our enormous wealth and ability to produce more and seeing an end to material want, or looking at our limited and malfunctioning political democracy and seeing everyone democratically running all of society, or looking at rising unemployment and seeing the possibility of people working fewer hours and enjoying more free time, and so on. Unfortunately, most others who encounter the same evidence don't see this potential, not even in the parts that have a socialist edge to them. And it is important to consider why they can't.

Investigating potential is taking the longer view, not only forward to what something can develop into but also backward to how it has developed up to now. This longer view, however, must be preceded by taking a broader view, since nothing and no one changes on its or his own but only in close relationship with other people and things, that is, as part of an interactive system. Hence, however limited the immediate object of interest, investigating its potential requires that we project the evolution of the complex and integrated whole to which it belongs. The notion of potential is mystified whenever it is applied to a part that is separated from its encompassing system or that system is separated from its origins. When that happens, 'potential' can only refer to possibility in the sense of chance, for all the necessity derived from the relational and processual character of reality has been removed, and there is no more reason to expect one outcome rather than another.

The crux of the problem most people have in seeing evidence for socialism inside capitalism, then, is that they operate with a conception of the present that is effectively sealed off from the future, at least any notion of the future that grows organically out of the present. There is no sense of the present as a moment through which life, and the rest of reality as the conditions of life, passes from somewhere on its way to somewhere. When someone is completely lost in the past or the future, we have little difficulty recognizing this as a mental illness. Yet, the present completely walled off from either the past or the future (or both) can also serve as a prison for thinking, though 'alienation' is a more accurate label for this condition than 'neurosis'. Here, people simply take how something appears now for what it really is, what it is in full, and what it could only be. With the exception of the gadgetry found in science fiction, what they call the 'future' is filled with social objects that are only slightly modified from how they appear and function in the present.

With this mind-set, there is no felt need to trace the relations any thing has with other things as part of a system – even while admitting that such a system exists – for, supposedly, there is nothing essential to be learned about it by doing so. Likewise, operating with narrow, independent parts that are also static, there is no difficulty in admitting that there was a past and will be a future while ignoring both when trying to understand anything in the present. If people can't see the evidence for socialism that exists all around them, therefore, it is not mainly, or even largely, because of an inability to abstract elements from capitalism and imaginatively project how they might function elsewhere. Rather, and more fundamentally, the conditions they see about them do not seem to belong to any social system at all, so there is no system to take them out of and, equally, no system to insert them into. The systemic and historical characters of both capitalism and socialism that would allow for such projections are simply missing.

IV

The dialectic enters this picture as Marx's way of systematizing and historicizing all the conditions of capitalism, so that they become internally related elements of an organic whole, which is itself but the most visible moment in how they got that way and what they may yet become. With this move, the present ceases to be a prison for thinking, and, like the past and the future, becomes a stage in a temporal process, with necessary and discoverable relations to the rest of the process. It is by analyzing a present conceived in this way that Marx believes he can discern the broad outlines of the socialist and communist societies that lie ahead.

The dialectical method with which Marx studies this future inside the capitalist present consists of four main steps. (1) He looks for relations between the main capitalist features of our society at this moment in time. (2) He tries to find the necessary preconditions of just these relations – viewing them now as mutually dependent processes – in the past, treating the preconditions he uncovers as the start of an unfolding movement that led to the present. (3) He then projects these inter-related processes, reformulated now as contradictions, from the past, through the present, and into the future. These projections move from the immediate future, to the probable resolution of these contradictions in an intermediate future, and on to the type of society that is like to follow in the more distant future. (4) Marx then reverses himself, and uses the socialist and communist stages of the future at which he has arrived as vantage points for re-examining the present extended back in time to include its real past, now viewed as the sum of the necessary preconditions for such a future.

Before elaborating on these steps, there are two qualifications and one clarification that need to be made. First, it should be clear that explaining how to study the future is not the same as actually making such a study. In the former, which is the case here, the details brought forward are meant to illustrate the approach and should not be taken as the results of an already completed study, though I have taken care to use only realistic examples. The second qualification has to do with Aristotle's warning that in undertaking any study we should not expect more precision than the nature of our subject permits. The potential within capitalism for socialism is real enough, but it is often unclear and always imprecise, both as regards the exact forms that will develop and as regards timing or the moment at which the expected changes will occur. In short, in investigating the future within the present, we must be careful not to insist on a standard for knowledge that can never be met.

The clarification has to do with the fact that the future that Marx uncovers by projecting the outcome of contradictions is not all of one piece. Marx's varied projections make it necessary to divide the future into four different stages, communism being but the last. Through his analysis of capitalism, as a system in the present that emerges out of its preconditions in the past, Marx also projects its immediate future (or its development over the next few years), the near future (or the coming of the crisis that results in a socialist revolution), a middle future or transition between capitalism and communism that we call 'socialism', and, finally, the far future or communism. How Marx uses his dialectical method for inquiring into what lies ahead varies somewhat depending on the stage of the future he is concerned with. While our interest here is limited to what I've called the 'middle' and 'far' futures, Marx's treatment of the 'immediate' and especially the 'near' futures cannot be wholly ignored, since the outcomes he projects for them enter into his expectations for socialism and communism.

V

Keeping these qualifications and this clarification clearly in mind, we can return to the four steps by which Marx sought to steal the secret of the future from its hiding place in the present. The first step, as I said, was to trace the main lines of the organic interaction that characterizes capitalist society – particularly as regards the accumulation of capital and the class struggle – at this moment of time. In order to focus on what is distinctively capitalist in our situation, Marx has to abstract out (omit) those qualities – equally real, and, for different kinds of problems, equally important – that belong to our society as part of other systems, such as human society (which takes in the whole history of the species), or class society (which takes in the entire period of class history), or modern capitalist society (which only takes in the most recent stage of capitalism), or the unique society that exists at this time in this place (which only takes in what is here and now). Every society and everything in them are composed of qualities that fall on these different levels of generality. Taken together – which is how most people approach them – they constitute a confusing patchwork of ill-fitting pieces that makes the systemic connections that exist on any single level very difficult to perceive. By starting with the decision to exclude all non-capitalist levels of generality from his awareness, to focus provisionally on the capitalist character of the people, activities, and products before him, Marx avoids tripping on what human society or class history or the other levels mentioned have placed in his way in carrying out his work as the systematizer of capitalism.[4]

The widespread view of capitalism as the sum of everything in our society rather than the capitalist 'slice' of it has been responsible for repeated complaints, most recently from postmodernists and social movement theorists, that Marx ignores the role of race, gender, nation, and religion. He ignores them, at least in his systematic writings, because they all predate capitalism, and consequently cannot be part of what is distinctive about capitalism. Though all of these conditions take on capitalist forms to go along with their forms as part of class society or the life of the species, their most important qualities fall on the latter levels of generality, and it is there (and on us in so far as we are subject to these levels) that they have their greatest impact. Uncovering the laws of motion of the capitalist mode of production, however, which was the major goal of Marx's investigative effort, simply required a more restricted focus.

With the distinctive qualities of capitalism in focus, Marx proceeds to examine the most important interactions in the present from different vantage points, though economic processes, particularly in production, are privileged, both as vantage points and as material to be studied. To avoid the overemphasis and trivialization that marks most one-sided studies, the relation between labor and capital is examined from each side in turn, and the same applies to all the major relations that Marx treats. Of equal significance is the fact that internal relations are taken to exist between all objective and subjective factors, so that conditions never come into Marx's study without umbilical ties to the people who affect and are affected by them, and the same applies to people – they are always grasped in context, with the essentials of this context taken as part of who and what they are. Capital, as Marx says, 'is at the same time the capitalist' (1973, 412).

After reconstituting the capitalist present in this manner, the second step Marx takes in his quest to unlock the future is to examine the preconditions of this present in the past. If the dialectical study of the present treats its subject matter as so many relations, a dialectal study of the past requires that we also view these relations as processes. History comes to mean the constant, if uneven, evolution of mutually dependent processes. The past, of course, takes place before the present, and in retelling the story one usually begins at the beginning and moves forward. But the correct order in inquiry is present first, and it is what Marx uncovers in his reconstruction of the present that guides him in his search into the past, helping him to decide what to look for as well as how far back to go in looking for it. The question posed is, What had to happen in the past for the present to become what it did? This is not to suggest that what occurred was preordained (though there may have been good reasons for it); only that it did in fact take place, and that it had these results. It is in following this approach that Marx is led to late feudalism as the period when most of the important preconditions for capitalism are first laid down.[5]

VI

After reconstructing the organic interaction of the capitalist present and establishing its origins in the past, Marx is ready to project the main tendencies that he finds there into one or another stage of the future. As part of this third step in his method, Marx re-abstracts (reorganizes, rethinks) these tendencies as 'contradictions', which emphasizes their interaction as processes that are simultaneously mutually supporting and mutually undermining one another. Over time, it is the undermining activities that invariably prevail. The fundamental assumption that underlies Marx's practice here is that reality is an internally related whole with temporal as well as spatial dimensions. Things that are separate and independent (if this is how one conceives them) cannot be in contradiction, since contradiction implies that an important change in any part will produce changes of a comparable magnitude throughout the system. Just as things that are static (again, if this is how one conceives them) cannot be in a contradiction since contradiction implies there is a collision up ahead. The use of 'contradiction' in formal logic and to refer to some relations within the categories of capitalist political economy (the province of systematic dialectics), rather than being true exceptions, offer instances of Marx's willingness – evident throughout his writings – to use a concept to convey only part of all that it can mean for him.[6] Finally, based on what has already been achieved in examining the present and the past, Marx's contradictions also contain both objective and subjective aspects as well as a high degree of economic content.

Marx's contradictions organize the present state of affairs in capitalism, including the people involved in them, in a way that brings out how this cluster of relations has developed, the pressures that are undermining their existing equilibrium, and the likely changes up ahead. With contradictions, the present comes to contain both its real past and likely future in a manner that allows each historical stage to cast a helpful light upon the others. Early in his career, Marx compared problems in society with those in algebra, where the solution is given once a problem receives its proper formulation (1967, 106). The solution to capitalism's problems, he believed, would also become clear once they were reformulated in terms of contradictions. It is chiefly by projecting such contradictions forward to the point of their resolution and beyond, where the character of the resolution gives shape to the elements of what follows, that Marx is able to catch a glimpse of both socialism and communism. The resolution of a contradiction can be partial and temporary or complete and permanent. In the former, as exemplified in the typical capitalist crisis, the elements involved are simply reordered in a way that puts off the arrival of the latter. Our concern here is with the kind of resolution that completely and permanently transforms all of capitalism's major contradictions.

Marx sees capitalism as full of intersecting and overlapping contradictions (1963, 218). Among the more important of these are the contradictions between use-value and exchange-value, between capital and labor in the production process (and between capitalists and workers in the class struggle), between capitalist forces and capitalist relations of production, between competition and cooperation, between science and ideology, between political democracy and economic servitude, and – perhaps most decisively – between social production and private appropriation (or what some have recast as the 'logic of production versus the logic of consumption'). In all of these contradictions, what I referred to earlier as the 'evidence for socialism' inside capitalism can be found reorganized as so many mutually dependent tendencies evolving over time. Viewed as parts of capitalism's major contradictions, their current forms can only represent a passing moment in the unfolding of a larger potential.

Whatever necessity (best grasped as likelihood) is found in Marx's projection of a socialist revolution in what I referred to as the near future is the result of his demonstrating that the conditions underlying capitalism have become more and more difficult to reproduce while the conditions that make socialism possible have developed apace. All this is contained in capitalism's main contradictions. According to Marx's analysis, these contradictions display capitalism as becoming increasingly destructive, inefficient, irrational, and eventually impossible, while at the same time socialism is presented as becoming increasingly practical, rational, conceivable, necessary, and even obvious – notwithstanding all the alienated life conditions and the enormous consciousness industry that work to distort such facts. Consequently, for Marx, it is only a matter of time and opportunity before the organization, consciousness and tactics of the rising class bring about the expected transformation.

VII

Marx's vision of what happens after the revolution is derived mainly from projecting the forms that the resolution of capitalism's major contradictions are likely to take in the hands of a new ruling class, the workers, who have already been significantly changed by their participation in a successful revolution, and who are now using their class interests as a guide in making all important decisions. The most important of these interests is to abolish their exploitation as a class along with all the conditions that underpin it. How quickly they could accomplish this, of course, is another matter. The question, then, is not 'Why would the workers do this?' but 'Why, when they come to power, would they do anything else?'

For class interest to bear the weight put on it by this account of future prospects, we need to place the relations among different classes, including their interests and the conditions of their lives and work that characterized earlier periods, inside the main contradictions that link the present with the past and the future. Only by understanding how capitalist class interests determine the forms and functions of what I called the 'evidence for socialism' inside capitalism (step one), and how, in response to these same interests, all this has evolved over time (step two), can we begin to grasp how quickly these forms and functions would change in response to the demands of a new ruling class with different interests (step three). If the workers' assumption of power together with the material conditions bequeathed by capitalism provide us with the *possibility* for socialism, it is the workers' class interests together with the removal of whatever interfered with the recognition of them earlier that supplies us with most of its *necessity*.

If Marx's vision of socialism (or the middle future) is derived mainly from the contradictions of capitalism, his vision of communism (or the far future) is derived not only from these contradictions (i.e., from projecting the resolution of these contradictions beyond the attainment of socialism), but also from the contradictions Marx sees in class history and even in socialism, in so far as it is a distinctive class formation. After socialism has developed to a certain point, the contradictions that have existed since the very beginning of classes (having to do with the general forms of the division of labor, private property, the state, etc.) come to a resolution. At the same time, and through the same processes, the contradictions that socialism still possesses as a class society (having to do with its own forms of the division of labor, private property, the state, etc.) are also resolved. It is the resolution of the contradictions from all these levels that marks the qualitative leap from socialism to communism, and that makes the latter so hard for most people today to conceive, let alone evaluate.

To summarize, Marx begins to study the future by tracing the main organic interconnections in the capitalist present. He then looks for their preconditions in the past; and he concludes by projecting the chief tendencies found in both, abstracted now as contradictions, to their resolution and beyond for the stage of the future with which he is concerned. The order of the moves is, present, past, future (unlike most futurological attempts to peer ahead that move from the present directly to the future or, as in many utopian efforts, that go directly to the future, dispensing with the present altogether).

VIII

Marx's method for studying the future is still not complete. In a fourth and final step, Marx reverses himself and uses the socialist and communist stages of the future at which he has arrived as vantage points for re-examining the present, now viewed (together with its own past) as the necessary preconditions for such a future. This last, though little understood, is the indispensable means by which Marx provides the 'finishing' touches to his analysis of capitalism. It is also part of his method for studying the future since the process I have described is an ongoing one. Building on what he learns from going through one series of steps, Marx begins the dance – the dance of the dialectic – all over again. For the work of reconstructing the present, finding its preconditions in the past, projecting its likely future, and seeking out the preconditions of this future in the present, now conceived of as an extension of the past, is never truly finished.

According to Marx, 'the anatomy of the human being is the key to the anatomy of the ape' (1904, 300). The same applies to the relations between later and earlier stages of society, and in the same way that our present provides the key for understanding the past, the future (i.e., the likely future, in so far as we can determine it) provides the key for understanding the present. It is Marx's grasp of communism, as unfinished as it is, for example, that helps him to see capitalism as the gateway to human history rather than its end, and makes it easier to distinguish the capitalist-specific qualities of current society (those that serve as the preconditions of socialism) from the qualities it possesses as an instance of class and human societies. Communism also provides Marx with a standard by which the greater part of what exists today is found wanting, as well as criteria for determining priorities for research and politics, distinguishing between the kind of changes capitalism can absorb, and those that set transitional forces into motion. The transparently class character of socialist society, epitomized in the dictatorship of the proletariat, also makes it easier to grasp the more hidden class character of capitalism. We shouldn't be surprised, therefore, that insisting that the capitalist state, whatever its democratic pretensions, is a dictatorship of the capitalist class is the most effective way to inoculate people against the dangers of reformist politics (hence the theoretical loss incurred when the French and other communist parties removed all references to the dictatorship of the proletariat from their programs).

But above and beyond all this, revisiting the present from the vantage point of its likely future concretizes and hence makes visible the potential that exists throughout the present for just such a future. To William Faulkner's supposed remark, 'The past is not dead – it is not even in the past', Marx could have added, 'And the future is not unborn – it is not even in the future.' Potential is the form in which the future exists inside the present, but until now it has been a form without a particular content, just because it was open to every conceivable content. Now, everywhere one looks, one sees not only what is but what could be, what really could be, not simply because one desires it but because the aforementioned analysis has shown it to be so. Seeing the 'facts' of capitalism as 'evidence' of socialism becomes so many 'arguments' for socialism. At the same time, informing workers of and sensitizing them to the extraordinary possibilities that lie hidden inside their oppressive daily existence greatly increases their power to act politically by indicating what, how, and with whom to act, just as it enhances their self-confidence that they can succeed. In sum, by enriching capitalism with the addition of communism, Marx's dialectical analysis 'liberates' potential to play its essential role in helping to liberate us.

Taken altogether, the future proves to be as important in understanding the present and past as they are in understanding the future. And always, the return to the present from the future instigates another series of steps from the present to the past to the future, using what has just been learned to broaden and deepen the analysis at every stage.

IX

Before concluding, it needs to be stressed that the projections of the future obtained through the use of the method outlined here are only highly probable, and even then the pace and exact forms through which such change occurs owe too much to the specificity of a particular place, the vagaries of class struggle, and also to accident to be fully knowable beforehand. Marx, himself, as we know, recognized 'barbarism' as a possible successor to capitalism, though he thought it very unlikely and devoted much less attention to this possibility than we need to after the bloodcurdling events of the last century.

To avoid other possible misunderstandings of what I have tried to do in this article, I would like to add that my account of Marx's method is not meant to be either complete or final, but rather – in keeping with Marx's own approach to exposition – a first approximation to its subject matter. Further, I do not believe that Marx's use of contradiction to project existing potential is the only means he uses to uncover the' socialist/communist future inside the capitalist present; it is simply the main one. Also, this approach to studying the future is not to be confused with Marx's strategies for presenting what he found, and hence with what he actually published, which always involved a certain amount of reordering that took the character of his audience into account. Nor am I maintaining that this is how Marx became a communist. That is a complex story in which Hegel's dialectic and Marx's unique appropriation of it are but part.

Once Marx constructed the chief elements of what came to be called 'Marxism', however, projecting capitalism's main contradictions forward became his preferred approach for studying the future, providing that future with just the degree of clarity and necessity needed for him to use it in elaborating his analysis of the present (in doing his version of 'Common From the Goose Studies'). It is also the best way that we today can learn about a socialist future that is more than wishful thinking. Only then, too, can the vision of socialism, which has been so battered by recent events, fulfill its own potential as one of our most effective weapons in the class struggle. Putting this weapon in the hands of the workers and other oppressed peoples, teaching them how to use it – to do *this*, to do this against all the pressures of the age – is largely why we need dialectics, and, with capitalism teetering on the brink, why we need dialectics now more than ever.

Appendix: Dance of the Dialectic

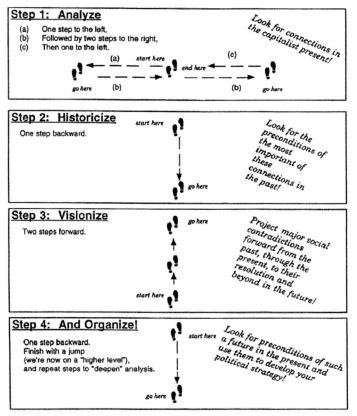

Step 1: Analyze

(a) One step to the left,
(b) Followed by two steps to the right,
(c) Then one to the left.

Look for connections in the capitalist present!

start here · end here · go here · go here

Step 2: Historicize

One step backward.

start here · go here

Look for the preconditions of the most important of these connections in the past!

Step 3: Visionize

Two steps forward.

go here · start here

Project major social contradictions forward from the past, through the present, to their resolution and beyond in the future!

Step 4: And Organize!

One step backward.
Finish with a jump
(we're now on a "higher level"),
and repeat steps to "deepen" analysis.

start here · go here

Look for preconditions of such a future in the present and use them to develop your political strategy!

Text and Choregraphy by Bertell Ollman   Layout by Fran Moran

Notes

1. For a fuller discussion of Marx's philosophy of internal relations, see Ollman, Bertell (1976) *Alienation: Marx's Conception of Man in Capitalist Society*, chapter 3.
2. For a fuller account of the different moments of Marx's dialectical method, see Ollman, Bertell (1978) *Social and Sexual Revolution*, chapter 4.
3. For an attempt to reconstruct Marx's vision of socialism and communism from his scattered comments on this subject, see Ollman, Bertell, *Social and Sexual Revolution*, chapter 3.
4. For a fuller account of Marx's practice of abstracting levels of generality, as part of his dialectical method, see Ollman, Bertell (1993) *Dialectical Investigations*, chapter 2.
5. For a fuller discussion of Marx's approach to studying the present through its preconditions in the past, see Ollman, Bertell, *Dialectical Investigations*, chapter 8.
6. For an explanation of the elasticity found in the meanings of Marx's key concepts, see Ollman, Bertell, *Alienation: Marx's Conception of Man in Capitalist Society*, chapters 2 and 3.

References

Bernstein, Eduard. 1961. *Evolutionary Socialism*, trans. Edith Harvey. New York: Schocken.

James, C. L. R. 1992. *The C. L. R James Reader*, ed. Anna Grimshaw. Oxford: Basil Blackwell.

Luxemburg, Rosa. 1966. *Reform or Revolution*, trans. Integer. Colombo, Ceylon: Young Socialist Publications.

Marcuse, Herbert. 1964. *Reason and Revolution*. Boston: Beacon.

Marx, Karl. 1904. *A Contribution to the Critique of Political Economy*, trans. N. I. Stone. Chicago: Charles Kerr.

Marx, Karl. 1963. *Theories of Surplus Value*, Part 1, trans. Emile Bums. Moscow: Progress Publishers.

Marx, Karl. 1967. ·*Writings of the Young Marx on Philosophy and Society*, ed. and trans. K. D. Easton and K. H. Guddat. Garden City, New York: Anchor.

Marx, Karl. 1973. *Grundrisse*, trans. Martin Nicolaus. London: Penguin.

Ollman, Bertell. 1976. *Alienation: Marx's Conception of Man in Capitalist Society*. Cambridge: Cambridge University Press.

Ollman, Bertell. 1978. *Social and Sexual Revolution: Essays on Marx and Reich*. Boston: South End Press.

Ollman, Bertell. 1993. *Dialectical Investigations*. New York: Routledge.

Rubel, Maximilien. 1987. 'Non-Market Socialism in the 20th Century'. In M. Rubel and J. Crump, eds, *Non-Market Socialism in the 19th and 20th Centuries*. London: Macmillan.

Wright, Erik Olin. 1995. 'Class Analysis and Historical Materialism'. Tape of talk at the New York Marxist School, February 23.

3
Dialectics and Systems Theory

Richard Levins

In a generally sympathetic review of *The Dialectical Biologist* (Maynard Smith, 1986), and in personal conversations, John Maynard Smith argued that the development of a rigorous, quantitative mathematical systems theory makes dialectics obsolete. Engels' awkward 'interchange of cause and effect' can be replaced by 'feedback', the mysterious 'transformation of quantity into quality' is now the familiar phase transition or threshold effect, while 'even in my most convinced Marxist phase, I could never make much sense of the negation of the negation or the interpenetration of opposites'. He could have added that hierarchy theory grasps some of the insights of 'integrated levels' or 'overdetermination'.

On the other hand, Mary Boger, a leader of the New York Marxist School, has been urging me for years not to allow dialectics to be subsumed under systems theory. Despite systems theory's concern with complexity, interconnection and process she has argued that it is still fundamentally reductionist and static, and despite the power of its mathematical apparatus it does not deal at all with the richness of dialectical contingency, contradiction or historicity. Finally, she added that systems-theoretic 'interconnection' does not grasp the subtleties of dialectical 'mediation'.

This essay is a first attempt to systematize my own views as they have evolved in discussions with Mary Boger, Rosario Morales, Richard Lewontin and other comrades.

As I entered this exploration I became aware of two opposing temptations. On the one hand, I wanted to emphasize the distinctness of dialectics from contemporary systems theory, to proclaim that our theoretical foundations are not obsolete and continue to have something important to say to the world of science that systems theory has not

already adopted. On the other hand, along with Engels I found it grat-
ifying to see science, grudgingly and haltingly and inconsistently but
nevertheless inexorably, becoming more dialectical. Both affirmations
are true, but their emotional appeal can also lead to errors of one-
sidedness. I attempted to use this awareness to question my conclusions
as I made one or another claim.

Any description of systems theory and of dialectical materialism is
subject to two kinds of problems: in both areas there are many prac-
titioners with quite divergent views. I will not attempt any kind of
comprehensive survey of systems theory or 'a systems approach', but
limit myself to systems theory in the narrow sense as a mathematical
approach to 'systems' of many parts. And second, systems theory and
dialectics are not mutually exclusive. Some systems theorists are also
Marxists or have been influenced by Marxism in their research contributions to the development of the theory. Other Marxists have had at least
a passing contact with systems theory and have used some of its notions
in their Marxist research. For example, Goran Therborn, a Swedish
Marxist social scientist influenced by systems theory, approached the
nature of the state from two perspectives: the traditional Marxist view
of the role of the state as an expression of class rule and the systems-
theoretic examination of its dynamics as a system with inputs and
outputs. The publisher's blurb for his book *What Does the Ruling Class Do
When it Rules?* (Therborn, 1978) summarizes the work: 'Therborn uses
the formal categories of systems analysis – input mechanisms, processes
of transformation, output flows – to advance a substantive Marxist
analysis of state power and state apparatuses...'

Nonetheless, the two are quite different in their origins, objectives and
theoretical underpinnings. In what follows I will discuss several general
themes that unite and differentiate them: wholeness and interconnection, selection of variables or parts, purposefulness and the outcomes of
processes. Materialist dialectics is not offered as a complete philosophy
of nature, a System in the classical sense.[1] Dialecticians are too aware
of the historical contingency of our thinking to expect that there will
ever be a final worldview. Rather it is first of all polemical, a critique
of the prevailing failings of both the mechanistic reductionist approach
and its opposite, the holistic idealist focus. Together these have dominated Euro-North American natural and social science since its emergence
in seventeenth-century Britain as a partner in the bourgeois revolution. They have also dominated politics as the broad liberal-conservative
consensus that has defined the 'mainstream' politics of democratic
capitalism.

Therefore dialectical materialism has focused mostly on some selected aspects of reality while ignoring others. At times we have emphasized the materiality of life against vitalism, as when Engels said that life was the mode of motion of 'albuminous bodies' (i.e., proteins; now we might say macromolecules). This seems to be in contradiction with our rejection of molecular reductionism, but simply reflects different moments in an ongoing debate where the main adversaries were first the vitalist emphasis on the discontinuity between the inorganic and the living realms, and then the reductionist erasure of the real leaps of levels. At times we have supported Darwin in emphasizing the continuity of human evolution with the rest of animal life, at other times the uniqueness of socially driven human evolution. We could classify our species as omnivores, along with bears, to emphasize that we are just another animal species that has to get its energy and substance by eating other living things, and are not limited to only one kind of food. Or we could underline our special status as 'productivores' who do not merely find our food and our habitat but produce them. Both are true; the relation of continuity and discontinuity in process is an aspect of dialectics that systems theory does not deal with at all.

But critique is not just criticism, and dialectics goes beyond the rejection of reductionist or idealist thinking to offer a coherent alternative, more for the way in which it poses questions than for the specific answers its advocates have proposed at any particular time. Its focus is on wholeness and interpenetration, the structure of process more than of things, integrated levels, historicity and contradiction. All of this is applied to the objects of the study, to the development of thought about those objects, and self-reflexively to the dialecticians ourselves so as not to lose sight of the contingency and historicity of our own grappling with the problems we study.

Dialectical materialism is unique among the critiques of science in that its roots are outside the academy in political struggle as well as within, that it directs criticism both at reductionism and idealism, that it is consciously self-reflexive, and that it rejects the goal of a final 'system'. But it is unlike postmodernist criticism of science which uses the contingency of scientific claims to deny the historically bounded but no less real validity of some claims over others, in favor of an acritical pluralism.

Systems theory has a dual origin, in engineering and in the philosophical criticism of reductionism. It comes out of engineering as cybernetics, the study of self-regulating mechanisms with often rather complex circuitry. Norbert Weiner introduced the term 'cybernetics' in his book of that name (*Cybernetics, or Control in the Animal and Machine*, 1961). The term became part of common usage in the Soviet Union, but was mostly replaced in the USA by control theory, the theory of servomechanisms, or systems theory. In this form it is the mathematics of feedback, the study of mathematical models. The preface to *The Theory of Servomechanisms*, one of the early classical texts in this field, states,

> The work on servomechanisms in the [Livermore] Radiation Laboratory grew out of its need for automatic radar systems. It was therefore necessary to develop the theory of servomechanisms in a new direction, and to consider the servomechanism as a device intended to deal with an input of known statistical character in the presence of interference of known statistical character. (ix.)

> A servomechanism involves the control of power by some means or other involving a comparison of the output of the controlled power and the actuating device. The comparison is sometimes referred to as feedback (James *et al.*, 1947, 2).

This form of systems theory is highly mathematical and formal. Its earlier versions assumed systems that were given, the equations known, and measurement precise. But soon systems analysis was taken up by military designers, with the idea of a weapons system replacing the development of particular weapons as the theoretical problem, and by management systems as the scientific aspects of directing large enterprises. Here the measurements are fuzzier, the equations not known and therefore other techniques become necessary. Herbert Simon at Carnegie Mellon University, Mesarovic at Case Western Reserve, the International Institute for Applied Systems Analysis in Austria as well as mathematicians and engineers in the Soviet Union and other centers worked to advance the conceptual frameworks and mathematics of many variables interacting at once and the computing routines for following what happens. More recently, the Santa Fe Institute has made the study of complexity itself the core intellectual problem.

The major role of engineering and management systems in developing systems theory is reflected in the assumption of goal-seeking. Thus Meadows *et al.* (1992) define a system as 'an interconnected set of elements that is coherently organized around some purpose. A system is more than the sum of its parts. It can exhibit dynamic, adaptive, goal-seeking, self-preserving and evolutionary behavior'.

But the 'system' of systems theory is not reality itself but a model of reality, an intellectual construct that grasps some aspects of the reality we want to study but also differs from that reality in being more manageable and easier to study and alter. Therefore models are not 'true' or 'false'. They are designed to meet a number of criteria that are in part contradictory, such as realism, generality and precision (Levins, 1966). It is the hope of systems analysts that the departures from reality that make them easier to study do not lead to false conclusions about that reality.

The wholeness, interconnectedness of parts and the purposefulness of systems are emphasized. The first two qualities are inherent in what we mean by a system.

Wholes

The other source of 'systems' theory has been in critical attempts to counter the prevailing reductionism in science since the last century. Here its boundaries are not well defined but shade off gradually into various holisms.

Holism is not new. The history of science is not the history of its mainstream, the succession of dominant paradigms popularized by Thomas Kuhn. There has always been dissidence in science, dissatisfaction with the dominant ideas, alternative approaches within the various disciplines and quite divergent 'mainstreams' among disciplines. 'Holistic' criticism has always coexisted with the dominant reductionism. It was expressed in such currents as vitalism in developmental biology, Bergson's 'emergence', in psychology (Bronfenbrenner, Perl, Piaget), ecology (Vernadsky's biosphere, the Soviet 'geo-biocoenosis', Clements' and later Odum's ecosystems), anthropology (Kroeber's 'superorganic') and other fields as a grasping for wholeness and interconnection. In this aspect it is usually referred to in the United States as a 'systems approach' or 'systems thinking'. Some authors engage in systems theory in both the narrow and the broad meanings. Especially ambitious and central was L. von Bertalanffy's General Systems Theory starting in the 1930s (von Bertalanffy, 1950). Biological complexity was usually a central challenge. W. Ross Ashby's *Design for a Brain* poses the problem as one of reconciling mechanistic structure and seemingly purposeful behavior:

We take as basic the assumptions that the organism is mechanistic in nature, that it is composed of parts, that the behavior of the whole is the outcome of the compounded actions of the parts, that organisms change their behavior by learning, and that they change it so that the later behavior is better adapted to their environment than the earlier. Our problem is, first, *to identify the nature of the change which shows as learning*, and secondly *to find why such changes should tend to cause better adaptation for the whole organism*. (1960, emphasis in original)

Ecology also has brought to public consciousness the rich interconnectedness of the world. Examples are regularly put forth of the unexpected, often counterproductive effects of interventions directed at solving a particular problem. Pesticides increase pest problems, draining a wetland can increase pollution, antibiotics provoke antibiotic resistance, clearing forests to increase food production may lead to hunger. And Barry Commoner's dicta that everything is connected to everything else and that everything goes somewhere have become part of the common sense of at least a part of the public.

The powerful impact of the realization that things are connected sometimes leads to claims that 'you cannot separate' body from mind, economics from culture, the physical from the biological or the biological from the social. Much very creative research has gone into showing the connectedness of phenomena that are usually treated as separate. It is even said that because of their interconnectedness they are all 'One', an important element of mystical sensibility that asserts our 'Oneness' with the Universe.

Of course you *can* separate the intellectual constructs 'body' from 'mind', 'physical' from 'biological', 'biological' from 'social'. We do it all the time, as soon as we label them. We have to in order to recognize and investigate them. That analytical step is a necessary moment in understanding the world. But it is not sufficient. After separating, we have to join them again, show their interpenetration, their mutual determination, their entwined evolution and yet also their distinctness. They are not 'One'. The pairs of mutualist species or predator and prey are certainly linked in their population dynamics. Sometimes the linkage is loose, as when each affects the life of the other but the effect is not necessary. Sometimes very tightly, as in the symbiosis of algae and fungi in lichens. Snowy owls and Arctic hares drive each other's population cycles in a defining feedback loop. Mutualists may evolve to become 'One', as Lynn Margulis has pioneered in arguing for the origins of cellular structures. But predator and prey are not 'One' until the last stages of digestion. Psychotherapists work both with asserting connection in examining family systems and with criticizing 'codependence', the pathological loss of boundaries and autonomy. There is a one-sidedness in the holism that stresses the connectedness of the world but ignores the relative autonomy of parts.

As against the atomistic and absolutized separations of reductionism, holists counterpose the unity of the world. That is, they align themselves at the 'oneness' end of a spectrum from isolated to 'One'. They look for some organizing principle behind the wholeness, some 'harmony' or 'balance' or purpose which gives the wholes their unity and persistence. In technological systems, there is a goal designed by the engineers that is the criterion for evaluating the behavior of the system and for modifying the design. To the extent that the development of systems theory has been dominated by designed systems, goal-seeking behavior appears as an obvious property of systems as such, and therefore it is sought also in the study of natural systems.

In the study of society, this may lead to a functionalism which assumes a common interest driving the society. But a society is not a servomechanism; its component classes pursue different, both shared and conflicting goals. Therefore it is not a 'goal-oriented' system, even when many of its components are separately goal-seeking.

Within the framework of static holism, it is difficult to accommodate change as other than destructive, so that conservation biology often emphasizes preservation of a particular species or ecological formation, rather than conditions that permit continued evolution.

Dialecticians value the holistic critique of reductionism. But we reject the sharp dichotomy of separation/connection or autonomy/wholeness and an absolute subordination of one to the other. This is not a complaint about being 'extreme'. 'Extreme' is a favorite reproach by liberals, for whom the desired condition is moderation, a middle ground 'somewhere in between', mainstream, compromise. Their favorite colors are 'not black or white but shades of gray'. In contrast the dialectical criticism is 'one-sidedness', the seizing upon one side of a dichotomous pair or a contradiction as if it were the whole thing. *Our spectrum is not a gradient from black through all the grays to white, but a fractal rainbow.*

Of course, despite Hegel's dictum that 'the truth is the whole' we cannot study The Whole. The practical value of Hegel's affirmation is twofold: First, that problems are larger than we have imagined so that we should extend the boundaries of a question beyond its original limits. Even systems theory construes problems too small, either because the domain is assigned to the analyst as a given 'system' or because additional variables known to interact with the initial system are not measurable or do not have known equations, or because of traditional boundaries of disciplines. Thus a systems analysis of the regulation of blood sugar may include the interactions among sugar itself, insulin, adrenalin, cortisol and other molecules but is unlikely to include anxiety, or the conditions that produce the anxiety such as the intensity of labor and the rate of using up of sugar reserves, whether or not the job allows a tired worker to rest or take a snack. Models of heart disease are likely to include cholesterol and the fats that are turned into cholesterol but not the social classes of the people in whom the cholesterol is formed and breaks down. Systems analysis would not know how to deal with the pancreas under capitalism or the adrenals in a racist workplace. Models of epidemics may include rates of reproduction of viruses and their transmission but not the social creation of a sense of agency that may allow people to take charge of their exposure and treatment.

The second application of the understanding that the truth is the whole is that after we have defined a system in the broadest terms we can at the time, there is always something more out there that might intrude to change our conclusions.

Dialectics appreciates the pre-reductionist kind of holism, but not its static quality, its hierarchical structure with a place for everything and everything in its place, nor the *a priori* imposition of a purposefulness that may or may not be there. Thus it 'negates' materialist reductionism's negation of the earlier holism, an example of the negation of the negation that Maynard Smith found so opaque but could have recognized as the non-linearity of change.

What are parts?

Wholes are thought of as made out of parts. Systems theory likes to take as its elements unitary variables that are the 'atoms' of the system, prior to it, and qualitatively unchanging as they ebb and flow. Their relations are then 'interactions' as a result of which the variables increase or decrease, emit 'outputs' and thus produce the properties of the wholes. But the wholes are not allowed to transform the parts, except quantitatively. The long distance conversation does not transform the telephone, the market does not change the buyer or seller, and power does not affect the powerful nor love the lover. It is the priority of the elements and along with it the separation of the structure of a system from its behavior – rational assumptions for designed and manufactured systems – that keeps systems theory still vulnerable to the reproach of being large-scale reductionism.

The parts of dialectical wholes are not chosen to be as independent as possible of the wholes but rather as points where properties of the whole are concentrated. Their relation is not mere 'interconnection' or 'interaction' but a deeper interpenetration that transforms them so that the 'same' variable may have a very different significance in different contexts and the behavior of the system can alter its structure. For instance temperature is important in the lives of most species. But temperature has many different meanings. It acts on the rate of development of organisms and therefore their generation time and also on the size of individuals; it limits the suitable locations for nesting or reproduction; it may determine the boundaries of foraging or the time available for searching for food. It influences the available array of potential food species and the synchrony between the appearance of parasites and their hosts. It modifies the outcomes of species encounters.

But temperature is not simply given to the organisms. The organisms change the temperature around them: there is a layer of warmer air at the surfaces of mammals; the shade of trees makes forests cooler than the surrounding grassland; the construction of tunnels in the soil regulates the temperatures at which ground nesting ants raise their brood; the color of leaf litter and humus determines the reflection and absorption of solar radiation. Through the physiology and demography of the organism, *effective* temperature, its range and its predictability are quite different from the weather box temperature of a place. On another timescale, temperature acts through various pathways as pressures of natural selection, changing the species, which again changes its effective temperature. Thus 'temperature' as a biological variable within an ecosystem is quite different from the more easily measured physical temperature that can be seen in the weather box as prior to the organisms.

Although systems theory is comfortable with the idea that a certain equation is valid only within some limits, it does not deal explicitly with the interpenetrations of variables in its models, their transformations of each other. In a sense, Marx's *Capital* was the first attempt to treat a whole system rather than merely to criticize the failings of reductionism. His initial objects of investigation in Volume I, commodities, are not autonomous building blocks or atoms of economic life that are then inserted into capitalism, but rather are studied as 'cells' of capitalism chosen for study precisely because they reveal the workings of the whole. They can be separated out for inspection only as aspects of the whole that called them forth. To Marx, this was an advantage because the whole is reflected in the workings of all the parts. But for large-scale reductionists the relationship goes from given, fixed parts to the wholes that are their product. The priority and autonomy of the part is essential to systems analysis. 'Autonomy' does not of course mean they have no influence on each other. The 'variables' of a system may increase and decrease but remain what they are.

Parts of a system may themselves be systems with their own structure and dynamics. This approach is taken by hierarchy theory in which nested systems each contribute as parts to higher level systems (O'Neill *et al.*, 1986). This allows us to separate domains for analysis. However, the reverse process, the defining and transforming of the subsystems by the higher level, is rarely examined. Much statistical analysis, for instance in epidemiology, separates the independent variables which are determined outside the system from the dependent variables which are determined by them. The independent variables might be rainfall or family income; the dependent variable might be the prevalence of malaria or the suicide rate. In contrast, systems approaches recognize the feedbacks that give mutual determination: predators eat their prey, prey feed their predators; prices increase production, production leads to surpluses that lower prices; snow cools the earth by reflecting away more sunlight, and then a cooler earth has more snow. In feedback loops, changes in each variable are in a sense the causes of the changes in the others. What then happens to causation? What makes one 'cause' more fundamental than another?

We can attempt to answer this question in two ways. First, we may ask where a particular pattern of change was initiated at a particular time. For instance we might ask of a predator/prey system, why does the abundance of both predator and prey vary over a five hundred mile gradient? We can analyze the feedback relationship to show that if the environmental differences along the gradient enter the system by way of the prey, say through temperature increases increasing its growth rate, this will increase the predator population so that the two variables are positively correlated. But if the environmental differences enter by way of the predator, perhaps because the predator is itself hunted more in some places than others, then increases in hunting reduce the predator and therefore increase the prey. This gives us a negative correlation between them. Therefore if we observe a positive correlation we can say that the variation is driven from the prey end and if a negative correlation then the variation is driven from the predator end. The prey mediates the action of the environment and is the 'cause' of the observed pattern in the one system, the predator in the other. Similarly in a study of the capitalist world economy, I examined production and prices during the 1960s and 1970s and found that the major agricultural commodities exhibited a positive correlation between production or yield per acre and prices on the world market. This supports the view that price fluctuations arise mostly in the larger economy and affect production decisions rather than appear as responses to fluctuations in production, and this despite obvious and dramatic changes of production due to the weather or pests.

Whether this is generally true or not is an empirical question. In a complex network of variables the driving forces for change may originate anywhere. When we attempt to ask, 'Does economics or geopolitics determine foreign policy?' or 'Is the content of TV driven by sales or ideology?' the question is unanswerable in general. The complex network of mutual determinations requires a complex answer that is hinted at in the awkward term 'overdetermination' which recognizes causal processes as operating simultaneously on different levels and through different pathways. Or it brings us back to Hegel: the truth is the whole.

Then where is the locus of historical materialism? Doesn't it require that the economy determine society?

No! 'The economy' as a set of factors in social life has no inherent priority over any of the other myriad interpenetrating processes. Sometimes it is determinant of particular events, sometimes not. As long as we remain within the domain of a system's network-tracing pathways, everything influences everything else by some pathway or other. Changes in the productive technology change economic organization and class relations and beliefs about the world, but changes in the technology arise through the implementation of ideas, and exist in thought before they are made flesh. Or as the founding document of UNESCO stated, 'Since wars are made in the minds of men...' Then is social life a product of intellect? Or is intellect an expression of class and gender? Approached in this way, each side mediates the other, and it would be dogmatic to assign absolute priority to either one.

But this is quite different from identifying *the mode of production and reproduction*, which is present not as a 'factor' in the network but as the network itself. It is the structure of that network, that mode, that defines workers and capitalists as the actors or 'variables' in the network, makes it possible for sexism to have commercial value, makes legislation a political activity, or allows major events to be initiated by the caprices of monarchs. It is the context within which the various mediations play themselves out and transform each other rather than a factor among factors.

Goal-seeking

The third quality of systems, purposefulness, also betrays the origin of systems theory. The outcomes are evaluated for their correspondence to the built-in purpose, while deviations from that purpose are seen as non-adaptive, contradictory and self-destructive behaviors. These appear as system failures. The engineer can discard or a manager can reorganize the structures that lead to them. But in reality only some systems are purposeful even when they are constructed to satisfy some purpose. In others, while the 'elements' are actors each with their own purposes and may be said to seek goals, the system as a whole does not.

Dialectical 'wholes' are not defined by some organizing principle such as harmony or balance or maximization of efficiency. In my view, a system is characterized by its structured set of contradictory processes that gives meaning to its elements, maintains the temporary coherence of the whole and also eventually transforms it into something else, dissolves it into another system, or leads to its disintegration.

Outcomes

Once mathematical systems theory defines a set of variables and inter-relations it then asks the simple mathematical question, What is the future trajectory of those variables starting from such and such initial conditions? From then on, all depends on the mathematical agility of the analyst or the computer program to come up with 'solutions' of the equations. A solution is the path of the variables. The desired result is prediction, the correspondence between the theoretical and observed values of the variables.

There are only a few possible outcomes of equations:

(a) The variables may increase or decrease out of bounds. This may mean a real explosion, disrupting the system. But it can also mean that past a certain point the equations are not valid.
(b) The variables may reach a stable equilibrium. It then remains there unless perturbed, and returns toward equilibrium after a perturbation. If the processes include randomness, then a solution may be a stable probability distribution.
(c) There may be more than one equilibrium, in which case not all of the equilibria are stable. Each stable equilibrium is the end result for the variables that start out 'near' that equilibrium, within some range called its basin of attraction. The basins of attraction around

the equilibria are separated by boundaries where there are unstable equilibria. The outcome then depends on the starting place, and the variables move toward the equilibrium in whose basin of attraction they start out.

(d) The variables may show or approach cyclic behavior, in which case how quickly the variables cycle and the magnitude of the fluctuations describe the solution. A cyclical pattern also has its basin of attraction, the range of initial conditions from which the variables approach that cycle.

(e) The trajectories may remain bounded but instead of approaching an equilibrium or a regular periodicity show seemingly erratic pathways, sometimes looking periodic for a while and then abruptly moving away, and different initial conditions no matter how similar may give quite different trajectories. This is referred to as chaos although in fact it has its own regularities.

The behavior of a system will depend on the equations themselves, the parameters and the initial conditions. Much of the content of systems theory is the description of the relations between the assumptions of the model and the outcomes for the variables, or identifying the procedures for validating the models.

The outcomes are expressed as quantitative changes in the variables. This is an extremely useful activity for making predictions or deciding upon interventions in the system or system design. But it is also limiting, and imposes constraints on the models. Most models require specifying the equations and estimating the parameters and variables. Therefore those that are not readily measureable are likely to be omitted. For instance, we can write compartment models for epidemics that take as variables the numbers of individuals in each compartment, those who are susceptible, infected but not infective yet, infective, or recovered and immune. We make some plausible assumptions about the disease (rates of contagion, duration of latent and infective periods, rate of loss of immunity) and turn the crank, watching as numbers shift from one compartment to another. Then we can ask questions such as these: Will the disease persist? How long will it take to pass the peak? How many people will die before it is over? What would be the effect of immunizing x percent of the children? We could add complications of differences due to age and even subdivide the population into classes with different parameters.

Contagion also depends on people's behavior, the level of panic in the population. This changes in the course of the epidemic as people observe acquaintances getting sick and dying, and may take protective action. But how much experience is needed to change behavior? How much panic before they will lose their jobs rather than face infection? What degrees of freedom do people have? How long will an altered behavior last? Do people really believe that what they do will affect what happens to them? Will they remember for next time? Since we have neither the equations for describing these aspects nor measurements of panic or historical horizon or economic vulnerability, such considerations will not usually appear in the models but at best only in the footnotes. In recent years, modeling has become a recognized major research activity. But this has had the effect of reducing modeling to the quantitative models described earlier.

Most systems modelers take it for granted that quantitative inform-ation ('hard' data) is preferable to qualitative ('soft') information and prefer prediction or fitting of data to understanding. In their view of science, progress goes simply from the vague, intuitive and qualitative to the precise, rigorous and quantitative. The highest achievement is the algorithm, the rule of procedure which can be applied automatically by anyone to a whole class of situations, untouched by human minds. That is the rationale behind Maynard Smith's suggestion that systems theory replaces dialectics. Marxists argue for a more complex and non-hierarchical relation between quantitative and qualitative approaches to the world.

A much smaller effort goes into qualitative systems modeling which would allow us to deal with these 'soft' questions. Instead of the goal of describing a system fully in order to predict its future completely or to 'optimize' its behavior, we ask how much we can get away with not knowing and still understand the system? Whereas the engineering systems presume rather complete control over the parameters so that we can talk about optimizing the parameters, the systems we are most concerned with in nature and in society are not under our control. We try to understand them in order to identify the directions in which to push but do not trust our models to be more than useful insights into the structure or process.

Dialecticians take as the objects of our interest the processes in complex systems. Our primary concern is understanding them in order to know what to do. We ask two fundamental questions about the systems: why are things the way they are instead of a little bit different and why are things the way they are instead of very different, and from these the practical questions of how to intervene in these complex processes to make things better for us. That is, we seek practical and theoretical understanding rather than a good fit. Precision and prediction may or may not be useful in this process, but they are not the goals of it.

The Newtonian answer to the first question is, things remain the way they are because nothing much is happening to them. Stasis is the normal state of affairs, and change must be accounted for. Order is the desired state, and disruption is treated as disaster. A dialectical view begins from the opposite end: change is universal and much is happening to change everything. Therefore equilibrium and stasis are special situations that have to be explained. All 'things' (objects or patterns of objects or processes) are constantly subject to outside influences that would change them. They are also all heterogeneous internally, and the internal dynamics is a continuing source of change. Yet 'things' do retain their identities long enough to be named and sometimes persist for very long times indeed. Some of them, much too long.

The dynamic answer to the first question is homeostasis, the self-regulation that is observed in physiology, ecology, climatology, the economy and indeed in all systems that show any persistence. Homeostasis takes place through the actions of positive and negative feedback loops. If an initial impact sets processes in motion that diminish that initial impact, we refer to it as negative feedback, while if the processes magnify the original change the feedback is positive. Thus positive and negative applied to feedback have nothing to do with whether we like them or not. When positive feedbacks have undesirable results that increase out of bounds, we refer to them as vicious circles.

It is often said that negative feedback stabilizes and positive feedback destabilizes a system. But this is not always the case. If positive feedback exceeds the negative then the system is unstable in the technical sense that it will move away from equilibrium. In that case, an increase of negative feedback is stabilizing. But if the indirect negative feedbacks by way of long loops of causation are too strong compared to the shorter negative feedbacks the system is also unstable and will oscillate. Then positive feedback loops can have a stabilizing effect by offsetting the excessive long negative feedbacks. Long loops behave like delays in the system. The significance of a feedback loop depends on its context in the whole. The complex systems of concern to us usually have both negative and positive feedbacks.

Homeostasis does not imply benevolence. A negative feedback loop should not be seen as the elementary unit of analysis or of design. A simple equation may give the appearance of 'self-regulation' in the sense that when a variable gets too big it is reduced and when it gets too small it is increased. But the reduction and the increase may have quite different causes. An increase in wages may lead to employers cutting the labor force, increasing unemployment and thus making it easier to reduce wages. A decrease in wages may lead to labor militancy that restores some of the cuts. The outcome (if nothing else happens) is a partial restoration of the original situation. Neither party is seeking homeostasis, and the wage/employment feedback is not designed or pursued by anyone to maintain economic stability. It is simply one possible manifestation of class struggle. Thus homeostasis does not imply functionalism, a view which assigns purpose to the feedback loop as such.

This distinction is important, especially when we examine apparently unsuccessful attempts to achieve socially recognized goals. Meadows *et al.* present the problem as follows:

> This book is about overshoot. Human society has overshot its limits, for the same reason that other overshoots occur. Changes are too fast. Signals are late, incomplete, distorted, ignored or denied. Momentum is great. Responses are slow ... (1992, 2).

From this systems-theoretic point of view, the socialized earth's error-correcting feedbacks are inadequate. And if you assume that social processes are aimed at sustainable, healthful, equitable relations among people and with the rest of nature, then the defect is in the feedback loops, the mechanisms for achieving these goals. But if agriculture fails to eliminate hunger, if resource use is not modulated to protect people's health and long-term survival, it is not because of the failings of a mechanism aimed at these goals. Rather, most of world agriculture is aimed at producing marketable commodities, resources are used to make profits and the welfare effects are side effects of the economy. It is the contradictions among opposing forces (and between those of the ecology and the economy) rather than the failure of a good try by inadequate information systems and deficient homeostatic loops that are responsible for much of the present suffering and the threat of more.

When a change occurs in a component (or variable) of a system, that initial change percolates through a network of interacting variables. It is amplified along some pathways and buffered along others. In the end, some of the variables (not necessarily the ones that received the initial change or those nearest the point of impact) have been altered, while others remain pretty much the way they were. Therefore we identify 'sinks' in the system, variables that absorb a large part of the impact of the external shock and other aspects of the system that remain unchanged, protected by the sinks. We can even have situations where things change in ways that contradict our common sense, where, for example, adding nitrogen to a pond can lower the nitrogen level or an inflated military budget undermines national security. (This outcome depends on the location of positive feedbacks within a system.)

But 'unchanged' requires some further examination. The 'variable' is not a thing but some aspect of a thing, perhaps the numbers of individuals in a population, not 'the population'.

One simple system consists of a predator that feeds on a single prey. All else is treated as 'external'. It is sometimes the case that the predator is regulated only by the prey. Then a change in conditions that acts on the reproduction or development rate or mortality of the prey directly, that is not due to the predator, will be passed along to the predator. Increased prey leads to increased predators and this reduces the prey back toward its original value. The 'prey' variable may remain unchanged while the predator population either increases in response to increased availability of prey or diminishes if fewer prey are produced. The predator variable acts as a sink in this system. Tracing the ups and downs of predator and prey finishes the tasks of the systems analysis.

But what I referred to as 'prey' is really only the numbers of prey. If prey reproduction has increased with more food but the population of prey has not changed, it is because the prey are being produced faster and consumed faster. That is, the prey population is younger. Individuals may be smaller and therefore more vulnerable to heat stress. They may be more mobile, migrating to find unoccupied sites. If the prey are mosquitoes, a shorter life span may mean that they do not spread as much disease even if there are more of them. They may spend more time in cool moist shelters where they meet additional predators and the model has to be changed. Natural selection in a younger population might focus more on those qualities that affect the survival and early reproduction of the young. Thus the variable, 'prey', that was unchanged in the model can be actively transformed in many directions not dealt with in the model.

The particulars of the dynamics, the relations among the positive and negative feedbacks in a system, sources and sinks, connectivity among variables, delays along pathways and their effects are all in the domain of systems theory in the narrow sense. The parts of the system become the variables of models, and equations are proposed for their dynamics. Systems theory studies these equations. Mathematical rules have been discovered for determining when the system will approach some equilibrium condition or oscillate 'permanently', that is, as long as the assumptions still hold.

Modern computational methods allow for the numerical solutions of large numbers of simultaneous equations. The parameters are measured, the initial conditions of the variables are estimated or assumed. (The distinction between parameters and variables is that the parameters are assumed to be determined outside the boundaries of the 'system' and are only inputs, while the variables change each other within the 'system'.) The computer then calculates successive steps in the process and comes up with numbers, the predicted states of the variables at different times. The numerical results are compared to observations. If the correspondence is good enough, it is assumed that the model is valid, that it 'accounts for' the behavior of the system being studied, or 90 percent of the behavior, or whatever level we decide is acceptable. If not, more data may be collected to get better estimates of parameters or the equations may be modified.

However, systems theory starts with the variables as givens. It deals with the problems of selecting variables only in a very limited way. When we approach any real system of any complexity, the question of what the right variables are to include in the model is itself quite complex. It is the classical Marxist problem of abstraction (see Ollman (1993) for a detailed examination of dialectical abstraction). Some practical systems modeling criteria are reciprocal interaction, commensurate timescales, measurability, variables that belong to the same discipline and can be represented by equations of change. The system should be large enough to include the major pathways of interaction, with identification of where external influences enter the network. Systems theory makes use of growing computing capacity to give numerical solutions to the differential or difference equations that describe the dynamics. In order to have precise outcomes it is necessary to have good estimates of the parameters, things like the reproductive rate of a population, the intensity of predation, the half-life of a molecule, or the cost/price ratio in an economic production function. The gathering of these measurements is difficult, so that estimates are often taken from the published literature rather than made afresh. Parameters that cannot be measured readily cannot be used.

Once variables are selected, they are then treated as unitary 'things', whose only property is quantity. The mathematics will tell us which quantities increase, which decrease, which fluctuate or remain unchanging. The source of change is either in the dynamics of the variables in interaction or in perturbation from outside the system. ('Outside the system' means outside the model. In a model of species interactions a genetic change within a species is regarded as an external event, since it is external to the demographic dynamics although it is located inside the cells of the bodies of individual members of a population.) But all variables are themselves 'systems' with internal heterogeneity and structure, with an internal dynamics that is influenced by events on the system scale and also changing the behavior of the variables. Thus dialectics emphasizes the provisional nature of the system and the transitory nature of the systems model.

The variables of a system change at different rates, so that some are indicators of long-term history while others are more responsive to the most recent conditions. Thus in nutritional surveys, we use the height of children for their age as an indicator of long-term nutritional status, the growth over a lifetime, while weight for height indicates food intake over recent months or weeks and therefore measures acute malnutrition. Because each variable reflects its history on its own timescale, they are generally not in 'balance' or harmony. Ideology need not 'correspond' to class position, political power to economic power or forests to climate. Rather, the links between variables in a system identify processes: ideology responding, not corresponding, to class position, economic power enhancing political power, political power being used to consolidate economic power, colder climate trees such as spruce and hemlock gradually displacing the oak and beech of a warmer period. But all of these processes take time, so that a system does not show a passive correlation among its parts but a network of processes constantly transforming each other. In Darwinian evolutionary theory both the adaptedness of a species to its surroundings and its non-adaptedness are required, the former showing the outcomes of natural selection and the latter identifying it as a process that is never complete and showing the history of the species. Complete adaptedness would have been an argument for special creation, not evolution, proclaiming a harmony that manifests the benevolent wisdom of the Creator.

The second question, why things are the way they are instead of very different, is a question of history, evolution and development. It is concerned with the long-term processes that change the character of systems. The variables involved in long-term change may overlap with the short-range ones, but are not in general the same. Many of the short-term processes are reversible, oscillating according to conditions without accumulating to contribute to the long run.

At any one moment the short-term events are strong processes, temporarily overwhelming some of the long-term directional changes that are imperceptible in the short run. Yet the two scales are not independent. The reversible short-term oscillations through which a system confronts changing circumstances have themselves evolved and continue to evolve as a result of their functioning in the long run. And they leave long-term residues: the breathing in and breathing out of ordinary respiration may also result in the accumulation of toxic or abrasive materials in the lung; the repetitive cycles of agricultural production can exhaust the soil; the periodicity of the tides also has its long-term effect of lengthening the day through tidal friction; the buying and selling of commodities can result in the concentration of capital. Long-term changes alter the circumstances to which the short-term system responds as well as the means available for that response.

Here mathematical systems theory is less useful, since the mathematics is much better developed for studying steady-state systems than evolving ones. (The work of Ilya Prigogine on dissipative systems is only a partial exception to this limitation.)

Conclusion

Systems analysis is one of the techniques for policy making. As its technical side becomes more sophisticated it also is usually less accessible to the non-specialist. Therefore it often reinforces a technocratic approach to public policy, and does that in the service of those who can afford to contract its services. The ruling class and its representatives are referred to in the trade by the more neutral term 'decision makers'. This is of course not unique to applied systems theory, but is a common correlate of its increasing use within a managerial framework. A special effort has to be made to counteract this tendency, to demystify the study of complexity and to democratize even complex decision making. The Soviet author Manasyev, before he embraced the 'free market', wrote an interesting book, *The Scientific Management of Society*, which emphasized the systems-theoretic aspects of planning as a technocratic procedure with only perfunctory nods in the direction of popular control of the planning process as a whole.

Systems theory can be understood as a 'moment' in the investigation of scientific problems within complex systems by means of mathematical models. Its value depends in large measure on the context of its use, and here dialectics has a broader role that can inform that use:

1. The posing of the problem, the domain to be explored, what is taken as the 'fundamental elements' and what as the givens of the

problem, the boundaries that are not questioned. To do this well requires not only a substantive knowledge of the objects of interest, their dynamics and history, and an understanding of process. There is also frank partisanship, since what is taken as given and what is assumed to be 'fundamental' is a political as much as a technical problem. For instance, a model of a society that consists of atomic individuals making decisions in the void cannot escape the dead end of bourgeois individualist reductionism no matter how elegantly the mathematics is developed. An economic model that consists of prices and production and profits and such can give projections of trajectories of prices and production and profits and such (at best; in reality they do this very badly). But it will never lead to an understanding of economics as social relations.

Sometimes the variables are given to the systems analyst: the species in a forest, the network of production and prices, the gizmos in a radio, the molecules in an organism. That is, the 'system' is presented to us as a problem to be solved rather than as an objective entity to be understood. But often it is presented more vaguely: How do we understand a rain forest or the health of a nation? The way in which a problem is framed, the selection of the system and subsystem is prior to systems theory but crucial to dialectics. A dialectical approach recognizes that the 'system' is an intellectual construct designed to elucidate some aspects of reality but necessarily ignoring and even distorting others. We ask what the consequences would be of different ways of formulating a problem and of bounding an object of interest.

2. Selection of the appropriate mathematical formalisms (equations, graph diagrams, random or deterministic models etc.). While technical criteria influence these choices there are also issues·of the purposes of the model, the partially conflicting goals of precision, generality, realism, manageability and understanding. The important thing here is not to be limited by the technical traditions of a field but to examine all these choices not only for hidden assumptions but also for their implications.

3. Interpretation of results. Here qualitative understanding is an important supplement to numerical results. In the course of an investigation, we may go from vague qualitative notions through quantitative explorations to more precise qualitative understanding. This is only one example of non-progressivist, non-linear thinking that is captured in our 'mysterious' negation of the negation.

Progress is not from qualitative to quantitative. Quantitative description of a system is not superior to qualitative understanding. When approaching complexity, it is not possible to measure 'everything', plug it all into a model and retrieve intelligible results. For one thing, 'everything' is too big. Qualitative understanding is essential in establishing quantitative models. It intrudes into the interpretation of the results. The task of mathematics is to make the arcane obvious and even trivial. That is, it must educate the intuition so that confronted with a daunting complexity, we can grasp the crucial features that determine its dynamics, know where to look for the features that make it what it is, suspect mainstream questions as well as answers.

A dialectical understanding of process in general looks at the opposing forces acting on the state of a system. This is now accepted more or less in ordinary scientific practice. Excitatory and inhibitory neurons, sympathetic and parasympathetic stimulation, opposing selection forces or an opposition between selective and random processes are all part of the tool kit of modern science. However, this has still not been generalized to thinking of process as contradiction.

4. When does the system itself change and invalidate the model?
   We need a permanent awareness of the model as a human intellec-tual construct that is more or less useful within certain bounds and then can become nonsense. The internal workings of the variables in a model, the dynamics of the model itself or the development of the science eventually reveals all models as inaccurate, limited and misleading. But this does not destroy the distinction between models that are terribly wrong from the start and those that have relative validity.

5. Structures doubts. Doubt is an essential part of the search for under-standing. There are areas of science that have been consolidated to the point of near certainty. Others are border regions of our knowledge where there is a plurality of insights and opinions and conflicting evidence. Here doubt and criticism are essential. And beyond that the unknown, where we have divergent intuitions and where our biases can roam freely. But where we have the same doubts persisting for long periods this is not a sign of a postmodern pluralist democracy but of stagnation. Useful doubt is not the expression of an esthetic of indecision or a response to the petulant reproach of 'you're so damn sure of yourself!' or an acknowledgement that truth is 'relative', but a historical perspective on error, bias, and limitation.

The art of modeling requires the sensitivity to decide when in the development of a science a previously necessary simplification has become a gross oversimplification and a brake to further progress. This sensitivity depends on an understanding of science as a social process and of each moment as an episode in its history, a dialectical sensitivity that is not taught in the 'objectivist' traditions of mechanistic systems analysis.

Thus systems theory is best understood as reflecting the dual nature of science: part of the generic evolution of humanity's understanding of the world and a product of a specific social structure that supports and constrains science and directs it toward the goals of its owners. On the one hand it is a 'moment' in the investigation of complex systems, the place between the formulation of a problem and the interpretation of its solution where mathematical modeling can make the obscure obvious. On the other hand it is the attempt of a reductionist scientific tradition to come to terms with complexity, non-linearity and change through sophisticated mathematical and computational techniques, a groping toward a more dialectical understanding that is held back both by its philosophical biases and the institutional and economic contexts of its development.

Note

1. The term 'dialectical materialism' is often associated with the particular rigid exposition of it by Stalin and its dogmatic applications in Soviet apologetics, while 'dialectical' by itself is a respectable academic term. At a time when the retreat from materialism has reached epidemic proportions it is worthwhile to insist on the unity of materialism and dialectics, and to recapture the full vibrancy of this approach to understanding and acting on the world. Here I use materialist dialectics and dialectical materialism as synonyms.

References

Ashby, W. Ross. 1960. *Design for a Brain*. New York: Wiley.

James, H. M., N. Nichols and R. S. Phillips, eds. 1947. *The Theory of Servomechanisms*. New York: McGraw-Hill.

Levins, Richard. 1966. 'The Strategy of Model Building in Population Science'. *American Scientist*, 54: 421–31.

Maynard Smith, John. 1986. 'Molecules are not Enough' (review of *The Dialectical Biologist*, by R. Levins and R. Lewontin). *London Review of Books*, 6 February.

Meadows, Donella H., Dennis L. Meadows and Jorgen Randers. 1992. *Beyond the Limits: Confronting Global Collapse Envisioning a Sustainable Future*. White River Jct., VT: Chelsea Green Publishing Company.

Ollman, Bertell. 1993. *Dialectical* Investigations. New York: Routledge.
O'Neill, R. V., D. L. DeAngelis, J. B. Waide and T. E. H. Allen. 1986. *A Hierarchical Concept of Ecosystems*. Princeton, New Jersey: Princeton University Press.
Therborn, Goran. 1978. *What Does the Ruling Class Do When it Rules?* London: New Left Books.
von Bertalanffy, L. 1950. 'An Outline of General Systems Theory'. *The British Journal for the Philosophy of Science*, 1: 2.

4

The Dialectics of Nature and Marxist Ecology

John Bellamy Foster

For 'Western Marxism' – a term introduced by Maurice Merleau-Ponty in 1955 in his *Adventures of the Dialectic* (1973) to describe the philosophical tendency stemming from Georg Lukács' *History and Class Consciousness* (1971; originally published in 1923) – no concept internal to Marxism has been more antithetical to the genuine development of historical materialism than the 'dialectics of nature'. Commonly attributed to Engels rather than Marx, this concept is often seen as the *differentia specifica* that beginning in the 1920s separated the official Marxism of the Soviet Union from Western Marxism. Yet, as Lukács, who played the leading role in questioning the concept of the dialectic of nature, was later to admit, Western Marxism's rejection of it struck at the very heart of the classical Marxist ontology – that of Marx no less than Engels.

The question of the dialectics of nature has therefore constituted a major contradiction within Marxist thought, dividing its traditions. On the one hand, the powerful dialectical imagination that characterized Western Marxism rested on a historical-cultural frame of analysis focusing on human praxis that excluded non-human nature. On the other hand, Marx's own dialectical and materialist ontology was predicated on the ultimate unity between nature and society, constituting a single reality and requiring a single science. Marx's original method had pointed to the complex interconnections between society and nature, utilizing a dialectical frame in analyzing both—although the nature dialectic was much less explicitly developed within his thought than the social dialectic. The unbridgeable chasm between nature and society that was to arise with Western Marxism was entirely absent in his work (as were the positivistic tendencies of what became official Marxism in the Soviet Union).

In recent decades, the larger consequences associated with the Western Marxist repudiation of the dialectics of nature have been highlighted by the growth of Marxist ecology, which is concerned with the complex coevolutionary relations between society and nature. Yet, even as it has brought this weakness of the Western Marxist tradition to the fore, the growth of Marxist ecology has provided new ways of transcending the contradiction, building on both classical Marxist thought and new understandings of the material relations between humanity and nature emerging in the context of a planetary ecological crisis.

Lukács and the dialectics of nature

The birth of 'Western Marxism' as a distinct philosophical tradition has commonly been traced to Georg Lukács' famous footnote 6 in Chapter 1 of *History and Class Consciousness*, in which he rejected any extension of the dialectical method from society to nature:

> It is of the first importance to realize that the method is limited here to the realms of history and society. The misunderstandings that arise from Engels' account of dialectics can in the main be put down to the fact that Engels – following Hegel's mistaken lead – extended the method to apply also to nature. However, the crucial determinants of dialectics – the interaction of subject and object, the unity of theory and practice, the historical changes in the reality underlying the categories as the root cause of changes in thought, etc. – are absent from our knowledge of nature (see also Jacoby, 1983, 525; Lukács, 1971, 24; and Vogel, 1996, 15).

Lukács suggests here that the dialectical method in its full sense necessarily involves reflexivity, the identical subject–object of history. The subject (the human being) recognizes in the object of his/her activity the results of humanity's own historical self-creation. We can understand history, as Vico said, because we have 'made' it. The dialectic thus becomes a powerful theoretical means of discovery rooted in the reality of human praxis itself, which allows us to uncover the totality of social mediations. Yet, such inner, reflexive knowledge arising from human practice, he insists, is not available where external nature is concerned. There one is faced with the inescapable Kantian thing-in-itself. Hence, the 'crucial determinants of dialectics' are inapplicable to the natural realm; there can be no dialectics of nature – as a method – equivalent to the dialectics of history and society. Engels – following Hegel's mistaken lead – was therefore wrong in extending 'the method to apply also to nature'.

As Lukács observed a few years later in a 1925 review of Bukharin's *Historical Materialism*, 'Engels reduced the dialectic to "the science of the general laws of motion, both of the external world and of human thought"' (1972, 139).[1] By applying the dialectical method to nature, Engels had overstepped its proper realm of application.

This prohibition against the extending dialectic to nature, which was to become a distinguishing feature of Western Marxism following Lukács' lead, had its counterpart in a prohibition against the undialectical introduction of the methods of natural science into the realm of the social science and humanities, that is against positivism. Engels' mistake, as Lukács suggested, was to have argued in *Anti-Dühring*, that 'nature is the proof of dialectics', and hence that the dialectic could be grasped by studying the development of natural science – thus the method of the latter could be a key to the method for the analysis of society itself (Marx and Engels, 1975, vol. 25, 23). In his critique of Bukharin's *Historical Materialism*, Lukács pointed to the way that Bukharin, following Engels' lead, had embraced a 'contemplative materialism' that drew largely on the external, objective view of nature – and then attempted to apply this to human society. 'Instead, of making a historical-materialist critique of natural sciences and their methods', Bukharin, Lukács wrote, extended 'these methods to the study of society without hesitation, uncritically, unhistorically, and undialectically' – thus falling prey to positivism and the reification of both nature and society (Lukács, 1972, 142).

Antonio Gramsci, who along with Lukács and Karl Korsch, helped found Western Marxism as a philosophical tendency in the 1920s, was likewise critical of Bukharin's *Historical Materialism* for its tendency to impose natural-scientific views on society. But Gramsci, though skeptical about the dialectics of nature, was nonetheless disturbed by the potential implications of what seemed to be Lukács' outright rejection of the concept in *History and Class Consciousness*:

> It would appear that Lukács maintains that one can speak of the dialectic only for the history of men and not for nature. He might be right and he might be wrong. If his assertion presupposes a dualism between nature and man he is wrong because he is falling into a conception of nature proper to religion and to Graeco-Christian philosophy and also to idealism which does not in reality succeed in unifying and relating man and nature to each other except verbally. But if human history should be conceived also as the history of nature

(also by means of the history of science) how can the dialectic be separated from science? Lukács, in reaction to the baroque theories of the *Popular Manual* [Bukharin's *Historical Materialism*], has fallen into the opposite error, into a form of idealism (Gramsci, 1971, 448).

Yet, for Gramsci too the dialectic of nature remained outside his analysis. He rejected any tendency to 'make science the base of life' or to suggest that the philosophy of praxis 'needs philosophical supports outside of itself' (1995, 293). In his philosophical practice the question of the dialectics of nature and the materialist conception of nature remain unexplored.

The seriousness of this contradiction for Marxist theory as a whole cannot be overstated. As Lucio Colletti observed in *Marxism and Hegel*, a vast literature 'has always agreed' that differences over (1) the existence of an objective world independent of consciousness (i.e. philosophical materialism or realism), and (2) the existence of a dialectic of matter (or of nature) constituted 'the two main distinguishing features between "Western Marxism" and "dialectical materialism"' (1973, 191–92). Lukács launched 'Western Marxism' in *History and Class Consciousness* by calling into question both of these epistemological propositions (the first through his critical identification of reification and objectification and hence his Hegelian-Marxist critique of the Subject–Object distinction, the second through his reservations about the dialectics of nature). Yet in a dramatic turnaround in his later years, Lukács was to reinstate the very principles that he had earlier rejected, on the grounds that he had violated Marx's own materialist ontology. Hence, Lukács was both the founder of Western Marxism and its most potent critic. Both through the contradictions of his thought and through his repudiation of his earlier views, he guaranteed that the problem of the dialectics of nature in Western Marxist thought would be raised primarily as a problem of his own philosophy.

Even in *History and Class Consciousness* itself there were signs that Lukács' rejection of the dialectic of nature was not absolute. Thus at the end of the most important essay in his book, 'Reification and the Consciousness of the Proletariat', Lukács wrote,

Hegel does perceive clearly at times that the dialectics of nature can never become anything more exalted than a dialectics of movement witnessed by the detached observer, as the subject cannot be integrated into the dialectical process, at least not at the stage reached hitherto.... From this we deduce the necessity of separating the merely objective dialectics of nature from those of society. For in the dialectics of society the subject is included in the reciprocal relation in which theory and practice become dialectical with reference to one another. (It goes without saying that the growth of *knowledge* about nature is a social phenomenon and therefore is to be included in the second dialectical type.) Moreover, if the dialectical method is to be consolidated concretely it is essential that the different types of dialectics should be set out in concrete fashion.... However, even to outline a typology of these dialectical forms would be well beyond the scope of this study (1971, 207).

From this it is clear that Lukács that did not entirely abandon the notion of the dialectics of nature even at the time of *History and Class Consciousness* but rather saw it as limited in the sense that it could never be 'more exalted than a dialectics of movement witnessed by the detached observer' and hence was 'merely objective dialectics', lacking an internal subject. Moreover, his criticism of this 'merely objective dialectics of nature' excluded the knowledge of nature, which was a social phenomenon and so fell within the dialectics of society. The larger 'typology' of 'dialectical forms' that Lukács referred to here was never concretely taken up in his analysis. To make matters even more complicated, in a review of the work of Karl Wittfogel published two years after *History and Class Consciousness*, Lukács stated, 'For the Marxist as a historical dialectician both *nature* and all the forms in which it is mastered in theory and practice are *social categories*; and to believe that one can detect anything supra-historical or supra-social in this context is to disqualify oneself as a Marxist' (1972, 144). But this would in itself seem to deny the possibility of an 'objective dialectics of nature' – or the Marxist nature of such an inquiry.

Recently, with the discovery of Lukács' *Tailism and the Dialectic*, written two or three years after the publication of *History and Class Consciousness*, and presenting a defense of that work in the face of the harsh criticisms to which it was subjected by Soviet Marxists associated with dialectical materialism, a more detailed and nuanced look at the early Lukács' position on the dialectics of nature has become available. By quoting extensively from the section on 'The Dialectics of Nature', we can see the full complexity of Lukács' position:

Self-evidently society arose *from* nature. Self-evidently nature and its laws existed *before* society (that is to say before humans). Self-evidently the dialectic *could* not possibly be effective as an *objective principle of development* of society, if it were not already effective as a principle of development of nature before society, if it did not already *objectively exist*. From that, however, follows neither that social development could produce no new, equally objective forms of movement, dialectical moments, nor that the dialectical moments in the development of nature would be *knowable* without the mediation of these new social dialectical forms....

This [metabolic] *exchange* of matter with nature [i.e. production] cannot possibly be achieved even on the most primitive level – without possessing a certain degree of objectively correct knowledge about the processes of nature (which exist prior to people and function independently of them).... The type and degree of this knowledge depends on the economic structure of society....

I am of the opinion that our knowledge of nature is socially mediated, because its material foundation is socially mediated; and so I remain true to the Marxian formulation of the method of historical materialism: 'it is social being that determines consciousness'....

The sentence [in footnote 6 of Chapter 1 of *History and Class Consciousness* where changes in concepts accompanying changes in reality are referred to] means that a change in material (the reality that underlies thought) must take place, in order that a change in thought may follow.... That objective dialectics are in reality independent of humans and were there before the emergence of people, is precisely what was *asserted* in this passage; but...for the dialectic as knowledge...thinking people are necessary (Lukács, 2000, 102–7).

Here Lukács contends that even in his controversial criticism of Engels in his footnote to Chapter 1 of *History and Class Consciousness* he assumed the existence of an objective dialectic of material change (both natural and social) that formed the condition for the change in concepts – the rise of *dialectical knowledge*. The issue for him then is not whether an objective dialectic exists as a process independent of human beings and containing within it matter and motion, contradiction, the interdependence of opposites, the transformation of quality and quantity, the mediation of totality, and so on. Rather he contends that this objective dialectic as such is inaccessible apart from the working out of the metabolic relation between human beings and nature as evident in the development of human social production. Dialectical knowledge is necessarily socially mediated, and does not constitute an immediate relation to nature. It is a product of human praxis. Moreover, the implic-ation of Lukács' whole argument up to this point is that insofar as the dialectic of nature does not arise directly out of the transformations resulting from the metabolic exchange with nature (i.e., in so far as it is not a social dialectic in which nature is simply a part) it can take no form 'more exalted' than a contemplative materialism or contemplative dialectic – 'merely objective dialectics'. There is thus a sense in which the dialectical method in its full sense can never be applied to nature except as mediated by social production, that is praxis (see Burkett, 2001).

Marx, Lukács observed in *Tailism and the Dialectic*, had suggested in letters to Ferdinand Lassalle (December 21, 1857 and February 22, 1858) that the ancient materialists Heraclitus and Epicurus created dialectical systems, but that these lacked self-conscious awareness of themselves as such. It is only with the emergence of historical materialism (i.e. with Marx himself), Lukács contends, that there arises a self-conscious dialect-ical conception resting on materialist foundations. And it is this mater-ialistically apprehended dialectic, which has now become 'for-us' and not 'only-in-itself', that is able to reveal for the first time the real basis of natural science and of knowledge in general. Such a self-conscious mater-ialist dialectic is knowledge that is aware that it is socially mediated by historical production or the '*capitalist* exchange of matter with nature'. It therefore becomes possible on this basis to apprehend how other societies with very different productive relations (different exchanges of matter with nature) would generate very different conceptual under-standings. The historical recognition of the material evolution of society and of human consciousness thus becomes possible (Lukács, 2000, 129–31; Marx, 1979, 418, 422).

In his 1967 'Preface to the New Edition' of *History and Class Conscious-ness*, in which he repudiated many of his earlier views, Lukács is less explicit on the question of the dialectic of nature, but condemns his early work for arguing 'in a number of cases that nature is a soci-etal category'. He strongly criticizes *History and Class Consciousness* for narrowing down the economic/materialist problem 'because its basic Marxist category, labour as the mediator of the metabolic interaction between society and nature, is missing.... It is self-evident that this means the disappearance of the ontological objectivity of nature' upon which the process of historical production/change is rooted. From this, he insisted, other mistakes arose, including (1) the confusion of objecti-fication with alienation (causing a lapse into Hegelianism), and (2) the tendency to 'view Marxism exclusively as a theory of society, as social philosophy, and hence to ignore or repudiate it as a theory of nature'.

These errors, he wrote, 'strike at the very roots of Marxian ontology'. Lukács thus suggested that what he had called the objective dialectics of nature existed. Moreover, he concedes that he was wrong in characterizing as a stance of 'pure contemplation' Engels' attempt to transcend the problem of subjectivity with respect to natural science by arguing that experimentation allowed a reconciliation of theory and practice. But Lukács points nevertheless to the continuing weaknesses of this argument of Engels, and leaves the question of the application of the dialectical method to nature hanging – implying that this is an insurmountable problem, that could not be solved as in his early work by 'an overextension of the concept of praxis' to all of reality (1971, ix–xviii).

There is in Lukács a different conception that recognizes that through the development of human labor, that is the developing metabolic exchange between nature and society, a historical transformation in the human consciousness of nature occurs that allows the expansion of the knowledge of nature, that is the genuine progress of the science of nature as dialectic. As he declared in his famous *Conversations* (Lukács, 1974) of 1967 – taking place the same year in which he wrote his new preface to *History and Class Consciousness* – 'You will remember how enthusiastically Marx greeted Darwin, despite many methodological reservations, for discovering the fundamentally historical character of being in organic nature. As for inorganic nature, it is naturally extremely difficult to establish its historicity.... The problem... is whether present-day physics is to be based on a so to speak obsolete standpoint – either that of vulgar materialism, or the purely manipulative conception of neo-positivism – or whether we are moving toward a historic and genetic conception of inorganic nature' (Lukács, 1974, 21). For Lukács such a historic and genetic understanding of nature (he gave the specific example of the breakthrough in the understanding of the origins of life introduced by Haldane and Oparin) clearly approached a dialectical conception (falling within his typology of 'dialectical forms') and captured in some way nature's own objective dialectic – without, however, representing the actual application of the full dialectical method in the sense that this pertained to human history and society. The problem of objectification remained and limited the pretensions of a dialectic of praxis. But 'since human life is based on a metabolism with nature, it goes without saying that certain truths which we acquire in the process of carrying out this metabolism have a general validity – for example the truths of mathematics, geometry, physics and so on' (1974, 43).

In summation, the 'Lukács Problem' as we have presented it here can be seen as consisting of: (1) the rejection of the notion that the dialectical method is applicable to nature, and (2) the assertion that a 'merely objective dialectic of nature' nonetheless exists and that this is essential to Marxist theory. Lukács, as we have seen, ended up by emphasizing this disjuncture within Marxist thought without being able to resolve it in any way, leaving behind a kind of Kantian dualism. Within Western Marxism generally the Lukács Problem is recognized only one-sidedly. The repudiation of the dialectics of nature and the rejection of any positivistic intrusion of natural science into social science is accepted. Yet the problem of the knowledge of nature and its relation to totality that persists in Lukács through his acknowledgement of an 'objective dialectics of nature' is largely ignored. Although for Lukács the dualism that seemed to emanate from his thought was a source of concern, Western Marxism in general has been more content to accept it – or else to adopt a more explicitly idealist way of resolving the contradiction through the subsumption of nature entirely under society.[2]

According to Herbert Marcuse, the dialectic of nature was part of the Hegelian dialectic of totality but was missing from Marx's own dialectical conception of social ontology rooted in labor – except insofar as nature entered into the social realm. Thus as he wrote in *Reason and Revolution*:

> The dialectical totality... includes nature, but only in so far as the latter enters and conditions the historical process of social reproduction.... The dialectical method has thus of its very nature become a historical method. The dialectical principle is not a general principle equally applicable to any subject matter. To be sure, every fact whatever can be subjected to a dialectical analysis, for example, a glass of water, as in Lenin's famous discussion. But all such analyses would lead into the structure of the socio-historical process and show it to be constitutive in the facts under analysis.... Every fact can be subjected to dialectical analysis only in so far as every fact is influenced by the antagonisms of the social process (1960, 314).

Marcuse's view did allow for a complex social-natural dialectic, if not a dialectics of nature separate from society. Yet, the rejection of the dialectics of nature characteristic of Western Marxism was so thoroughgoing in general as to leave very little room for the consideration of nature outside of human nature. In *From Hegel to Marx* the early Sidney Hook wrote,

> Galileo's laws of motion and the life history of an insect have nothing to do with dialectic except on the assumption that all nature is

spirit.... Whether natural phenomena are continuous at all points or discontinuous at some is an empirical question. It is strictly irrelevant to the solution of any *social* problem.... The natural objective order is relevant to dialectic only when there is an implied reference to the way in which it conditions historical and social activity. (1950, 75–6)

For Jean-Paul Sartre in the *Critique of Dialectical Reason*:

In the historical and social world... there *really* is dialectical reason; by transferring it into the 'natural' world, and forcibly inscribing it there, Engels stripped it of its rationality: there was no longer a dialectic which man produced by producing himself, and which, in turn, produced man; there was only a contingent law, of which nothing could be said except *it is so* and not otherwise. (2004, 32)

Pathway I: Classical Marxism and the dialectics of nature

'Western Marxism', in the sense referred to earlier, therefore provided little or no answer other than the dismissal of the question itself to the larger Lukács Problem on the status of the dialectic of nature within Marxist thought. It is therefore necessary to turn to pathways out of this dilemma offered by those whose position on the dialectic of nature and society is more complex. Here we will briefly and schematically consider mainly two such pathways, those offered by: (1) classical Marxism (mainly Marx and Engels themselves) and (2) the development of Marxist ecology.

Within classical Marxism the concept of the dialectic of nature stemmed largely from Engels' heroic, if not always successful, attempt, first in *Anti-Dühring* and then in *The Dialectics of Nature*, to extend the dialectical method beyond society to nature – in ways consistent with a materialist outlook and developments in nineteenth-century science. The extant evidence suggests that Marx was broadly supportive of the efforts on Engels' part and regarded it as part of their overall collaboration. Yet, Marx's philosophical background was far deeper than that of Engels, and his treatment of nature and the dialectic in many ways more philosophically complex. This became evident with the publication of Marx's early philosophical writings.

Still, rather than searching in Marx's expanded corpus for solutions to the problem of a materialist dialectical method extending to both society and nature, Western Marxists insisted instead that Marx's greater philosophical sophistication had led him to adopt a social ontology cordoned

off from nature and natural science – and all questions of philosophical materialism. A wedge was thus driven between Marx and Engels
and between Marx and nature. Marx's early naturalism and humanism
became humanism alone – and if Marx was faulted it was for giving way
unduly to naturalism in his later writings. Materialism, like the dialectic
related only to society and was narrowed down to an abstract concept of
economic production – abstract since removed from all natural conditions. Sebastiano Timpanaro, a lone voice against this trend, was thus
inspired to open his book *On Materialism* with the ironic statement:
'Perhaps the sole characteristic common to virtually all contemporary
varieties of Western Marxism is their concern to defend themselves
against the accusation of materialism' (1975, 29). In rejecting dialectical
materialism, Western Marxism rejected materialism (and with it nature)
rather than the dialectic, attempting to find a way to define Marxism
exclusively as a dialectic of social praxis.

Marx's materialism, as he developed it first in his earlier writings –
in particular his dissertation on Epicurus, the *Economic and Philosophical
Manuscripts* of 1844, the *Theses on Feuerbach, The Holy Family* and *The
German Ideology* – had the distinction that it sought to transcend the division between materialism and idealism, by creating a new materialism
embodying the active principle previously developed best by idealism,
while retaining a materialist starting point and emphasis. From the
materialist side he drew upon Epicurus and Feuerbach, on the idealist
side from Hegel. It was the immanent dialectic that he found in Epicurus
that first allowed Marx to envision a materialism rooted in human
sensuous activity. Epicurus, in insisting on the truth of the senses, while
also emphasizing the role of the human mind in assessing the data of
sense experience, laid the grounds for a sophisticated materialism that
rejected God, teleology, determinism, and skepticism, all at the same
time. Epicurus, Marx wrote, always sought to break through 'the bonds
of fate' (Marx and Engels, 1975, vol. 1, 49). As Jean-Paul Sartre wrote
in 'Materialism and Revolution', 'The first man who made a deliberate
attempt to rid men of their fears and bonds, the first man who tried to
abolish slavery within his domain, Epicurus, was a materialist' (1955,
207).

This gave rise in Marx's thought to what might be called a 'natural
praxis' underlying his social praxis. For Marx the materialist method was
rooted in the senses, but the senses played an active, constitutive role,
and were not simply passive instruments, reflective of a passive nature.
'Human sensuousness', Marx argued in his dissertation on Epicurus
(introducing a philosophical viewpoint that although emanating from

Epicurus' physics was to be fundamental to his own materialist dialectic throughout his life), 'is...embodied time, the existing reflection of the sensuous world in itself'. Mere perception through the senses is only possible because it expresses an active and therefore changing relation to nature – and indeed of nature to itself. 'In hearing nature hears itself, in smelling it smells itself, in seeing it sees itself' (Marx and Engels, 1975, vol. 1, 64–5).

Epicurus had stated that 'death is nothing to us' – referring to the fact that once there is no sensation there is nothing for us. Marx was to echo this in the *Economic and Philosophic Manuscripts* by saying, 'Nature... taken abstractly, for itself, and fixed in its relation to man, is *nothing* for man.... Nature as nature', as a mere abstraction devoid of sense, is 'nothing proving itself to be nothing' (Marx, 1974, 398–99).

For Marx all human activity has a basis in nature, is sensuous activity, which does not prevent the development of distinctly human species characteristics, that is, 'human-social activity'. The senses are nature touching, tasting, seeing, hearing, and smelling itself. The tools with which human beings seek to transform the natural world around them constitute the 'inorganic body of man' – the social technology that extends the 'natural technology' of the human organs and capacities. (Here Marx followed the ancient Greek notion of the bodily organs as tools or natural technology, reflected in the dual meaning of the Greek term *organon*, which referred both to the organs and to tools – see Foster and Burkett, 2000). Labor and production constituted the active human transformation of nature, but also of human nature, the human relation to nature and of human beings themselves. The alienation of human beings from themselves and their production is also the alienation of human beings from nature, and the alienation of nature itself, since human beings are 'a part of nature' (Marx, 1974, 328).

The 'first fact' (Marx and Engels, 1975, vol. 5, 31–2) to be established in analyzing human beings, Marx argued in *The German Ideology*, was their dependence on nature to meet their physical needs – and hence the necessity of production for human subsistence. Human labor (and production) according to Marx in *Capital* was a metabolic exchange between nature and society without which human beings could not exist and history could not develop. 'The fact that man is an *embodied*, living, real, sentient, objective being with natural powers', Marx wrote,

> means that he has *real, sensuous objects* as the objects of his being, or that he can only *express* his life in real, sensuous objects.... Hunger is a natural *need*; it requires, therefore, a *nature* outside itself, an *object*

outside itself, in order to be satisfied and stilled.... A being which does not have its nature outside itself is not a *natural* being and does not share in the being of nature. (1964, 207)

At every point in his analysis, therefore, Marx insisted on the complex material relation between human beings and nature. The relation was in fact a dialectical one in that it was an internal relation within a single totality. Rather than positing a dualistic relation between human beings and nature, he suggested that the two opposing poles existed radically separated from one another only insofar as alienation in the realm of appearance separated human beings from their essential human capacities as both natural and social beings – beings actively constituting nature's relation to itself through natural and social praxis. As Alfred Schmidt wrote,

The hidden nature speculation in Marx [holds that]...the different economic formations of society which have succeeded each other historically have been so many modes of nature's self-mediation. Sundered into two parts, man and material to be worked on, nature is always present to itself in this division.... Only in this way [as the self-mediation of nature through human activity] can we speak meaningfully of a 'dialectic of nature'. (1971, 79)

In his references to Marx's argument that labor-production was the metabolic relation between society and nature, Lukács had implicitly recognized this while never elaborating it, and nevertheless retaining the notion of nature as an 'exalted' sphere not entirely subject to the dialectical method.

Andrew Feenberg has argued that 'Marx's theory suggests a solution to some of the problems in Lukács.... Specifically, Marx's way of conceiving the relation of man to nature promises to overcome the split between history and nature which mars Lukács' theory' (1981, 213). Lukács had pointed to labor and production or the metabolic exchange between human beings and nature as the means of overcoming the subject–object duality. Human beings in Vico's terms can understand nature as history because they have made it. As more and more of nature is transformed by history the externality of this part of nature disappears and nature becomes subsumed within production. Objectification becomes for human beings the objectification of themselves. Yet, this requires an enormous extension of what constitutes the realm of production, of social praxis. Seen merely in terms of production, moreover, such a conception seems absurd. As Feenberg, quoting Marx, asks, 'Under what conditions can "man himself become *the* object?" Will not the realm of independent nature always transcend society, hence the human subject?' (1981, 214).

Marx's theory of social praxis rooted in production thus requires what will be referred to here as *natural praxis* – a much larger concept of human praxis that encompasses human activity as a whole, that is, the life of the senses. Here Marx's new materialism rests much more on the old materialism extending back to Epicurus. Feenberg suggests that Marx attempted to overcome these difficulties

> by elaborating a remarkable new theory of sensation in which the senses 'become directly theoreticians in practice', acting on their objects as does the worker on his raw materials. The senses, unlike labor, have traditionally been conceived by philosophy as a potentially universal mode of reception, relating to all possible (real) objects. The senses can therefore take over where actual labor leaves off, supporting the assertion of a universal identity of subject and object in nature. (1981, 217–18; Marx, 1964, 160)

This was the argument that Marx had in fact found in Epicurus' 'immanent dialectics' (Voden, n.d., 332–3) and that had been developed (not always as radically) up through Feuerbach. Thus it was the latter who said, 'Only sense and only sense perception give me something as *subject.*' And 'only sensuous beings act upon one another' (Feuerbach, 1972, 213, 224).

This was a point of view that was both materialistic and holistic, aimed at a complex totality. Indeed, in commenting on the materialist tradition in philosophy, which he associated in particular with Epicurus and his modern adherents, Hegel had gone so far as to concede that the aim of materialism was in his terms a dialectical one: 'We must recognize in materialism the enthusiastic effort to transcend the dualism which postulates two different worlds as equally substantial and true, to nullify this tearing asunder of what is originally One' (1971, 34).

Marx's theory, according to Feenberg, provides a 'meta-theoretical reconstruction of sense knowledge as a historically evolving dimension of human being. Marx argues that the object of sensation contains a wealth of meaning available only to the trained and socially developed sense organ' (1981, 218). Indeed, Marx insists, in Epicurean-materialist terms, but in ways that display a more active principle or a natural praxis, that 'The *distinctive character* of each faculty is precisely its *characteristic* essence and thus also the characteristic mode of its objectification, of its *objectively real*, living *being*. It is therefore not only in thought, but through *all* the senses that man is affirmed in the objective world.... The cultivation of the five senses is the work of all previous history.' Emancipation from the alienation of private property is for Marx also 'the complete emancipation of the human qualities and senses' (Marx, 1964, 160–1).

Underlying Marx's argument is the proposition, previously advocated most radically by Epicurus, that the senses (if rationally trained and developed) are the source of enlightenment and that the object of sense perception is real, and not a product of human consciousness. Treating Locke as belonging to the materialist tradition in the line of descent from Epicurus, Marx stated that Locke in his *Essay on Human Understanding* had suggested 'indirectly that there cannot be any philosophy at variance with the healthy human senses and reason based on them' (Marx and Engels, 1975, vol. 4, 129). There is a necessary relation between the senses and the object of sense perception, which forms the basis for human knowledge. 'Sense experience (*see* Feuerbach)', Marx wrote,

> must be the basis of all science. Science is only genuine science when it proceeds from sense experience, in the two forms of *sense perception* and *sensuous* need; i.e. only when it proceeds from nature.... Natural science will one day incorporate the science of man, just as the science of man will incorporate natural science; there will be a *single* science.... The first object for man – man himself – is nature, sense experience; and the particular sensuous human faculties, which can only find objective realization in *natural* objects, can only attain self-knowledge in the science of natural being (1964, 164).

In Marx's notion of natural praxis, sense perception develops in history in accord with the development of human production. By actively and rationally sensing the world in wider and wider dimensions human beings are able historically to experience the world as the objectification of their praxis – but only insofar as they are able to emancipate the senses by overcoming alienation of nature. As Feenberg explains Marx's position:

> Marx cannot allow, as does British empiricism, that the sense object is merely a sign, causally (or otherwise) connected with a 'real' object that would only be accidentally related to sensation.... If the sensed object is only a sign or image, then no real unity of subject and object

is achieved in sensation, as Kant's first *Critique* makes abundantly clear....

Marx's... epistemological atheism insists on locating both appearance and reality in the sphere of sensation, as levels or degrees in the unveiling of what is perceived. The truth of the object does not lie beyond sensation in thought but in truer and deeper sensation itself, in the developed and liberated senses of social man. Only on this assumption can Marx overcome the split between man and nature which threatens his philosophy of praxis at every turn (1981, 219–20).

The active mind, or abstract human consciousness, in Marx's materialism – building on ancient Greek materialism and its modern developers, such as Bacon, Gassendi, Hobbes, Locke, Condillac, and so on – depends on an act of preconception/anticipation, first introduced in Epicurus' concept of *prolepsis*, whereby thought and higher language arise out of preconceptions or anticipatory generalizations drawn upon sense perception (Diogenes Laertius, 1925, 563; Marx and Engels, 1975, vol. 1, 405–6).[3] In Feenberg's words, 'The early Marx can be seen to approach and anticipate the phenomenological concept of a "pre-reflexive" unity of subject and object' (1981, 220–21).[4] Illustrative of this is the way Marx explained the development of higher thought or language at the end of his life in *Notes on Adolph Wagner* (following an argument introduced by Epicurus/Lucretius). Human beings in the development of their natural praxis, he argues,

> begin, like every animal, by *eating, drinking etc* .... *by relating themselves actively*, taking hold of certain things in the external world through action, and thus satisfying their need[s] .... Through the repetition of this process, the property of those things, their property 'to satisfy needs', is impressed upon their brains; men, like animals, also learn to distinguish theoretically' from all other things the external things which serve for the satisfaction of their needs. At a certain stage of this evolution, after their needs, and the activities by which they are satisfied, have, in the meantime, increased and developed further, they will christen these things linguistically as a whole class, distinguished empirically from the rest of the external world .... But this linguistic designation only expresses as an idea what repeated corroboration in experience has accomplished, namely, that certain external things serve man already living in a certain social connection (this is a neces-

sary presupposition on account of language) for the satisfaction of their needs (1975, 190–91).

In like fashion, the later Lukács was to state,

We must start from the fact that man is first and foremost, like every organism, a being that responds to his environment – which brings me back to the ontological question. In other words, man reconstructs the problems arising from his real existence as questions, and then responds to them; there is no such thing at all as a free-floating consciousness, existing on its own basis, and working purely from the inside outwards, and no one has managed to demonstrate such a thing. (1974, 42)

Although dedicated to ontological materialism in his emphasis and his starting point, Marx also saw his 'new materialism' of praxis (both natural and social) as a synthesis of materialism with the active component of idealism. The possibility of this seems to have first emerged in his thought as a result of his encounter with Epicurus' materialism, which broke the 'bonds of fate' by starting with materialist postulates and then ending up with an immanent dialectic and the principle of human freedom. The weakness that remained in Epicurus' philosophy and in all other materialist views leading up to and encompassing Feuerbach, however, was that the argument remained 'contemplative' – without a sufficient development of social praxis. As Marx stated in the first of his 'Theses on Feuerbach':

The chief defect of all hitherto existing materialism (that of Feuerbach included) is that the thing, reality, sensuousness, is conceived only in the form of the *object or of contemplation*, but not as *sensuous human activity, practice*, not subjectively. Hence, in contradistinction to materialism, the *active* side was developed abstractly by idealism – which, of course, does not know real, sensuous activity as such. (1974)

What Marx called 'contemplative materialism' – that is materialism as it existed from Epicurus to Feuerbach – has the failing that it 'does not comprehend sensuousness as practical human-sensuous activity' (1974, 421–23).

Marx never abandoned materialism or realism. Nature always existed to some extent independent of human beings and prior to human beings – though human beings and their relations were ultimately conceived as a part of nature within a complex set of internal relations.

The senses were limited in the extent to which they could apprehend the world. But this constituted no insuperable obstacle to the understanding of nature since human sense perception and scientific inference based on it was capable of historical development. Moreover, materialism could be combined with the dialectical method – the way in which basic laws of nature (of matter and motion) were handled – in order to develop reasoned science based on sense experience. In a June 27, 1870, letter to his friend Dr L. Kugelmann Marx observed that Frederick 'Lange [addressing Marx's *Capital*] is naïve enough to say that I "move with rare freedom" in empirical matter. He hasn't the least idea that this "free movement in matter" is nothing but a paraphrase for the *method* of dealing with matter – that is, the *dialectic method*' (1934, 112).

For Marx, like Hegel, the 'true is the whole', and could therefore not be understood apart from its development, making *dialectical reason* necessary (Hegel, 1977, 11). All was transitory, a passing away. Time itself was, as Epicurus had first stated and Marx later repeated, the 'accident of accidents'. Thus the only immutable reality, according to Epicurus (and later Marx) was 'death the immortal' – all reality was time and process – there were no set positions in the world, nothing was static (Marx and Engels, 1975, vol. 1, 65, 473, 478; Marx, 1963, 110; Lucretius, 1997, 93). Contingency (symbolized by Epicurus' famous atomic swerve) was everywhere.

It is no mere coincidence that this notion of 'death the immortal' that Marx took from Epicurus as a fundamental description of his own philosophy has recently been characterized by Ann Fairchild Pomeroy in her *Marx and Whitehead* as 'the only general statement made possible by Marx's dialectics' and as the point of convergence of Alfred North Whitehead's process philosophy with Marx (Pomeroy, 2004, 9, 50). It constitutes the recognition that reality is to be conceived as process or as internal relations – and for Marx, especially, *historically* – since 'death the immortal' (what we now would call the arrow of time) is built into the 'nature of things'. As Marx wrote in relation to Epicurus: 'the temporal character of things and their appearance to the senses are posited as intrinsically one' (Marx and Engels, 1975, vol. 1, 65).

Marx's basic ontological scheme for understanding the world, as with Hegel, was one of internal relations. This is far removed from what Engels following Hegel had termed the 'metaphysical' view, in which the world is a collection of things, isolated from one another, creating an understanding that is necessarily limited and partial – reductionist, determinist, and dualist (Marx and Engels, 1975, vol. 25, 21–4). According to the philosophy of internal relations, as Bertell Ollman put it in his *Dialectical Investigations* , 'each part is viewed as incorporating in what it is all its relations with other parts up to and including everything that comes into the whole' (1993, 35). In Marx's case this was not a question simply of thought relating to itself as in the case of idealism, but represented the complex, changing, contingent, contradictory, and coevolutionary nature of the world itself – that is, the world and each 'totality' within it was characterized by internal relations. The common 'metaphysical' mistake of translating it into a world of separate things rigidly cut off from each other is therefore wrong. For Marx, each thing consists of the totality of its relations. Faced with a world of reality of this kind, the only rational way of 'dealing with matter' was the dialectic method. As Ollman stated,

> Dialectics is an attempt to resolve this difficulty [of comprehending a world that is ever changing and interacting] by expanding our notion of anything to include, as aspects of what it is, both the process by which it has become that and the broader interactive context in which it is found . . . . Dialectics restructures our thinking about reality by replacing the common sense notion of 'thing', as something that *has* a history and *has* external connections with other things, with notions of 'process', which *contains* its history and possible futures, and 'relation', which *contains* as part of what it is its ties with other relations (1993, 11; 2003).

Hence, characteristic of Marx's thought was the tendency to see all of reality as historical – not just human society but the natural world itself. Natural history had to be studied along with social history – neither was to be viewed as passive; both were characterized by complex laws of change and contradiction. How Marx viewed natural history is most concretely evident in his broader ecological discussions – that is, in his considerations of evolution and of what he called the 'metabolic relation' between human beings and nature embodied in production. In the 1850s and 1860s European and North American agriculture was threatened by the impoverishment of the soil due to the failure to replace the nutrients (nitrogen, phosphorus, and potassium) removed from the soil and shipped to the cities in the form of food and fiber, where these nutrients ended up as waste polluting the cities. Following Justus von Liebig, the great German chemist, Marx argued that this robbing of the soil constituted a crisis for agriculture. But Marx went further than any other thinker of his time in terms of treating this as a metabolic rift in the human relation to nature based on capitalist relations of production. This theory emphasized the 'nature-imposed' conditions of human production outside of society itself, the historical (geological) evolution of the soil, and its complex interaction with the evolution of human society and production (Foster, 2000, 141–77).

Marx specifically employed the word 'metabolism', as he stated in his *Notes on Adolph Wagner*, to capture 'the "natural" process of production as the material exchange between man and nature' – in accordance with a complex, dialectical, coevolutionary scheme (1975, 209). Human labor itself was defined as the metabolic relation exchange between human society and nature, within a context of material permanence. Marx quoted Epicurus (via Lucretius) to emphasize the materialist axiom that nothing in the material world comes from nothing or is in the end reduced to nothing (1976, 323). Rather than standing in a pure theoretical relation to the world, human beings, Marx had stressed in *Notes on Adolph Wagner*, apprehended the world through their senses activated in the context of their real practical activity in meeting their essential needs. Communist society was itself seen as the historical resolution of the contradiction between nature and society, as well as of the class contradictions internal to society, 'by organizing the human metabolism with nature in a rational way' via unalienated human production (1981, 959).

At every point therefore Marx's dialectic sought to break the bonds of fate associated with the notion of an objective world separate from and dominating human beings – along with the alienation of the external world and attempts to dominate it on the part of human beings. His materialist dialectic sought to embody both genuine humanism and genuine naturalism, while also adopting a realistic conception of the world beyond humanity – in relation to which human beings evolved in complex, coevolutionary ways. The material world was experienced by human beings as a sensuous reality and hence the liberation of the world required the emancipation of the senses and of the sensuous relation to nature along with the emancipation of society. But this in turn required as its basis the rational regulation of the metabolic relation between nature and society.

Marx's explicit treatment of nature in terms of the dialectical method focused on those realms in which nature was objectified through actual human praxis – both natural and social. It was Engels who tried to provide the philosophical extension of this in terms of science and nature more broadly – treating nature as a system of internal relations characterized by its own dialectical 'laws'. Thus Engels famously wrote in *Anti-Dühring*: 'Nature is the proof of dialectics' (Marx and Engels, 1975, vol. 25, 23). This deceptively simple statement, the truth of which was taken for granted within Marxism for the next few decades – but that later emerged as perhaps the single greatest point of contention within Marxist theory – stood for the thesis that there existed a dialectic of nature side by side with (or even anterior to) the dialectic of society.

Just as Marx and Engels viewed the materialist conception of history as inseparably bound to the materialist conception of nature, they viewed the dialectics of society as inseparably bound to the dialectics of nature. Both society and nature had to be viewed materialistically and dialectically, since they embodied a dialectical motion in their very being. Without materialism dialectics led to dialectical idealism, of which Hegelianism was the highest form. Without dialectics, materialism led to abstract empiricism and mechanism, as embodied in British political economy and in the so-called 'scientific materialism' then prevalent in Germany.

The first systematic case for a distinct dialectics of nature was made by Engels while Marx was still alive in the late 1870s in *Anti-Dühring* – a work that he read to Marx in full prior to its publication and to which Marx contributed a chapter. This was followed by Engels' *Dialectics of Nature* – a voluminous, incomplete manuscript, consisting mainly of fragments, parts of which were written between 1873 and 1882 (thus overlapping in time with *Anti-Dühring*). *The Dialectics of Nature* was not published in its entirety until 1925, three decades after Engels' death. Engels' analysis is often seen in terms of the three laws of dialectics that he outlined in these works: (1) 'the transformation of quantity into quality and vice versa'; (2) 'the law of the interpenetration of opposites', and (3) 'the law of the negation of the negation' (Marx and Engels, 1975, 356). Although these 'laws', taken from Hegel, constituted pathways to dialectical thinking, their formalization as abstract laws tended to lead to an approach, when turned into a rigid schema by later thinkers, that militated against dialectic. Hence, Engels' analysis has been widely criticized on this basis.

Rejection of Engels' position on the nature dialectics was, as we have seen, crucial to the genesis of Lukács' dialectic and 'Western Marxism'. There is no doubt that 'dialectical materialism' as it developed in the Soviet Union in the 1930s frequently turned into a mechanical, and extremely undialectical, way of thinking that all too often gave way to crude positivism. Nevertheless, it is much harder to criticize Engels of such a failing – nor, as we shall see, is it possible to place such criticisms at the door of all those who, inspired by his example, tried to extend the materialist dialectic, applying it in the natural and physical sciences. Indeed, Marx himself, as we have noted, was supportive of Engels' efforts.

Engels' outlook has been criticized most extensively in terms of his rendition of physics, which was still dominated by the mechanistic Newtonian worldview. By the time Engels' *Dialectics of Nature* was actually published, several decades after being written, physics had gone through several revolutions making his work seem dated – although his dialectical view had caused him to question mechanism at every point. Yet, it was in the biological sphere that Engels' dialectical naturalism was most developed. Here he drew heavily upon the Darwinian revolution and explored lines of coevolution. Applying a dialectical-materialist method to the theory of evolution Engels wrote,

> *Hard and fast lines* are incompatible with the theory of evolution. Even the border-line between vertebrates and invertebrates is now no longer rigid, just as little is that between fishes and amphibians, while that between birds and reptiles dwindles more and more every day.... Dialectics, which likewise knows no *hard and fast lines*, no unconditional, universally valid 'either-or' and which bridges the fixed metaphysical differences, and besides 'either-or' recognizes also in the right place 'both this – and that' and reconciles the opposites, is the sole method of thought appropriate to the highest degree to this stage [in the development of science]. (Marx and Engels, 1975, vol. 25, 493)

In this view, then, the fluid, changing, interpenetrating forms that clearly characterize nature (as it is given to us as natural beings through our sense experience – both sense perception and sensuous need) demand a method of reasoning (the dialectic) capable of dealing with this. Under the influence of Hegel, Darwin, and the work of the German scientist (electrophysiologist) Emil Du Bois-Reymond, Engels developed a view of the evolution and the origins of life as a *process of emergence*. The idea of emergence has been traced back to Epicurus and was clearly a part of Marx's conception of nature as well. As Z. A. Jordan explained in *The Evolution of Dialectical Materialism*,

> The doctrine of emergent evolution is a hypothesis concerned with novelties which are not mere combinations of their component elements and which are supposed to occur in the course of natural development, such as the emergence of life or of mind.... The fact cannot be denied that the central idea of emergent evolution is to be

found in *Anti-Dühring* and *Dialectics of Nature*.... In the case of Engels, the emphasis is clearly upon the ontological conception, upon the gradual emergence of the atomic, chemical, and biological level, the latter with its numerous emergent transitions to higher and higher forms of life' (Jordan, 1967, 165–6).

Engels' dialectics of nature thus can be seen as a genetic-historical approach rooted in a philosophy of emergence. The natural world is conceived as an interconnected fabric with an arrow of time (since involving irreversible transformations) that can only be envisioned in terms of qualitative (beyond merely quantitative) transformations, the interpenetration of opposites (i.e. internal relations that encompass mutually determining processes), and the negation of the negation (emergence). Our understanding of this world for Engels is dialectical and made possible by human praxis, including the methods of experimentation introduced by science.

The brilliance of Engels' dialectical conception of nature, when he turns specifically to nature-society relations, can be seen in his understanding of the rupture in the evolutionary process and the ecological disaster resulting from the alienated society of capitalism, which goes against all 'laws' of natural reproduction and sustainability. Human history, according to Engels, continually comes up against ecological problems that represent contradictions in the human relation to nature – contradictions in nature introduced by society and undermining its own natural conditions. These contradictions can only be transcended by relating to nature rationally through nature's laws, and thus organizing production accordingly – a possibility not open to capitalist society. Warning of the ecological consequences of the alienation of nature in history Engels writes in *The Dialectics of Nature*,

> Let us not, however, flatter ourselves overmuch on account of our human victories over nature. For each such victory nature takes its revenge on us. Each victory, it is true, in the first place brings about the results we expected, but in the second and third places it has quite different, unforeseen effects which only too often cancel the first.... Thus at every step we are reminded that we by no means rule over nature like a conqueror over a foreign people, like someone standing outside nature – but that we, with flesh, blood and brain, belong to nature, and exist in its midst, and all that all our mastery of it consists in the fact that we have the advantage over all other

creatures of being able to learn its laws and apply them correctly (Marx and Engels, 1975, vol. 25, 460–1).

Marx and Engels strove to comprehend the dialectic of nature and society, in which natural relations – not simply social relations – were taken seriously as embodying necessity and contradiction. As a result, they were able to perceive in ways far more penetrating than their contemporaries a dialectic of ecology involving new historical contradictions. This is no less true of Marx than Engels. As Marx analyzing the alienation of nature, was to observe in the *Grundrisse*:

> It is not the *unity* of living and active humanity with the natural, inorganic conditions of their metabolic exchange with nature, and hence their appropriation of nature, which requires explanation or is the result of a historic process, but rather the *separation* between these inorganic conditions of human existence and this active existence, a separation which is completely posited only in the relation of wage labor and capital. (1973, 489)

This separation both in material reality and human consciousness was, as Marx and Engels argued, to have disastrous ecological consequences manifested in what Marx called the 'irreparable rift' between nature and society (Marx, 1981, 949).

Pathway II: The development of Marxist ecology

Given the direction of Marx and Engels' own thought, which pointed to the disastrous material consequences arising from the alienation of nature along with the alienation of humanity under capitalism, it is not surprising that later advances in the development of the conception of the dialectic of nature were to be inseparable from the emergence of a Marxist ecological worldview. As recent investigations both into Marx's ecology and into subsequent Marxist and materialist thought have shown, ecological insights of the kind depicted here were not only intrinsic to Marx and Engel's worldview but were deeply rooted in the materialist tradition going back to the ancient Greeks. Moreover, they extended beyond Marx and Engels to some of their early followers. This included figures such as: August Bebel, William Morris, Karl Kautsky, Rosa Luxemburg, V. I. Lenin, and Nikolai Bukharin. In the Soviet Union in the 1920s wider ecological analyses blossomed in the work of scientists such as V. I. Vernadsky, N. I. Vavilov, Alexander Oparin, and Boris Hessen (Foster, 2000, 236–54).

In contrast, Western Marxism beginning with Lukács' *History and Class Consciousness*, as we have seen, became extremely critical of application of the methods of natural science to the realm of human history and society, while also rejecting the application of the dialectical method to science and nature. Hence, an enormous theoretical firewall was erected separating the two spheres and limiting any ecological insights. The Frankfurt School's considerations of nature and the domination of nature in the work of Max Horkheimer and Theodore Adorno tended to attribute these problems to the Enlightenment and its modern positivistic heir – and to be concerned much more with the domination of human nature than nature as a whole (Horkheimer and Adorno, 1972). Hence, its critique was carried out without any genuine ecological knowledge. In the Soviet Union too the pioneering role of scientists in this area largely vanished in the 1930s with the purges, which took the lives of such important figures as Bukharin, Vavilov, and Hessen.

Nevertheless, a powerful engagement with materialist science and the dialectic of nature developed in Britain in the 1930s and 1940s in the work of such important figures, most of them scientists such as, J. B. S. Haldane, Hyman Levy, Lancelot Hogben, J. D. Bernal, Joseph Needham, Benjamin Farrington, and Christopher Caudwell. These thinkers self-consciously united a materialist philosophy with roots extending as far back as Epicurus with modern science, dialectical conceptions, and Marxist revolutionary praxis. They all struggled to overcome conceptions of an unbridgeable gulf between nature and society and furthered ecological notions. One of the most important figures in this period was the mathematician Levy, whose early system theory as developed in his 1933 *The Universe of Science* helped inspire British ecologist Arthur Tansley (a Fabian-style socialist and former student of Marx's friend, the biologist E. Ray Lankester) to introduce the concept of 'ecosystem' in 1935 (see Foster, 2002).

Levy's 1938 work *A Philosophy for a Modern Man* advanced a philosophy of internal relations intended to explain the significance of dialectical conceptions for science. In analyzing changes in forest succession as illustrative of dialectical processes Levy wrote, 'Vegetation ... transforms the environment, and the environment in its turn the vegetation. It is almost like a society of human beings. We may expect, therefore, to find in the growth of vegetation dialectical changes manifesting themselves over and over again, whereby the whole isolate passes from phase to phase' (1938, 126). Levy's analysis of dialectical interrelations of nature and society led him to point to environmental rifts resulting from capitalism's intrinsic disregard for this connectedness. Thus the largely unforeseen effects of the steam engine on the coal region of South Wales; the consequences of the unthinking introduction of a pair of rabbits into Australia without any recognition of the ecological consequences; and how red deer could in one context be diminished by the destruction of their forest environment, while in another context they could proliferate and destroy their environment (with both cases attributable to human interference related to profit-making) – were all points emphasized in his analysis. He also alluded to the unequal exchange affecting poor countries as the rich countries rapaciously extracted their limited raw materials (pp. 91, 125–30, 199, 227).

A materialist dialectic therefore could be applied to elucidate both nature-nature and people-nature (or people-nature-people) relations/metabolisms (see Burkett, 1997). All material relations of social change between people necessarily involved the changing of natural relations. A fundamental 'phase change' in nature or society is a manifestation of 'irreversible historical change' involving coevolutionary processes and the changing of conditions. Basic to a materialist dialectical conception, according to Levy, is the notion that the universe not only exists but is constantly changing. And with this arises changes in language (thinking, science) and consciousness. All history was interactive in complex sequences: 'We change and alter under the impact of the environment; the environment is changed and altered under our impact. We are its environment.' It is characterized by emergence, beginning with 'the emergence of living properties in matter' as 'a very distinctive step in the natural process'. There is an arrow of time at work in the world: 'The traffic of the universe flows in one direction only.' Yet, the underlying contingency of relations prevents a deterministic outlook (Levy, 1938, 19, 24, 100, 130).

The ecological conceptions emanating from dialectical Marxist scientists of this period resulted in what has been the leading materialist theory of the origins of life (overcoming earlier laboratory-based refutations of spontaneous generation). Thus the dialectical-materialist Haldane–Oparin hypothesis on the origins of life (based on Vernadsky's earlier work on the biosphere) argued that the conditions that had allowed for the origins of life were altered by life itself, which created an atmosphere rich in reactive oxygen (Levins and Lewontin, 1985, 277). This act of life itself so altered the base conditions of the biosphere that, in the words of Rachel Carson, 'this single extraordinary act of spontaneous generation could not be repeated' (1998, 230). Commenting on this, J. D. Bernal was to observe in his *Origins of Life*, 'The great liberation of the human mind, of the realization, first stressed by Vico and then put into practice by Marx and his followers that *man makes himself,* will now be enlarged with the essential philosophical content of the new knowledge of the origin of life and the realization of its self-creative character' (1967, 182).

It was this ecological conception of world of life that was itself in many ways reflexive and self-creating, arising out of materialist dialectics, that was to give birth to many of the most powerful insights associated with the development of modern ecology. Moreover, it can now be argued more generally, extending Engels' early proposition with respect to nature, that 'ecology is the proof of dialectics'. No other form of thinking about nature and society has so conclusively shown the importance of irreversible change, contingency, coevolution, and contradiction.

As two noted ecological scientists David Keller and Frank Golley have observed,

> Ecology is captivating due to the sheer comprehensiveness of its scope and complexity of its subject matter; ecology addresses everything from the genetics, physiology and ethology of animals (including humans) to watersheds, the atmosphere, geologic processes, and influences of solar radiation and meteor impacts – in short, the totality of nature .... An ecological worldview emphasizes interaction and connectedness. (Keller and Golley, 2000, 1–2)

With the growth of ecology dialectical forms of thinking have necessarily advanced, giving new force to a dialectics of nature that at first was limited and at times distorted by the dominant mechanistic conceptions of science. Mechanism, as Whitehead had said, made nature 'a dull affair, soundless, scentless, colourless; merely the hurrying of material, endlessly meaninglessly' (1967, 54). In contrast, the dialectical view emerging from ecology is anything but lifeless or mechanical; it has generated a view of nature no longer shorn of life, interconnection, and sensuous reality – no longer deterministic – but a world of coevolution, contradiction, and crisis.

Dialectical thinking in ecology was more a question of necessity than choice. Neither mechanism nor vitalism, neither determinism nor teleology were adequate in the ecological realm – a realm that demanded an understanding that was at once genetic and relational. The inability to conceive of an ecology that left humans out meant that ecology was from the first at once natural and social.

In the post–Second World War era the center for the study of the evolutionary sciences shifted from Britain to the United States, which also became the center for work in dialectical biology for those scientists influenced by dialectical materialism. In particular the work of Richard Levins, Richard Lewontin, and Stephen Jay Gould, along with many other scientific colleagues with materialist and dialectical orientations, has shown the power of such forms of thinking when applied to fields such as genetics, paleontology, evolutionary biology, and ecology itself (Levins and Lewontin, 1985; Gould, 2002). Lacking the epistemological surety of the dialectic of social praxis, ecological science is nonetheless able to make up for this in part through a genetic or historical form of analysis, together with experiments that in isolating phenomenon for study are nonetheless non-reductionistically designed to understand the larger processes of which they are a part. In this analysis scientific inference is directed at uncovering complexity. Change is to be considered to be constant, opposing forces create change, and life rather than simply responding to its environment also generates its environment – the organism is conceived as both subject and object of evolution.

As Brett Clark and Richard York have explained in 'Dialectical Nature: Levins and Lewontin's *Dialectical Biologist* Reconsidered – 20 Years On':

> Evolution is not an unfolding process with predictable outcomes, but a contingent, wandering pathway through a material world of constraints and possibilities. In *The Dialectical Biologist* Levins and Lewontin contend that the larger, physical world in which an organism is situated is filled with its own contingent history and structural conditions – i.e. caught up in what might be described as historical processes. Interaction (the collision of atoms as Epicurus wrote) are part of the fabric of life, because objects throughout the physical world are interconnected. Multiple pathways or channels exist, in relation to the structural integrity of organisms, for evolutionary processes – in fact, they are part of what created life and makes its continuance possible. Even when the external conditions are fixed, multiple pathways exist, as life creates its own path, in its interaction with opposing forces. Emergence is an outgrowth of life, given the active experience of its heterogeneous organization. The constant interactions and interpenetration of opposites, at all levels of existence, provide the means for the mutability of life.... The dialectical interchange between the environment and the organism is a central tenet of the coevolutionary position. Both the environment and organism are integrated levels, 'partly autonomous and

reciprocally interacting' in both directions. ... Thus, both the parameters of change and the nature of transformation are subject to
change given the ongoing development of life.... So long as genes,
organisms, and environments are studied separately, our knowledge
of the living world will not advance. (2005, 20–1)

Ecological dialectics in this complex variegated sense, seems a far cry
from Lukács' notion of a 'merely objective dialectics of nature' in which
human beings, entirely removed from praxis in this realm, simply look
on from the outside at a distance – able only to derive very general
external 'exalted' laws regarding a passive nature. Instead the changing conditions of human existence and of natural life as a whole are
teaching us that human beings as living, sensuous beings are part of the
ecological world – that the biosphere is constitutive of our own existence even as we transform it through our actions. Scientific inference
rooted in developing praxis – both natural and social – is providing the
intellectual basis for a reflexive ecological science that constantly seeks
to transcend the boundaries between natural and social science – and in
ways that are dialectical rather than reductionist. This is now altering in
many ways our view of the social world itself – expanding its scope in
a universe of internal relations, forcing broader dialectical conceptions
on society in relation to an evolving ecological crisis. We can see a new
revolutionizing of Marxist materialism so as to take into account these
wider ecological conceptions – as well as an attempt to reconnect this
to the deep materialist roots of historical materialism (see Levins and
Lewontin, 1985; Burkett, 1999, Foster, 2000, Dickens, 2004).[5]

The historical basis of this new dialectics of ecology has been the
development of human production, of what Marx called the metabolic
relation between human beings and nature, which has made ecology
the most vital of the sciences since our changing relation to the environment (which humankind has too long viewed as a mere external
relation rather than an internal relation) is threatening to undermine
both the conditions of production and of those of life itself. Hence, it is
an increasingly dialectical conception forced on humanity as a result of
its own myopic intrusion into the universe of nature – a result of alienated social praxis. To recapture the necessary metabolic conditions of
the society–nature interaction what is needed is not simply a new *social
praxis*, but a revived *natural praxis* – a reappropriation and emancipation
of the human senses and human sensuousness in relation to nature.

This in fact is what revolutionary materialist dialectics has always
been about. From the beginning, materialism drew its impetus from

its revolutionary character – revolutionary in relation to all aspects of human existence. 'Epicurus', Sartre wrote, 'reduced death to a fact by removing the moral aspect it acquired from the fiction of seats of judgment in the nether world.... He did not dare do away with the gods, but reduced them to a mere divine *species*, unrelated to us; he removed their power of self-creation and showed that they were the products of the play of atoms, just as we were' (1955, 218). But a merely contemplative materialism, which relies on mechanism, can be as destructive as idealism. A materialism unrelated to praxis and divorced from dialectical conceptions is, as Sartre emphasized, a mere mechanical myth and can itself be a tool of domination. What is needed is an expansion of our knowledge of the universe of praxis (or to adopt Sartre's term the universe of concrete 'totalizations'). What is required in other words is a more unified understanding of the dialectics of nature and society – recognizing that the dialectical method when applied to nature is our way of handling the complexity of a constantly changing nature. The development of ecology as a unifying science is pointing irrefutably to the validity of Marx's original hypothesis that in the end there will only be 'a single science' covering a complex reality in which the dialectic of change subverts all reductionisms.

Notes

1. In fact, Engels' statement, which Lukács must have quoted from memory, was considerably more complex: 'Dialectics ... is nothing more than the science of the general laws of motion and development of nature, human society and thought' (Marx and Engels, 1975, vol. 25, 131).
2. An example of the latter is Vogel (1996) who argues in a cross between critical theory and post-structuralism that in rejecting the positivistic 'misapplication' of science to society, Lukács left natural science and nature itself (i.e. the domain of natural-physical science) unquestioned. For Vogel the object should be to extend the argument by deconstructing natural scientific conceptions of 'nature', which should be viewed as mere discursive constructions.
3. Marx was not only aware of the epistemological bases of Epicurus' thought but also of the way in which this was incorporated (often in less sophisticated forms) in early modern philosophy and science. Although in the history of philosophy Epicurus' epistemology and system of scientific inference was typically underestimated, in recent decades there has been a dramatic turnaround as new sources of Epicurean philosophy drawn from the library of papyri in Herculaneum have increased the knowledge of this philosophy. Much of this has verified what Marx deduced in the analysis in his dissertation. See Fitzgerald, 2004; Asmis, 1984; Foster, 2000, 21–65.
4. The 'phenomenological' element in Marx's thought derives from his brand of materialism, which sees human existence and consciousness as corporeal,

based on the body, the sense organs and sense perception. Merleau-Ponty is in accord with Marx when he writes: 'The body...is wholly animated, and all its functions contribute to the perception of objects—an activity long considered by philosophy to be pure knowledge' (Merleau-Ponty, 1964, 5). On the corporeal aspects of Marx's materialism see Frachia, 2005.

5. Not all Marxist ecologists are willing to embrace the notion of the dialectics of nature, even when qualified by a critical realism/critical materialism. For example Joel Kovel, editor of the ecological socialist journal *Capitalism, Nature, Socialism*, while making some valid points, clearly learns toward the early Lukácian rejection of the concept:

> Efforts to read dialectic directly into non-human nature are undialectical. Since a 'dialectic of anything' must include praxis, a dialectic of nature posits that nature directly manifests the relation between theory and practice characteristic of human beings. This would make the human and non-human worlds identical in their most fundamental feature....The disjunction between humanity and nature extends to the knowing of nature, which can never be fully realized. (1998, 479)

References

Asmis, Elizabeth. 1984. *Epicurus' Scientific Method*. Ithaca: Cornell University Press.

Bernal, J. D. 1967. *The Origins of Life*. New York: World Publishing Co.

Burkett, Paul. 1997. 'Nature in Marx Reconsidered: A Silver Anniversary Assessment of Alfred Schmidt's *Concept of Nature in Marx*', *Organization & Environment*, 10:3, 164–83.

Burkett, Paul. 1999. *Marx and Nature*. New York: St. Martin's Press.

Burkett, Paul. 2001. 'Lukács on Science: A New Act in the Tragedy', *Economic and Political Weekly*, 36:48, December 1, 4485–89.

Carson, Rachel. 1998. *Lost Woods*. Boston: Beacon Press.

Clark, Brett and Richard York. 2005. 'Dialectical Nature: Levins and Lewontin's *Dialectical Biologist* Reconsidered – 20 Years On', *Monthly Review*, 57:1, 13–22, May.

Colletti, Lucio. 1973. *Marxism and Hegel*. London: Verso.

Dickens, Peter. 2004. *Society and Nature*. Cambridge: Polity.

Diogenes Laertius. 1925. *Lives of Eminent Philosophers*, vol. 2. Cambridge, Mass.: Harvard University Press.

Feenberg, Andrew. 1981. *Lukács, Marx and the Sources of Critical Theory*. Totowa, New Jersey: Rowan and Littlefield.

Feuerbach, Ludwig. 1972. *The Fiery Brook*. Garden City, New York: Doubleday.

Fitzgerald, John T. 2004. 'Introduction: Philodemus and the Papyri from Herculaneum'. In Fitzgerald, John T., Dirk Obrinsk, and Glenn S. Holland, eds, *Philodemus and the New Testament World*. Boston: Brill, 1–12.

Foster, John Bellamy. 2000. *Marx's Ecology*. New York: Monthly Review Press.

Foster, John Bellamy. 2002. 'Marx's Ecology in Historical Perspective', *International Socialism*, 96, 71–86, Autumn.

Foster, John Bellamy and Paul Burkett. 2000. 'The Dialectic of Organic/Inorganic Relations', *Organization & Environment*, 13:4, 403–25, December.

Frachia, Jospeh. 2005. 'Beyond the Human-Nature Debate: Human Corporeal Organization as the "First Fact" of Historical Materialism', *Historical Materialism*, 13:1, 33–61.

Gould, Stephen J. 2002. *The Structure of Evolutionary Theory*. Cambridge, Mass.: Harvard University Press.

Gramsci, Antonio. 1971. *Selections from the Prison Notebooks*. New York: International Publishers.

Gramsci, Antonio. 1995. *Further Selections from the Prison Notebooks*. Minneapolis: University of Minnesota Press.

Hegel, G. W. F. 1971. *The Philosophy of Mind*. Oxford: Oxford University Press.

Hegel, G. W. F. 1977. *The Phenomeonology of Spirit*. Oxford: Oxford University Press.

Hook, Sidney. 1950. *From Hegel to Marx*. Ann Arbor: University of Michigan Press.

Horkheimer, Max and Theodor Adorno. 1972. *The Dialectic of Enlightenment*. New York: Continuum.

Jacoby, Russell. 1983. 'Western Marxism'. In Tom Bottomore, ed., *A Dictionary of Marxist Thought*. Oxford: Blackwell.

Jordan, Z. A. 1967. *The Evolution of Dialectical Materialism*. New York: St. Martin's Press.

Keller, David R. and Frank B. Golley. 2000. 'Introduction'. In Keller and Golley, ed., *The Philosophy of Ecology*. Athens: University of Georgia Press.

Kovel, Joel. 1998. 'Dialectic as Praxis', *Science & Society*, 62:3, 474–82.

Levins, Richard and Richard Lewontin. 1985. *The Dialectical Biologist*. Cambridge, Mass: Harvard University Press.

Levy, Hyman. 1938. *A Philosophy for a Modern Man*. New York: Alfred A. Knopf.

Lucretius. 1997. *On the Nature of the Universe*. Oxford: Oxford University Press.

Lukács, Georg. 1971. *History and Class Consciousness*. London: Merlin Press.

Lukács, Georg. 1972. *Tactics and Ethics*. New York: Harper and Row.

Lukács, Georg. 1974. *Conversations with Lukács*, ed. Theo Pinkus. Cambridge, Mass: MIT Press.

Lukács, Georg. 2000. *A Defence of History and Class Consciousness: Tailism and the Dialectic*. London: Verso.

Marcuse, Herbert. 1960. *Reason and Revolution*. Boston: Beacon Press.

Marx, Karl. 1934. *Letters to Kugelmann*. New York: International Publishers.

Marx, Karl. 1963. *The Poverty of Philosophy*. New York: International Publishers.

Marx, Karl. 1964. *Early Writings*. New York: McGraw Hill.

Marx, Karl. 1973. *Grundrisse*. London: Penguin.

Marx, Karl. 1974. *Early Writings*. London: Penguin.

Marx, Karl. 1975. *Texts on Method*. Oxford: Basil Blackwell.

Marx, Karl. 1976. *Capital*, vol. 1. New York: Vintage.

Marx, Karl. 1979. *The Letters of Karl Marx*, ed., Saul Padover. Englewood Cliffs, New Jersey: Prentice-Hall.

Marx, Karl. 1981. *Capital*, vol. 3. New York: Vintage.

Marx, Karl and Friedrich Engels. 1975. *Collected Works*. New York: International Publishers.

Merleau-Ponty, Maurice. 1964. *The Primacy of Perception*. Evanston, Illinois: Northwestern University Press.

Merleau-Ponty, Maurice. 1973. *Adventures of the Dialectic*. Evanston, Illinois: Northwestern University Press.

Ollman, Bertell. 1993. *Dialectical Investigations*. New York: Routledge.
Ollman, Bertell . 2003. *Dance of the Dialectic*. Urbana: University of Illinois Press.
Pomeroy, Anne Fairchild. 2004. Albany: State University of New York Press.
Sartre, Jean-Paul. 1955. *Literary and Philosophical Essays*. New York: Criterion Books.
Sartre, Jean-Paul. 2004. *Critique of Dialectical Reason*, volume 1. London: Verso.
Schmidt, Alfred. 1971. *The Concept of Nature in Marx*. London: Verso.
Timpanaro, Sebastiano. 1975. *On Materialism*. London: New Left Books.
Voden, Alexei Mikhailovich. No date. In Institute of Marxism-Leninism, *Reminiscences of Marx and Engels*. Moscow: Foreign Language Publishing House.
Vogel. Steven. 1996. *Against Nature*. Albany: State University of New York Press.
Whitehead, Alfred North. 1967. *Science and the Modern World*. New York: Free Press.

5
I'll Make You an Offer You Can't Refuse

Bill Livant

In all the gangster movies I saw as a kid, there was always a moment when one of the gangsters said, 'I'll make you an offer you can't refuse.' My reaction was to smile, just as I'm sure you did when you saw *The Godfather* and other movies like it.

There are two meanings to this sentence: (1) I'll make you an offer that is so good that if you accept it you will receive many benefits-and therefore any rational person would accept it. (2) I'll make you an offer that you better accept, because if you don't, terrible things will happen to you. To think that this sentence means only one or the other of these two possibilities is wrong, because it means both at the same time. But which one is dominant? Historically? In the totality?

One of the difficulties people have in acquiring a dialectical understanding of the world is due to the one-sided way in which most contradictions are presented to us in language. But occasionally a sentence comes along that perfectly captures the uneasy equilibrium between the opposing elements in a contradiction. This is the case here where the gangster's offer contains both true and false accounts of the history of the market, the nature of power, and the logic of the market.

History: The false history of the market is that people have voluntarily come together to freely exchange goods and services. They are free to enter and leave as they wish. No one on this account was forced to enter the market or became trapped once he or she was there. No land was ever seized and its occupants forced to seek a living elsewhere. The true history, of course, is just the opposite.

Nature of power: The false story is that inside the market no one has more power than another. Whatever inequality exists must come from outside the market. The true story is that the market does not simply transmit power from outside; it also makes some people more powerful than others and uses this power as well as the power that comes from outside in all its transactions.

Logic: The false picture is that all movement in the market occurs symmetrically. Everyone gets value for value. The real logic is asymmetrical. Using the greater power given them by their position in the market (as well as the power derived from other not unrelated sources), certain groups (guess which?) always get a lot more than they give.

The gangster who made the offer that was too good to refuse understood all this very well. The smile that invariably accompanied his offer was made through clenched teeth. The fact that the movie audience smiled as well suggests that here was a contradiction that even we could easily understand – though we may not have been able to explain it.

6
Dialectics of Emergence*

Lucien Sève

One of the central paradoxes with which we are confronted in non-linear thinking is that of emergence. It can be formulated as follows: while a whole is generally thought of as a sum of its parts, a *spontaneous* generation of properties that do not belong to the parts seems to occur in the non-linear passage of the parts to the whole. This compels us to re-examine with greater philosophical care the seemingly simple categorical couple of whole/parts, where the whole – to para-phrase Kant – is any kind of multiplicity taken as a unity.

From the whole to totality

According to the traditional view, whole and part are two opposed determinations, each taken as external to the other, that can be related in two different ways: either through disjunction or through conjunction. In the first way, the whole is a prior unity capable of division into parts, or, depending on the case, into fragments, segments and so on. These parts are homogenous with the whole from which they originate, like the portions of a cake or pieces from a crumbling rock. The very word 'part' itself (from the Latin 'parterre', to divide) expresses the logic-ally secondary character of what has been separated from an already existing whole. In the second way, parts are prior entities capable of forming a whole – like a construction of some sort combining pieces that, depending on the context, can be called 'elements', 'components', 'ingredients' and so on. Such a whole is not necessarily homogenous with the parts that make it up, but is more like a molecule in respect to its atoms. Here, the whole is presented as logically secondary in relation to its parts.

Although they differ in one significant respect, these two logics share a fundamental feature: they suggest that both whole and part are conceivable without the other. The whole can remain undivided, and thus without parts. Likewise, the elements can remain independent, so that they never form a whole. Whole and part are conceived, therefore, as two aspects of a pair while remaining more or less autonomous, that is 'without a necessary internal connection'. The same whole can be divided into various kinds of parts, and the same parts can be recomposed into different wholes – so that neither the whole nor the parts can be said to contribute anything essential to the sense of the other. The possible non-homogeneity of the whole and the parts in the second of these logics, therefore, cannot be rationally accounted for. It is impossible to understand the new properties of the whole on the basis of its prior parts or from anything that occurs in the whole itself. Thus, the emergence of these new properties must remain a mystery.

Mechanical and dialectical relationships

In some typically difficult pages devoted to these two categories in his *Science of Logic*, Hegel reformulates the problem before us in a dialectical manner. The approach to understanding that pretends to be able to think of the whole prior to its parts and of the parts prior to the whole is simply nonsense. Treated independently of the whole, parts cannot be 'parts'. Likewise, taken independently of the parts, the whole cannot be a whole. To say of atoms that exist in a free state that they are 'parts' would be absurd. They become parts only when they enter into the composition of a whole, that is only in relation to a molecule. And the atoms in turn are only wholes in relation to the nucleuses and electrons (or parts) into which they can be broken down. 'Whole' and 'part', therefore, are not really concepts that refer to two 'different' kinds of things. As Hegel points out regarding other categorical couples (like cause and effect), whole and part form but one and the same concept:[1] that of the *whole/part relationship*.

This dialectical view finds corroboration in every area of contemporary science where – at the deepest level – what we find are not things but relations. In quantum physics, for example, in contrast to what is suggested by the inaccurate expression 'elementary particles', it is not the particle that is elementary but the *fundamental interaction* in which it participates. [2] One can easily draw examples of this sort from the other sciences. The whole, therefore, is in its essence a totalization of parts, which in their turn are constitutive elements of a whole. What we have here is a typical *dialectical unity of opposites* – there is no top without a bottom, or identity without a difference (a formal difference that becomes real in human beings, where it can remain identical to itself only by constantly differing from itself through metabolic exchanges, cellular renewal, immunitary adaptations, etc.). Whole and part always mutually presuppose and imply each other.

This attempt to rethink the whole/part relation in a dialectical manner, however, encounters a limit in the very form of its object. The basis of dialectics is the unity of opposites, a unity that encompasses their concrete identity, which is to say, includes their differences. But whole and part cannot be thought of as a typical example of this unity. As Hegel points out, 'the whole is equal to the parts', but – he adds – 'it is not equal to them as parts.'[3] The whole is equal to the parts only insofar as they are 'taken together', and taken 'together' they are precisely nothing but the whole. To claim that the whole is equal to the parts is thus a mere tautology: the whole is equal to itself. This is equally true as regards the parts. They are equal to the whole insofar as it is an ensemble of parts – they are therefore equal to themselves. Even when it is conceived dialectically, however, the relation of the whole to the parts remains haunted by the abstract understanding; it still seems to be an external relation in which the diversity of the parts and the unity of the whole are to a certain extent alien to each other. If the pieces of a building set, for example, have shapes that seem to prescribe how the set should be assembled, they still don't predetermine the whole that one can construct with them. Furthermore, a given whole can be constructed in more or less the same way with different pieces.

The idea of an organic whole

If we follow the development of this problem in Hegel's *Science of Logic*, the relation of the whole to the parts, which was initially understood as 'external and mechanical', gets transformed into a dialectical relation in which the parts and the whole are not 'indifferent' to each other. Now, each component of the relation *entirely internalizes the other* – they have become identical in their difference: whole of parts and parts of the whole.[4] When one passes from the mechanical and from the physical to the chemical, to the biological and to anything that manifests a 'spiritual life', the simple whole gets transformed by degrees into something quite different: an authentic 'totality' that we would qualify as 'organic'. At this point, we are not in the presence of a haphazard assemblage of pieces but of a synthetic unity made up of 'limbs and organs' that belong to it, and can only revert to being parts in the hands of an anatomist who deals not with living bodies but with corpses.[5] The organic totality is thus the *dialectically achieved* form of the whole/part relation.

It is by such means that the ordinary logico-philosophical view of the relation between part and whole is overturned. For if the parts are integral to the whole, they can no longer be viewed as preexisting it as pieces in a construction game that enable the whole to be put together. Rather, in an organic totality, the whole *forms its parts* and is simultaneously formed by them through embryological or historical processes. Playing in this way an active role in the production of its parts, the whole also leaves its imprint on them. Hence a paradox that is inconceivable from a non-dialectical point of view: in a certain sense, the whole *is present in each of its parts*, which can then be said to belong to the whole in a very unusual way. Thus, in quantum cosmology, the history as well as the present state of the universe can be read out of every particle; the cellular program that permitted the birth of the cloned ewe Dolly from a mammal tissue also shows the extent to which the entire biological individual is present in each of his cells and so on. Marx, whose analysis of a social formation presupposes its nature as an organic totality, pointed out that in urban societies a town is not a 'simple multiplicity of individual houses. Here, the whole is not constituted by its parts. It is a kind of autonomous organism.... The economic totality is, in a fundamental way, present in each individual house.'[6] The categorical vocabulary itself must change, for this totality is not, properly speaking, *composed of parts* but *organically formed* of limbs, organs and functions. Put in still another way, rather than the simple addition of homogenous parts, the whole here is, before all else, a new *emergent* reality.

From totality to emergence

It is time to attack the question head-on: Doesn't the term 'emergence' designate, more or less judiciously, a category that is in its essence dialectical? This suggestion is all the more plausible since even the best non-dialectical works on emergence never come to grips with what they purport to explain.

The limits to explaining the superior by the inferior

An outstanding article by the Danish philosopher Claus Emmeche and his scientific co-authors Simo Koppe and Frederic Stjernfelt, 'Explaining Emergence: Towards an Ontology of Levels', is a case in point (Emmeche *et al.*, 1997). Drawing on C. Lloyd Morgan's (1923) definition of 'emergence' as a 'creation of new properties', they carefully analyze each of these terms in order to bring out the relation between emergence and determinism, making no concessions to either vitalistic irrationalism or to the simplifications inherent in a mechanical determinism. The aim of the article is to achieve a 'final devitalization of emergence'. It seeks to expunge the concept of emergence, in other words, from all its finalist and theological connotations, so that it can become part of a scientific view of reality that has been expanded to include all that we've learned from the dynamics of non-linear systems. The research program is admirable, and we want to underline how interested we are in what they have presented. However, the conclusions they come to are very disappointing.

For example, after a long and interesting study of the relationship between the levels and sub-levels of reality, Emmeche and his co-authors assert that if the laws of a lower level cannot explain the specific laws of a higher one, the latter, in turn, 'cannot alter the laws of the lower level'. Thus, 'biological phenomena cannot alter physical laws', nor can psychical phenomena alter biological laws. This claim in undeniably true – that 'natural laws cannot be abolished' is a crucial materialist thesis for Marx.[7] While undeniable, this claim would result in an indefensible fatalism if it were not completed. For, as Marx pointed out, if the laws of nature cannot be abolished, the *form* under which they manifest themselves can change. Every law expresses a certain necessity, but it is a universal necessity that doesn't prescribe by what singular processes and under what unique conditions it will be realized. In other words, the law only circumscribes a range of both *formal possibilities* and real impossibilities. This is why a given level of organization of matter, while respecting the laws of the lower level(s) on which it rests, will nonetheless *superimpose its own logic* on the lower level (s) and select what actually takes place out of the formal possibilities that are available.

An important *dialectical reversal* occurs here in which the general determination of the superior by the inferior has to accommodate itself to a particular determination of the inferior by the superior. It is precisely the understanding of this reversal that takes us from a simple materialism, closed within a one-sided view of things, to a complex materialism that has a place for all the dialectics of reciprocal action. A quick example illustrates this point: in general, the evolution of biological species depends on conditions in the natural environment. But with historically developed humanity, as much as people try to create a particular way of life, various social logics impose themselves, for better or worse, on the underlying natural conditions. In this way, industrial activities that aim to increase the return of private capital end up polluting the environment to such an extent that they have altered the world's climate; in the developed societies, various conditions and social practices have also affected the average height, life expectancy, brain functions and more of many individuals. This indicates something of the exceptional range of application of Hegel's – and also Marx and Engels' – analysis of the important, though often confused, distinction between 'base' and 'support' (in German, *Grund* and *Grundlage*). The support of anything is the condition of its possibility, while the base is what gives it its fundamental character. For example, if a territory provides a nation with a support, it is its history that gives it a base and explains what it has become.

In the various levels of organization found in matter, one must expect that the initial base of whatever process is being considered (e.g., the natural conditions required for the appearance of our species) tends to get reduced to a mere supporting function once the specific qualities of the higher level begin to develop (in this case, the socially and historically formed capacities of human beings). This specificity does not emerge any longer from its support (though the latter remains a determining condition of its possibility), but in the logic of its own internal relations, which also becomes the explanatory base of this new level. One can measure here the extent to which the claim, in a sense undeniable, that the higher level cannot 'alter' the laws of the lower level still fails (through lack of dialectics) to capture a crucial aspect of reality. And it is just this missing aspect that is decisive for dispelling the obscurity that surrounds the logico-philosophical question of emergence.

For if the phenomenon of emergence results in the creation of new properties, what is the origin of such properties? The question appears insoluble. Two possibilities suggest themselves. The first is that these properties originate in preconditions located at an inferior level or in a previous situation. In other words, the new properties were already in existence somewhere and somehow, but this explanation seems to say that there really was no emergence. The second view starts by rejecting the idea that new properties originate from any initial conditions, but this amounts to asserting that these new properties have been created *ex nihilo*. Both of these positions are equally absurd. Confronted with an irreducible paradox of this sort, our only option is to start to think dialectically. This is what Hegel does in a long section of the first book of his *Science of Logic* when he reflects on the dialectics of quality and quantity. At the center of this reflection is the category of 'qualitative jump', and it is here that we find the key to our problem.

Quantity and quality

Is it necessary to resort to dialectics to capture such a notion? If a lot of scientists are still cautious or even hostile to the very idea of non-linearity, many are led in their own work to make use of such notions as limited value, threshold effect, transition phase... Should one claim that, unless they have studied the *Science of Logic*, these scientists don't know what they are doing? Doubtless, they know what they are doing, but, philosophically speaking, they often do not know what they know, and beyond a certain point this limitation cannot but have a regret-table influence on their work. It is this second order knowledge of the dialectics of quality and quantity that we will rely on now to arrive at a plausible explanation of the concept of emergence and an account of the processes it designates. This is a difficult task, for we have to express in a few paragraphs some of the complex thoughts that takes up about 70 pages in the first book of the *Science of Logic*. At best, we can only hope to provide a very simplified overview, and it should be taken as such if we are to avoid countless misunderstandings and as many irrelevant objections.

A thing is only what it is in so far as it is not something else. This negation establishes an internal as well as external limit that constitutes the difference between one thing and another, and at the same time determines its *identity*. The determinateness of the thing (its identity-difference) is its *quality*, which in turn manifests itself in a particular set of properties. In this way, quality forms a body with the thing as determined by its limits; it cannot change without changing it, without making it 'different'. In contrast, quantity is what Hegel calls the 'suppressed (*aufgehobene*) quality', that is the *indifferent* change, the change that does not make a thing differ from itself. A house is a house, whether it is bigger or smaller; the color red remains red, whether it is paler or deeper.

Thus, quality and quantity are *dialectical opposites*, and not – as most people view them – two dimensions of being that are more or less foreign to one another, which would make it inconceivable that a quantitative change could trigger a qualitative change. It is because they form a couple of opposites that there is a dialectics of quantity and quality, a dialectic in which their concrete unity is the *measure*. Hegel under-stands 'measure' not as the subjective activity of measuring, but as an objective determinate mode of being, as *qualitative quantum*, such as the specific weights or fusion points of substances, the proportions of the solar system or of living organisms.[8] In this way, the whole of nature can be said to be 'measured'. And when the quantum inherent in each measure 'develops beyond a certain limit', the corresponding quality that is enclosed in this limit is also suppressed by a 'jump to a different quality'. As this gets repeated again and again, the relationship involved takes on the form of 'a nodal line connecting differences', like the scale of harmonic sounds or the ordered series of chemical compounds. According to this analysis, the threshold effect and the qualitative jump only exist because there is an inseparable union of the two opposites, quantity and quality, such that a definite quality belongs to the same body as a given 'quanta' (which is itself bounded by certain limits).

Let us advance now to the heart of the analysis. Hegel does not say that qualitative change is always sudden. This interpretation does not do justice to his meaning, and only makes his position easier to contest. Instead, Hegel holds that qualitative change is *punctuated*, that is to say, always occurs at a definite point in quantitative change, or when the latter reaches the threshold beyond which the conditions for the existence of a particular quality can no longer be maintained.[9] Thus, one can think of continuity and rupture together, or, better still, *one can only think of them together* as aspects of the same movement of passage or of change in which one quality becomes another. When considered from the angle of quantity, this passage or process is in fact 'gradual' but 'this gradualness only applies to the exterior facet of change and not to its qualitative side'. From the vantage point of quality, however, change is a jump, since it only occurs when the quantum arrives at a new measure.[10] Thus, the change in anything is like a medal with two faces that the ordinary understanding overlooks in obstinately sticking to one side or the other without investigating the relation between the two, and hence not noticing that a *continuous variation* of the quantity results in a *punctuated mutation* of the quality.

Let's examine more closely what the Hegelian text – at once so speculative and at the same time so profound – actually says: what brings on a qualitative *difference* (the passage to another quality) is a quantitative change, one that is foreign to the qualitative aspect of the thing. Consequently, the two qualities, the one that exists before the change and the one that comes into existence after it, are *indifferent to each other*. And here then is the really crucial point: *the one is not born out of the other*. In other words, all that the 'new thing' shares with the thing that existed before is 'the external difference of the quantum: it did not emerge out of the previous thing but *immediately out of itself.*'[11]

Where do the novel properties of a new quality come from?

Let us recall that the central question posed by emergence is, "Where do the novel properties of a new quality come from?" and that this question appeared insoluble because they can't come from either what preceded it – without appearing to deny that there is any emergence – or from the novel properties themselves – without falling into the nonsense of seeming to explain a thing by itself. Yet, most of the philosophically minded scholars who have examined the enigma of emergence have consistently overlooked that for almost two centuries a sketch of a third option can be found in Hegel's *Science of Logic*. Hegel's answer, which is fundamentally different from the two examined earlier, would appear to resolve our problem.

The novel properties of a new quality do not originate in the preceding quality, either logically or chronologically. Taking direct aim at the dogma that claims 'there is no jump in nature', Hegel mocks the conventional view according to which the novel properties of a new quality are already contained in whatever it was that preceded it but are unnoticed 'because they are too small'. As Hegel points out, in a chemical series illustrating Dalton's law of multiple proportions, each substance exhibits 'particular qualities' that are completely absent in the preceding stage; they are linked solely to the 'particular points' of the scale at which they emerge. To those who think it is possible to account for the change in quality by singling out the progressive character of the transformation, Hegel responds that progressive change is 'just the opposite of qualitative change'. We can add to Hegel's analysis, of course, that in so far as the new quality does not alter the thing entirely (the vaporization of water does not change its chemical composition) or severe its ties with what in the preceding form has become its support (the construction of an architect doesn't do away with the affect of gravity on his materials), some determinations of the former subsist in the latter as common properties. But, contrary to what ordinary understanding seems to suggest, it is important to acknowledge that the novel properties of a new quality, which is the only aspect of the problem that interests us here, can never be accounted for by starting from either anterior or posterior forms. A key merit of the dialectical category of 'jump' is that it completely rejects any attempt to dismiss or trivialize the *newness of the new*. At the same time, it takes full account of the disturbing fact that, while the acquisition of new properties by the new quality is necessary and therefore foreseeable from a quantitative point of view, it may nonetheless be qualitatively unpredictable. One can see how this aspect of dialectical analysis also illuminates another fundamental paradox of non-linearity, which is the disconcerting coincidence it gives rise to between determinism and unpredictability.

This is the first negation contained in Hegel's response to the question that we posed. The second is as follows: to claim that the new thing emerges 'immediately from itself' does not amount to getting trapped in the logical mystery that would treat the thing as its own explanation, or, even worse, in the irrational belief of a creation *ex nihilo*. What does the expression 'from itself' mean then? If we understand it in a resolutely materialist manner, it means that the novel properties of the qualities considered arose out of the *new quantum* at which the qualitative leap occurred, this quantum carrying with it a *new measure* in the Hegelian sense of the term, that is to say a new unity of quantity and quality. It is the passage to a new quantum that generates whatever is distinctive of the new whole. One should not try to make sense of a qualitatively new whole, therefore, by calling up the old one, but by *analyzing the new one*.

And what needs to be analyzed there? What exactly is the thing in the whole that has to be discerned that is not the simple sum of its parts and yet is not so foreign to them that it suggests a *deus ex machina*? This something is its *organization* as a whole, the *overall connection of its elements* and its *logic*, which together constitute precisely what is novel about the new measure that has emerged at the tipping point. As indicated by the double negation, this is, in the last analysis, the dialectical affirmation to which we are led by Hegel: the new thing cannot be accounted for either by its elements or without them. It can only be explained by its *relations*, which are the real basis of the qualities that mutate according to the level of quantity involved.[12] Another important insight associated with the above is that not only does the organization of the new whole not derive from the old one, but the disorganization of the latter is a prerequisite for its reorganization on a new basis. Isn't it this essentially dialectical logic that assumes such spectacular forms in such non-linear phenomena as chaos, bifurcation and auto-organization?

Various contemporary forms of knowledge as well as the analyses of some scientists who possess an authentic logico-philosophical culture, one that includes dialectics, show that these are not merely hypothetical philosophical considerations. A case in point is the great biologist and Nobel Prize winner Francois Jacob in his old but still extremely stimulating work *The Logic of Life* (Jacob, 1970). Expounding 'the architecture in stages' of the cell, an 'articulation of structures subordinated to each other', he presents the general principle as follows: 'new properties and logics appear with every level of organization'. Thus, one understands that 'what evolves is not matter... it is the organization itself.' The properties of a given level of organization remain dependent on its parts, and yet they cannot merely be deduced from them (1970, 323, 328, 344). This theoretical approach partakes of a lineage that goes back to Hegel, and belongs squarely within the culture of dialectics, 'a dialectics in which opposites interpenetrate and quality emerges out of quantity' (1970, 170). Anterior to what we learned from the discovery of the intrinsic non-linearity of reality, however, these theses – as relevant as they are even today – could not offer an adequate explanation for the paradox that preoccupies us in this essay, the paradox which the great majority of living scientists try to make sense of using the concept of 'emergence'.

Dialectics and emergence

The meaning of the very notion of 'emergence' remains very controversial. Neither etymology nor common usage provides much support for the analysis made above. Instead, they suggest two common but equally untenable interpretations of the origins of what is novel in the new situation. In one case, to speak of emergence – as in the emergent part of an iceberg, for example – merely refers to the extension of a pre-existing reality; here, the term seems to exclude any authentic newness in what is new. In the other – as in the case of something that surges out of nothing – the notion implies that the result is completely separate from whatever came before. Taken in this sense, the emergent reality appears to be embedded in an irrational vitalism that eschews any organic link to its previous form. The choice, then, seems to be between the impossible occurrence of anything that is authentically new on one hand, and an unthinkable creation *ex nihilo* on the other. If scientific and philosophical reticence to accept the importance of the idea of emergence remains as strong as ever, therefore, the unfortunate resonance of the term itself must bear some of the responsibility for this state of affairs. But if the interpretation given to the process of emergence by non-linear thinking really succeeds in bypassing these criticisms, the meaning of 'emergence' for which we have been arguing may yet acquire wide acceptance. And this new meaning will place it squarely within the culture of dialectics.

Notes

* This is an abridged and edited version of a work that appeared in Sève 2005.

1. Hegel, 1981b, vol. II, 'La Logique du concept', section I, chap. 1, B.
2. In their overview of the particule universe, the physicists Gilles Cohen-Tannoudji and Jean-Pierre Baton wrote, 'The smallest entity of matter is no longer an object. It is a relation, an interaction, what we call a quantum of action' (1989, 9). And these authors in their book make explicit use of the vocabulary of dialectics.
3. Hegel, 1981b, vol. II, 'La Logique de l'essence', section II, chap. 3, A.
4. Hegel, 1981a, *Encyclopédie des Sciences philosophiques*, vol. I: *'La Science de la logique'*, Addition to § 135.
5. Ibid.
6. Marx, *Manuscrits de 1857–1858*, the chapter on capital, V, I.
7. See letter of July 11, 1868, in K. Marx and F. Engels, *Letters to Kugelmann*, Éditions sociales, Paris, 1971.
8. The idea of a *non-accidental 'measure'* of living matter has had a great career in contemporary science without, it would seem, any input from Hegel. See, for example, Erwin Schrödinger,*Qu'est-ce que la vie?*, or Stephen Jay Gould, *Darwin et les grandes énigmes de la vie*, chap. 21.
9. Hegel, it is true, mentions water here as an example of a substance that becomes 'solid all at once when it freezes'. But, if cases of more or less sudden qualitative change in nature are plentiful, numerous examples to the contrary could be mentioned. Furthermore, the suddenness of the qualitative jump, for Hegel, is only a consequence of its punctuality (he does not say whether he considers it necessary). It is punctuality alone that constitutes its basic truth: a qualitative change spread over time does not contradict it as long as it takes place at a determined threshold. The so-called 'dialectical law' according to which qualitative change has to *be sudden* – as if, to take a trivial example, water could not evaporate very slowly at ordinary temperature but only at boiling point. This 'law', which belongs to Stalin's 1937 vulgarization of dialectical Marxism, is nothing but ideological support for the belief that 'to avoid being wrong in politics, one must be a revolutionary and not a reformist', an assertion all the more groundless since it mistakenly assimilates suddenness with the revolutionary essence of social transformations.
10. In what contemporary physics refers to as phase transitions 'of the second order' – such as boiling water under very high pressure – *the clear distinction* between phases (between the liquid and the vapor state) *fades away*, giving rise to 'critical states' where the two forms interpenetrate on every scale (water bubbles containing liquid droplets that in turn contain vapor bubbles, and so on). The Hegelian notion of 'nodal point', therefore, cannot be credited with absolute validity. Nevertheless, at the same time, thresholds are omnipresent, since, for example, the erasure of clear-cut limits between the phases of a second order transition takes place at a *precise point* – in the case of water, at a pressure of 218.3 atmospheres. This should make clear the great importance of Hegel's analysis as well as the error of taking it as the last word in a closed theoretical system. All categorical (*catégoriel*) knowledge, no matter how advanced it is for a given time, may still have surprises

in store for us. We must be willing to dialectize dialectics without limits. Thus, because he only considered isolated contradictions, for example, Hegel ended up ignoring the *statistical* dimension of things, whose importance is fundamental for understanding the complexity of transitions from one phase to the next.

11. Hegel, 1981b, *Science of logique*, vol. I, section III, chap. 2, B.
12. Physicists who work on phase transitions have raised the question – Can we explain the discontinuities observed on the macroscopic scale, as in the vaporization of a liquid, from its microscopic structure? Does a quick transformation at the atomic level take place at the temperature of transition, making the change of phase no more than its 'reflection'? According to the physicist Roger Balian, this question has now been answered: 'On the atomic scale, nothing distinguishes water from vapor or ice; their mutual transformations correspond to *a change in the organisation of the total structure* that is controlled by two macroscopic parameters, temperature and pressure.' (See Klein and Spiro, 1995, 177–8.)

References

Cohen-Tannoudji, Gilles and Jean-Pierre Baton. 1989. *L'Horizon des particules*. Paris: Gallimard.

Emmeche, C., S. Koppe and F. Stjernfelt. 1997. 'Explaining Emergence: Towards an Ontology of Levels', *Journal for General Philosophy of Science*, 28: 83–119.

Hegel, G.W.F. 1981a. *Encyclopédie des Sciences philosophiques*, vol. I: '*La Science de la logique*'. Addition to § 135. Paris: Aubier Montaigne.

Hegel, G.W.F. 1981b. *Science de la logique*, vol. I, II. Paris: Aubier Montaigne.

Jacob, F. 1970. *La Logique du vivant*. Paris: Gallimard.

Klein, Etienne and Michel Spiro. 1995. *Le Temps et sa fleche*. Paris: Flammarion.

Marx, Karl. 1980. *Manuscrit de 1857–1858*. Paris: Éditions socials.

Marx, Karl and Friedrich Engels. 1971. *Letters to Kugelmann*. Paris: Éditions socials.

Sève, Lucien. (ed.) 2005. *Dynamics and Dialectics of Non-Linear Systems*. Paris: Odile Jacob Éditions.

7
The Dialectics of Spacetime

David Harvey

One of the more frustrating aspects of Marxian approaches to dialectics is the seemingly blind indifference to understanding the role of the basic concepts of space and time. It is even more irritating to find that some of the most interesting dialectical approaches to space and time can be found in the writings of those, such as Leibniz and Alfred North Whitehead, who otherwise have little or no place in the Marxian canon. So why this lacuna in Marxian theorizing? And how can we begin to make up for the absence?

Of course, I exaggerate somewhat when I say there is a *total* absence of consideration of these topics. Lenin's critique of Mach touches on such matters and Lukács ruminated long and hard on the nature of temporality and history as did Benjamin, while Lefebvre's copious writings on spatiality, most notably *The Production of Space*, have been widely cited (though, indicatively, not so much by Marxists). Deleuze and Guattari, clearly influence by, though working tangentially to the Marxian tradition, have much of interest to say on the topic also. And since 1970 or so, geographers within or close to the Marxian tradition such as Soja, Smith, Massey, Merrifield, Thrift, Sheppard, Castree and myself have explicitly sought to lift the veil on what for us has always been a pressing practical as well as a theoretical problem (Crang and Thrift, 2000; Massey, 2005; Merrifield, 2002; Sheppard, 2005; Soja, 1989; Smith, 1984). Since spatiotemporal framing is always overtly or covertly present in any form of inquiry, there are also innumerable places in Marxian theorizing where the issue arises tacitly or tangentially. If, for example, Whitehead is only half correct to insist that the determination of the meaning of nature reduces itself to questions of the character of space and time, then the copious recent writings on environmental questions from a Marxist perspective are necessarily underpinned by some tacit conceptions of space and time. (Burkett, 1999; Whitehead, 1964, 33). But this then poses a problem for Marxian critical theory: Can these tacit and unstated conceptions as to the nature of space and time impose limitations or even lead into gross errors without our knowing it? The only way we can begin to answer such a crucial question is through overt critical engagement with the dialectics of space and time.

In what follows, I outline a view of the dialectics of space and time as a starting point for further debate. This view has been derived from my own practical work on issues of urbanization, uneven geographical development at a variety of scales (from imperialism to spatial fragmentation in the city) and from attempts to extend Marxian political economy to encompass specific understandings of capitalism's workings within and through space and time.

The basic framework I propose operates across two fundamental dimensions. On the first dimension we see three distinctive definitions of space and time: absolute, relative and relational. On the second dimension, due mainly to Lefebvre, we see another three definitions: experienced, conceptualized and lived. I will then examine what happens when we merge these two dimensions. I begin, however, with a consideration of each dimension in isolation.[1]

The first dimension

Absolute space is fixed and we record or plan events within its frame. Space is distinct from time (history is distinct from geography). Time is also absolute and fixed, generally depicted as linear, stretching infinitely from the past into the future. This is the space and time of Newton, Descartes and Kant. Space is usually represented as a pre-existing and immoveable grid amenable to standardized measurement and open to calculation. Geometrically, this is the space of Euclid and therefore the space of cadastral mapping and engineering practices. It is a primary space of individuation – res extensa as Descartes put it – and this applies to all discrete and bounded phenomena. You and me as individual persons are clearly identified in terms of our unique location in absolute space and time. No other person can be exactly in your or my space at a given time. Socially this is the exclusionary space of private property in land and other bounded territorial designations (such as states, administrative units, city plans and urban grids). Within this space and time, measurement and calculability thrive. When Descartes' engineer looked upon the world with a sense of mastery, it was a world of absolute space (and time) from which all uncertainties and ambiguities could in principle be banished and in which human calculation could uninhibitedly flourish. Absolute space and time is pre-eminently the space and time of *things*.

Relative space is mainly associated with the name of Einstein and the non-Euclidean geometries that began to be constructed most systematically in the nineteenth century. This is pre-eminently the space of *processes and of motion*. Space cannot here be understood separately from time (history and geography cannot be separated and so we have to deal in historical geography). This mandates an important shift of language from absolute space *and* absolute time to relative space-time. At the mundane level of geographical work, we know, for example, that the relative space-time of transportation relations looks and is very different from the absolute spaces of private property. The uniqueness of location and individuation defined by bounded territories in absolute space gives way to a multiplicity of locations that are equidistant from, say, some central city location. Relative identity is multiple rather than singular. Many people can be in the same place relative to me and I can be in exactly the same place as many other people relative to someone else. We can create completely different maps of relative locations by differentiating between distances measured in terms of cost, time, modal split (car, bicycle or skateboard) and even disrupt spatial continuities by looking at networks and topological relations (the optimal route for the postman delivering mail or the airline system operating through key hubs). We know, given the differential frictions of distance encountered on the earth's surface, that the shortest distance (measured in terms of time, cost, energy expended) between two points is not necessarily given by the way the legendary crow flies. Furthermore the standpoint of the observer plays a critical role. The typical New Yorker's view of the world, as the famous Steinberg cartoon suggests, fades very fast as one thinks about the lands to the west of the Hudson River or east of Long Island.

All of this relativization does not necessarily reduce or eliminate the capacity for individuation or control, but it does indicate that special rules and laws are required for the particular phenomena and processes under consideration. Measurability and calculability become more complicated. There are multiple geometries from which to choose. The spatial frame varies according to what is relativized and by whom. When Gauss first established the rules of a non-Euclidean spherical geometry to deal with the problems of surveying accurately upon the curved surface of the earth, he also affirmed Euler's assertion that a perfectly scaled map of any portion of the earth's surface is impossible. If maps accurately represent directions then they falsify areas (Greenland looks larger than India on the Mercator map). Einstein took the argument further by pointing out that all forms of measurement depended upon the frame of reference of the observer. The idea of simultaneity in the physical universe, he taught us, has to be abandoned. It was, of course, Einstein's achievement to come up with exact means to examine such phenomena as the curvature of space when examining temporal processes operating at the speed of light (Osserman, 1995). But in Einstein's schema, time remains fixed while it is space that bends according to certain observable rules. Difficulties do arise, however, as we seek to integrate understandings from different fields into some more unified endeavor. The spatiotemporal frame required to represent energy flows through ecological systems may not be compatible with that of capital flows through global financial markets. Understanding the spatiotemporal rhythms of capital accumulation requires a quite different framework to that required to understand global climate change. Such disjunctions, though difficult to work across, are not necessarily a disadvantage, provided we recognize them for what they are. Comparisons between different spatiotemporal frameworks can illuminate problems of political choice (do we favor the spatiotemporal frame defined by financial flows or that of the ecological processes they would and do disrupt, for example). We also see more clearly how processes of capital accumulation, incorporating a drive both to speed up turnover time and to erase the barriers of distance, produce time-space compression in the world market (Harvey, 1989, Part III).

The relational concept of space is most often associated with the name of Leibniz who, in a famous series of letters to Clarke (effectively a stand-in for Newton) objected vociferously to the absolute view of space and time so central to Newton's theories.[2] His primary objection was theological. Newton made it seem as if even God was inside of absolute space and time rather the maker of a particular version of space and time. In the relational view, matter and processes do not exist *in* space-time or even mold it (as in the case of relative space-time). Space and time are internalized within matter and process. It is therefore impossible to disentangle space from time. They fuse into spacetime (the hyphen disappears). This relational notion of spacetime implies the idea of internal relations (a fundamental category in Ollman's dialectics, though even he refrains from any specific examination of its spatiotemporal meanings; Ollman 1992, 2003). An event or a thing at a point in space cannot be understood by appeal to what exists only at that point. It internalizes everything else going on around it in past, present and even future (much as many individuals assembled in a room to discuss bring with them a vast array of experiential data accumulated from the world). A wide variety of disparate influences congeal at a certain point (e.g. within a conference room) to define the nature of that point. Identity, in this argument, means something quite different from the sense we have of it from absolute space. Indeed, individuation and identity become indistinct and immaterial even though objective. This conception appears at first blush rather difficult to absorb within Marxian theory. But, I shall later argue, it is fundamental to the Marxian concept of value. For the moment I merely point to many areas in which the relational conception makes a lot of sense. If we ask, along with Whitehead, where is a thought located, then we are hard-pressed to find a material answer. We cannot dissect someone's brain to identify their thoughts, for example. But if thoughts are immaterial they more often than not have material and objective consequences. Relationality is therefore in the first instance about events and phenomena that are immaterial (like collective memories) but objective.

Measurement becomes more and more problematic the closer we move toward a world of relational spacetime. But why would it be presumed that spacetime only exists if it is measurable and quantifiable in certain traditional ways? This leads to some interesting reflections on the failure (perhaps better construed as limitations) of positivism, empiricism and traditional materialism to evolve adequate understandings of spatial and temporal concepts beyond those that can be measured. In a way, relational conceptions of spacetime bring us to the point where mathematics, poetry and music merge. And that, from a scientific (as opposed to aesthetic) viewpoint, is anathema to those of a positivist or simple materialist bent. Kant, recognizing space as real and absolute but only accessible to the intuitions, tries to build a bridge between Newton and Leibniz by incorporating the concept of space within the theory of Aesthetic Judgment. But Leibniz's return to popularity and significance not only as the guru of cyberspace, but also as a foundational thinker in relationship to more dialectical approaches to mind-brain issues and quantum theoretical formulations signals some sort of urge to go beyond absolute and relative concepts and their more easily measurable qualities as well as beyond the Kantian compromise. But the relational terrain is an extremely challenging and difficult terrain upon which to work. Einstein, for one, could never accept it and so denied quantum theory until the end. There are, however, many thinkers who, over the years, have applied their talents to reflecting upon the possibilities of relational thinking. Alfred North Whitehead was fascinated by the necessity of the relational view and did much to advance it (Fitzgerald 1979). Deleuze likewise has made much of these ideas both in his reflections on Leibniz (with reflections on baroque architecture and the mathematics of the fold in Leibniz's work) as well as on Spinoza (Deleuze 1992). David Bohm's explorations of quantum theory focus heavily on relational thinking (Bohm 2002; Hiley and Peat, 1991).

But why and how would I, as a working geographer, find the relational mode of approaching spacetime useful? The answer is quite simple that there are certain topics, such as the political role of collective memories in urban processes, that can only be approached in this way. I cannot box political and collective memories in some absolute space (clearly situate them on a grid or a map) nor can I understand their circulation according to the rules, however sophisticated, of circulation of ideas in relative space-time. If I ask the question, What does the Basilica of Sacre Coeur in Paris, Tiananmen Square or 'Ground Zero' *mean*? Then the only way I can seek an answer is to think in relational terms (Harvey 2003). And, as I shall shortly show, it is impossible to understand Marxian political economy without engaging with relational perspectives.

So is space (space-time and spacetime) absolute, relative or relational? I simply don't know whether there is an ontological answer to that question. In my own work I think of it as being all three. I reached this conclusion 30 years ago and I have found no particular reason (nor heard any arguments) to make me change my mind. This is what I then wrote,

Space is neither absolute, relative or relational in itself, but it can become one or all simultaneously depending on the circumstances. The problem of the proper conceptualization of space is resolved through human practice with respect to it. In other words, there are no philosophical answers to philosophical questions that arise over the nature of space – the answers lie in human practice. The question 'What is space?' is therefore replaced by the question 'How is it that different human practices create and make use of different conceptualizations of space?' The property relationship, for example, creates absolute spaces within which monopoly control can operate. The movement of people, goods, services, and information takes place in a relative space because it takes money, time, energy, and the like to overcome the friction of distance. Parcels of land also capture benefits because they contain relationships with other parcels...in the form of rent relational space comes into its own as an important aspect of human social practice (Harvey 1973, 13).

Are there rules for deciding when and where one spatial frame is preferable to another? Or is the choice arbitrary, subject to the whims of human practice? The decision to use one or other conception certainly depends on the nature of the phenomena under investigation. The absolute conception may be perfectly adequate for issues of property boundaries and border determinations but it helps me not a whit with the question of what is Tiananmen Square, Ground Zero or the Basilica of Sacre Coeur. I therefore find it helpful – if only as an internal check – to sketch in justifications for the choice of an absolute, relative or relational frame of reference. Furthermore, I often find myself presuming in my practices that there is some hierarchy at work among them in the sense that relational space can embrace the relative and the absolute, relative space can embrace the absolute, but absolute space is just absolute and that is that. But I would not confidently advance this view as a working principle let alone try to defend it theoretically. I find it far more interesting in principle to keep the three concepts in dialectical tension with each other and to constantly think through the interplay among them. Ground Zero is an absolute space at the same time as it is in relative space-time and of relational spacetime. From this I derive the first preliminary determination: the dialectics of space and time entails keeping all three conceptions of absolute, relative and relational in dialectical tension with each other.

The second (Lefebvrian) dimension

Lefebvre constructs a quite different dimension to understanding spatiality out of considerations of human practices (Lefebvre, 1991). He derives (almost certainly drawing upon Cassirer, though, as usual in French intellectual circles, without acknowledgment; see Cassirer, 1944) a tripartite division of material space (the space of experience and of perception open to physical touch and sensation); the representation of space (space as conceived and represented); and spaces of representation (the lived space of sensations, the imagination, emotions and meanings incorporated into how we live day by day).

Material space is, for us humans, quite simply the world of our tactile and sensual interaction with matter, it is the space of physical and sensual experience. The elements, moments and events in that world are constituted out of a materiality of certain qualities. How we represent this world is, however, an entirely different matter. We usually seek some appropriate if not accurate reflection of the spatial and temporal qualities that attach to the material realities that we experience. We use abstract representations (words, graphs, maps, diagrams, pictures, geometry and other mathematical formulations, etc.) to do this. The correspondence between the materiality and the representation is always in question and frequently fraught with dangerous illusions. But Lefebvre, along with other Marxists like Benjamin, insists that we do not live as material atoms floating around in a materialist world; we also have imaginations, fears, emotions, psychologies, fantasies and dreams (Benjamin, 1999). These form what Lefebvre calls, rather awkwardly, spaces of representation. This depicts the way we humans live – physically, affectively and emotionally – in the world. We may also seek to represent the way this space is lived emotively and affectively as well as materially by means of poetic images, photographic compositions and artistic reconstructions. The strange spatiotemporality of a dream, a fantasy, a hidden longing, a lost memory or even a peculiar thrill or tingle of fear as we walk down a street can be given representation through works of art that ultimately always have a mundane presence in absolute space and time.

So, according to Lefebvre, we experience space, conceptualize and represent space and live space. It is tempting, as with the first tripartite division of spatial terms we considered, to treat of Lefebvre's three categories as hierarchically ordered, but here too it seems most appropriate to keep the three categories in dialectical tension. The physical and material experience of spatial ordering is mediated to some degree by the way space and time are represented. The oceanographer/physicist swimming among the waves may experience them differently from the poet enamored of Walt Whitman or the pianist who loves Debussy. Reading a book about Patagonia will likely affect how we experience that place when we travel there even if we experience considerable cognitive dissonance between expectations generated by the written word and how it actually feels upon the ground. The spaces and times of representation that envelop and surround us as we go about our daily lives likewise affect both our direct experiences and the way we interpret and understand representations. We may not even notice the material qualities of spatial orderings incorporated into daily life because we adhere to unexamined routines. Yet it is through those daily material routines that we absorb a certain sense of how spatial representations work and build up certain spaces of representation for ourselves (e.g. the visceral sense of security in a familiar neighborhood or of being 'at home'). We only notice when something appears radically out of place. It is, I want to suggest, the dialectical relation between the categories that really counts, even though it is useful for purposes of understanding to crystallize each element out as a distinctive moment to the experience of space and time.

This mode of thinking about space helps me interpret works of art and architecture. A picture, like Munch's *The Scream*, is a material object but it works from the standpoint of a psychic state (Lefebvre's space of representation or lived space), and attempts through a particular set of representational codes (the representation of space or conceived space) to take on a physical form (the material space of the picture open to our actual physical experience) that says something to us about the qualities of how Munch lived that space. He seems to have had some sort of horrific nightmare, the sort from which we wake up screaming. And he has managed to convey something of the sense of that through the physical object. Many contemporary artists, making use of multimedia and kinetic techniques, create experiential spaces in which several modes of experiencing space-time combine. Here, for example, is how Judith Barry's contribution to the Third Berlin Biennial for Contemporary Art is described in the catalogue:

> Judith Barry investigates the use, construction and complex interaction of private and public spaces, media, society, and genders. The themes of her installations and theoretical writings position themselves in a field of observation that addresses historical memory, mass communication, and perception. In a realm between the viewer's imagination and media-generated architecture, she creates imaginary spaces, alienated depictions of profane reality.... In the work *Voice Off*...the viewer penetrates the claustrophobic crampedness of the exhibition space, goes deeper into the work, and, forced to move through the installation, experiences not only cinematic but also cinemaesthetic impressions. The divided projection space offers the possibility of making contact with different voices. The use and hearing of voices as a driving force, and the intensity of the psychic tension – especially on the male side of the projection, – conveys the inherent strength of this intangible and ephemeral object. The voices demonstrate for spectators how one can change through them, how one tries to take control of them and the loss one feels when they are no longer heard. (2004, 48–9)

The ultimate dialectics of space and time

There is much in this description of Barry's work that escapes the Lefebvrian categories and refers back to the distinctions between absolute space and time (the cramped physical structure of the exhibit), relative space-time (the sequential motion of the visitor through the space) and relational spacetime (the memories, the voices, the psychic tension, the intangibility and ephemerality, as well as the claustrophobia). Yet we cannot let go of the Lefebvrian categories either. Her constructed spaces have material, conceptual and lived dimensions.

I propose, therefore, a speculative leap in which we place the threefold division of absolute, relative and relational space-time up against the tripartite division of experienced, conceptualized and lived space identified by Lefebvre. The result is a three-by-three matrix (Figure 7.1).

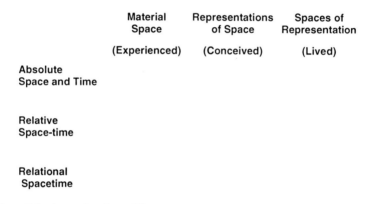

Figure 7.1 A matrix of possible spatio temporalities (note that across the first line indentities can be clearly assigned, across the second they are multiple and across the third they become uncertain and immaterial).

The points of intersection within the matrix suggest different modalities of understanding the meanings of space, space-time and spacetime. It may properly be objected that I am here restricting possibilities because a matrix mode of representation is self-confined to an absolute space. This is a perfectly valid objection. Insofar as I am here engaging in a representational practice (conceptualization), I cannot do justice to either the experienced or the lived realms of spatiality either. By definition, therefore, the matrix I set up and the way I can use it has limited revelatory power. But with all that conceded, I find it helpful to consider the combinations that arise at different intersections within the matrix provided, that is we construe this as a beginning rather than as an endpoint.

The virtue of representation in absolute space is that it allows us to individuate phenomena with great clarity. With a bit of imagination it is possible to think dialectically across all the points defined within the matrix so that each is imagined as an internal relation of all the others. I find it helpful to read across or down the matrix of categories and to imagine complex scenarios of combination. It proves impossible to confine oneself to just one modality of spatial and spatiotemporal thinking. The actions taken in the absolute space only make sense in relational terms. Even more interesting, therefore, is the situation in which moments in the matrix are in more explicit dialectical tension. Let me illustrate.

In what space or spacetime is the site known as 'Ground Zero' in Manhattan located and how does this affect our understanding of that site and of what should be built? It is, of course, an absolute space that can be materially reconstructed and to this end engineering calculations (informed by Newtonian mechanics) and architectural designs must be made. There is much discussion about retaining walls and the load-bearing capacities of the site. Aesthetic Judgments on how the space, once turned into a material artifact of some sort, might be lived as well as conceptualized and experienced are also influential. The problem is to so arrange the physical space as to produce an emotive effect while matching certain expectations (commercial as well as emotive and aesthetic) as to how the space might be lived. Once constructed, the experience of the space may be mediated by representational forms (such as guide books and plans) that help us interpret the intended meanings of the reconstructed site. But moving dialectically across the dimension of absolute space alone is much less rewarding than the insights that come from appealing to the other spatiotemporal frames. Capitalist developers are keenly aware of the relative location of the site and judge its prospects for commercial development according to a logic of exchange relations and the flows of capital that relate to it and give it its commercial value. Its centrality and proximity to the command and control functions of Wall Street are important attributes and if transportation access can be improved in the course of reconstruction, then so much the better since this can only add to land and property values. For the developers the site does not merely exist *in* relative space-time: the re-engineering of the site offers the prospect of transforming relative space-time so as to enhance the commercial value of the absolute spaces (by improving access to airports, for example). The temporal horizon would be dominated by considerations of the amortization rate and the interest/discount rate applying to fixed capital investments in the built environment.

But there would almost certainly be popular objections, led by the families of those killed at that site, to thinking and building only in these absolute or relative spatiotemporal terms. Whatever is built at this site has to say something about individual and collective memory. Memory is immaterial but objective and hence relational. There will likely also be pressures to say something about the meanings of community and nation as well as about future possibilities (perhaps even a prospect of eternal truths). Nor could the site ignore the issue of relational spatial connectivity to the rest of the world. Can something experienced as a local and personal tragedy be reconciled with an understanding of the international forces that were so powerfully condensed within those few shattering moments in a particular place? Will we get to feel in that space the widespread resentment in the rest of the world toward the way US hegemony was so selfishly being exercised throughout during the 1980s and 1990s? Will we get to know that the Reagan administration played a key role in creating and supporting the Taliban in Afghanistan in order to undermine the Soviet occupation and that Osama bin Laden turned from being an ally of the US into an enemy because of US support for the corrupt regime in Saudi Arabia? Or will we only learn of cowardly, alien and evil 'others' out there who hated the US and sought to destroy it because of all it stood for in terms of the values of liberty and freedom? The relational spatiotemporality of the event and the site can be exhumed with enough dedicated digging. But the manner of its representation and of its materialization is uncertain. The outcome will clearly depend upon political struggle. And the fiercest battles will have to be fought over what relational spacetime the rebuilding will invoke. Capitalist developers would not be averse to combining their mundane commercial concerns with inspiring symbolic statements (emphasizing the power and indestructibility of the political-economic system of global capitalism that received such a body blow on 9/11) by erecting, say, a towering phallic symbol that spells defiance. They, too, seek expressive power in relational spacetime. But there are all manner of other relationalities to be explored. What will we know about those who attacked and how far will we connect? The site is and will have a relational presence in the world no matter what is built there and it is important to reflect on how this presencing works: will it be lived as a symbol of US arrogance or as a sign of global compassion and understanding? Taking up such matters requires that we embrace a relational conception of spacetime.

The dialectics of space and time in Marxian theory

What has all this to do with Marxian theory? The Marxist tradition, I began by observing, has not been deeply engaged upon such issues and this general failure (although there are, of course, numerous exceptions) has more often than not meant a loss of possibilities for certain kinds of transformative politics. If, for example, socialist realist art fails to capture the imagination and if the monumentality achieved under past communist regimes was so lacking in inspiration, if planned communities and communist cities often seem so dead to the world, then one way to engage critically with this problem would be to look at the modes of thinking about space and spacetime incorporated in the communist project and the unnecessarily limiting and constricting roles they may have played in socialist planning practices.

There has not been much explicit debate about such issues within the Marxist tradition. Yet Marx himself is a relational thinker. In revolutionary situations such as that of 1848, Marx worried that the past as memory might weigh like a nightmare on the brain of the living and forthrightly posed the question as to how a revolutionary poetry of the future might be constructed in the then and there (1963). At that time he also pled with Cabet not to take his communist-minded followers to the new world. There, Marx averred, the Icarians would only re-plant the attitudes and beliefs internalized from out of the experience of the old. They should, Marx advised, stay as good communists in Europe and fight through the revolutionary transformation in that space, even though there was always the danger that a revolution made in 'our little corner of the world' would fall victim to the global forces ranged around it (see Marin 1984).

Furthermore, in the works of Thompson, Williams and others, we find different levels of appreciation of spatiotemporality (Thompson 1967; Williams, 1989). In Williams' novel *People of the Black Mountains* the relationality of spacetime is central. Williams uses it to bind the narrative together and directly emphasizes the different ways of knowing that come with different senses of spacetime:

> If lives and places were being seriously sought, a powerful attachment to lives and to places was entirely demanded. The polystyrene model and its textual and theoretical equivalents remained different from the substance they reconstructed and simulated .... At his books and maps in the library, or in the house in the valley, there was a common history which could be translated anywhere, in a community of evidence and rational enquiry. Yet he had only to move on the mountains for a different kind of mind to assert itself; stubbornly native and local, yet reaching beyond to a wider common flow, where touch and breadth replaced record and analysis; not history as narrative but stories as lives (1989, 10–12).

For Williams the relationality comes alive walking on the mountains. It centers a completely different sensibility and feeling than that constructed from the archive. Interestingly, it is only in his novels that Williams seems able to get at this problem. So how then can the broader perspectives I have outlined on the dialectics of space and spacetime become more closely integrated into our reading, interpretation and use of Marxian theory? Let me lay aside all concern for caveats and nuances in order to present an argument in the starkest possible terms.

In the first chapter of *Capital*, Marx introduces three key concepts of use value, exchange value and value. Everything that pertains to use value lies in the province of absolute space and time. Individual workers, machines, commodities, factories, roads, houses and actual labor processes, expenditures of energy and the like can all be individuated, described and understood in themselves within the Newtonian frame of absolute space and time. Everything that pertains to exchange value lies in relative space-time because exchange entails movements of commodities, money, capital, labor power and people over time and space. It is the circulation, the perpetual motion, that counts. Exchange, as Marx observes, therefore breaks through all barriers of (absolute) space and time (1976, 209). It perpetually reshapes the geographical and temporal coordinates within which we live our daily lives. It gives different meaning to the use values we command in absolute space. With the advent of money, this 'breaking through' defines an even grander and more fluid universe of exchange relations across the relative space-time of the world market (understood not as a thing but as continuous movement and interaction). The circulation and accumulation of capital occurs, in short, in relative space-time. Value is, however, a relational concept. Its referent is, therefore, relational spacetime. Value, Marx states (somewhat surprisingly), is immaterial but objective. 'Not an atom of matter enters into the objectivity of commodities as values' (1976, 138; see also 167). As a consequence, value does not 'stalk about with a label describing what it is' but hides its relationality within the fetishism of commodities (1976, 165–77). The only way we can approach it is via that peculiar world in which material relations are established between people (we relate to each other via what we produce and trade) and social relations are constructed between things (prices are set for what we produce and trade). Values are, in short, social relations and these are always immaterial but objective. They are impossible to measure except by way of their effects (try measuring any social relation of power directly and you always fail). Value, according to Marx, internalizes the whole historical geography of innumerable labor processes set up under conditions of or in relation to capital accumulation in the spacetime of the world market. Many are surprised to find that Marx's most fundamental concept is 'immaterial but objective' given the way he is usually depicted as a materialist for whom anything immaterial would be anathema. But he roundly condemns the materialism of those scientists who cannot incorporate history (and, I would add, geography) into their understandings. This relational definition of value, I note in passing, renders moot if not misplaced all those attempts to come up with some direct and essentialist measure of it. I repeat, social relations can only ever be measured by their effects.

If my characterization of the Marxian categories is correct, then this shows no priority can be accorded to any one spatiotemporal frame. The three spatiotemporal frames must be kept in dialectical tension with each other in exactly the same way that use value, exchange value and value dialectically intertwine within the Marxian theory. There would, for example, be no value in relational spacetime without concrete labors constructed in innumerable places in absolute spaces and times. Nor would value emerge as an immaterial but objective power without the innumerable acts of exchange, the continuous circulation processes, that weld together the global market in relative space-time. Value is, then a social relation that internalizes the whole history and geography of concrete labors in the world market. It is expressive of the social (primarily but not exclusively class) relations of capitalism constructed on the world stage. It is crucial to mark the temporality involved, not only because of the significance of past 'dead' labor (fixed capital including all of that embedded in built environments) but also because of all the traces of the history of proletarianization, of primitive accumulation, of technological developments that are internalized within the value form. Above all, we have to acknowledge the 'historical and moral elements' that always enter into the determination of the value of labor power (Marx, 1976, 275). We then see Marx's theory working in a particular way. The spinner embeds value (i.e. abstract labor as a relational determination that has no material measure) in the cloth by performing concrete labor in an absolute space and time. The objective power of the value relation is registered when the spinner is forced to give up making the cloth and the factory falls silent because conditions in the world market are such as to make this activity in that particular absolute space and time valueless. While all of this may seem obvious, the failure to acknowledge the interplay entailed between the different spatiotemporal frames in Marxian theory often produces conceptual confusion. Much discussion of so-called 'global–local relations' has become a conceptual muddle, for example, because of the inability to under-stand the different spatiotemporalities involved. We cannot say that the value relation causes the factory to close down as if it is some external abstract force. It is the changing concrete conditions of labor in China when mediated through exchange processes in relative space-time that transforms value as an abstract social relation in the world market in such a way as to bring the concrete labor process in Mexico to closure. A popular term like 'globalization' functions relationally in exactly this way at the same time as it disguises the value form and its reference to class relations. If we ask where is globalization, then we cannot find a material answer.

So far, I have largely confined attention to a dialectical reading of Marxian theory down the left hand column of the matrix. What happens when I start to read across the matrix instead? The materiality of use values and concrete labors in the factory is obvious enough when we examine the laborer's experience in absolute space and time. But how should this be represented and conceived? Physical descriptions are easy to produce but Marx insists that the social relations (themselves not directly measurable) under which work is performed are critical also. Under capitalism the wage laborer is conceptualized (second column) as a producer of surplus value for the capitalist and this is represented as a relation of exploitation. This implies that the labor process is lived (third column) as alienation. Under different social relations, for example those of socialism, work could be lived as creative satisfaction and conceptu-alized as self-realization through collective endeavors. It may not even have to change materially in order for it to be reconceptualized and lived in a quite different way. This was, after all, Lenin's hope when he advoc-ated the adoption of Fordism in Soviet factories. Fourier, for his part, thought that work should be about play and the expression of desire and be lived as sublime joy, and for that to happen the material qual-ities of work processes would need to be radically restructured. At this point we have to acknowledge a variety of competing possibilities. In his book *Manufacturing Consent*, for example, Burawoy (1982) found that the workers in the factory he studied did not generally experience work as alienation. This arose because they smothered the idea of exploitation by turning the workplace into a site for role and game-playing (Fourier style). The labor process was performed by the workers in such a way as to permit them to live the process in a non-alienated way. There are some advantages for capital in this, since unalienated workers often work more efficiently. And, we have to admit, if there is no prospect of any radical revolutionary change, workers might just as well try to live their lives in an unalienated and even fun way. Capitalists have therefore acceded to various measures, such as calisthenics, quality circles and the like, to try to reduce alienation and to emphasize incorporation. They have also produced alternative conceptualizations that emphasize the rewards of hard work and produce ideologies to negate the theory of exploitation. While the Marxian theory of exploitation may be formally correct, therefore, it does not always or necessarily translate into alienation and political resistance. Much depends on how it is conceptualized. Part of class struggle is therefore about driving home the significance of exploitation as the proper conceptualization of how concrete labors are accomplished under capitalist social relations. Again, it is the dialectical tension between the material, the conceived and the lived that really matters. If we treat the tensions in a mechanical way then we are lost.

While working through matters in this way is helpful, I earlier argued that the 'matrix thinking' offers limited opportunities unless we are prepared to range freely and dialectically over all the moments of the matrix simultaneously. Let me give an example. The primary form of representation of value is through money. This too is an immaterial concept with objective power but it must also take on material form as an actual use value. This it does in the first instance through the emergence of the money commodity (e.g. the thing gold). The emergence occurs, however, through acts of exchange in relative space-time and it is this that allows tangible money forms to become an active presence in absolute space and time. This creates the paradox that a particular material use value (such as gold or a dollar bill) has to represent the universality of value, of abstract labor. An absolute representation and materialization must be found for relational meanings. It further implies that social power can be appropriated by private persons and from this the very possibility of money as capital placed in circulation in relative space-time arises.

There are, as Marx points out, many antinomies, antitheses and contradictions in how money is created, conceptualized, circulated and used as both a tangible means of circulation and a representation of value on the world market. Precisely because value is immaterial and objective, money always combines fictitious qualities with tangible forms. It is subject to that reversal Marx describes in the fetishism of commodities such that material relations arise between people and social relations are registered between things. Money as an object of desire and as an object of neurotic contemplation imprisons us in fetishisms while the inherent contradictions in the money form inevitably produce not only the possibility but also the inevitability of capitalist crises. Money anxieties are frequently with us and have their own spatiotemporal locations (the impoverished child that pauses before the vast panoply of capitalist commodities perpetually beyond reach in the window of the store). The spectacles of consumption that litter the landscape in absolute space and time can generate senses of relative deprivation. We are surrounded at every turn with manifestations of the fetish desire for money power as the representation of value on the world market. But the currents that swirl round relationally in world financial markets produce frequent crises – many devastating as in Indonesia in 1998 and Argentina in 2002. The relational tensions are registered in the absolute spaces and times of neighborhood, cities and whole countries.

Now let me range widely (and perhaps wildly) across the whole matrix to see what can be gained when we think dialectically across its various combinations. Consider, for example, a category such as class consciousness. In what space and time can it be found and how can it be articulated across the spatiotemporal matrix in ways that lead to fruitful results? Let me suggest in the first instance that it resides primarily in the conceptualized relational space of Marxian theory, that it must therefore be regarded as abstract and universal. But in order for that conception to have meaning, it must be both relationally lived (be part of our emotive and affective being in the world) at the same time as it operates as an immaterial but objective force for change. But in order for this to be so, workers have to internalize class consciousness in their lived being and find ways to put it into motion across relative space-time. But it is only when the presence of a class movement is registered in the absolute space and time of streets, factories, corporate headquarters and the like that the movement becomes a direct material force. No one really understood what the anti-globalization movement stood for until bodies appeared on the streets of Seattle at a certain time.

But who is in fact to say what workers' dreams and beliefs are actually about? Ranciére, for example, provides a good deal of substantive evidence that workers' dreams and hence aspirations in the 1830s and 1840s in France were far from what many Marxist labor historians have inferred from a study of their material circumstances (1989). They longed for respect and dignity, for partnership with capital not its revolutionary overthrow. We can, of course, dispute Ranciére's findings, but the world of utopian dreams is a complicated world and we cannot make automatic presumptions as to how it may be actually constituted and the ways in which it came to be. But what we can say with certainty is that it is only when those dreams are converted into an active force that these immaterial longings and desires take on objective powers.

And for that to happen requires a dialectical movement across and through the whole matrix of spatiotemporal positionings. Blockages can be thrown up at any point. Hegemonic neoliberal representations of market exchange as both efficient and just place barriers to reconstructions of actual labor processes because that conception of the market leads people to live their lives as if anything and everything wrong is their own individual responsibility. Transformations in spatial and temporal relations through technological innovations alter identities and political subjectivities at the same time as they shift terrains across which the circulation of capital and labor can occur. Time horizons of capital circulation shift with the discount rate which is in turn sensitive to the circulation of speculative capital in financial markets. The effects are registered in the absolute spaces of neighborhoods, factories, shopping malls and entertainment centers. But the interpretation is that what happens is both inevitable and just because the market is the avatar of individual freedom.

In all of these ways we see how the churning and ephemerality of capital accumulation across and through space and time become a means for rendering opaque that which should be clear. If our task is to both understand the world and change it, then grappling with the dialectics of space and time becomes a crucial starting point.

Notes

1. Much of what follows is drawn from D. Harvey, 2005, 'Space as a Key Word' in Castree, N. and Gregory, D. (eds), *David Harvey: A Critical Reader* (Oxford: Basil Blackwell).
2. I reviewed some of this in Harvey, 1996, particularly chapter 10.

References

Benjamin, Walter. 1999. *The Arcades Project*. Cambridge, Mass: Belknap Press.
Bohm, David. 2002. *Wholeness and the Implicate Order*. New York: Routledge.
Burawoy, Michael. 1982. *Manufacturing Consent: Changes in the Labor Process under Monopoly Capitalism*. Chicago: Chicago University Press.
Burkett, Paul. 1999. *Marx and Nature: A Red and Green Perspective* . New York: St Martin's Press.
Cassirer, Ernst. 1944. *An Essay on Man*. New Haven: Yale University Press.
Crang, Mike, and Nigel Thrift. 2000. *Thinking Space (Critical Geographies)*. London: Routledge.
Deleuze, Gilles. 1992. *The Fold: Leibniz and the Baroque*. Minneapolis: Minnesota University Press.
Fitzgerald, Janet. 1979. *Alfred North Whitehead's Early Philosophy of Space and Time*. New York: Rowman and Littlefield.

Harvey, David. 1973. *Social Justice and the City*. London: Edward Arnold.

Harvey, David. 1989. *The Condition of Postmodernity*. Oxford: Basil Blackwell.

Harvey, David. 1996. *Justice, Nature and the Geography of Difference*. Oxford: Basil Blackwell.

Harvey, David. 2003. *Paris, Capital of Modernity*. New York: Routledge.

Harvey, David. 2005. 'Space as a Key Word'. In Castree, N. and Gregory, D. (eds), *David Harvey: A Critical Reader*. Oxford: Basil Blackwell.

Hiley, Basil and F. David Peat (eds). 1991. *Quantum Implications*. New York: Routledge.

Lefebvre, Henri. 1991. *The Production of Space*. Oxford: Basil Blackwell.

Marin, Louis. 1984. *Utopics: A Spatial Play*. Atlantic Heights, NJ: Humanities Press.

Marx, Karl. 1963. *The Eighteenth Brumaire of Louis Bonaparte*. New York: International Publishers.

Marx, Karl. 1976. *Capital, Volume 1*. New York: Viking Press.

Massey, Doreen. 2005. *For Space*. London: Sage Publications.

Merrifield, Andy. 2002. *Dialectical Urbanism*. New York: Monthly Review Press.

Ollman, Bertell. 1992. *Dialectical Investigations*. New York: Routledge.

Ollman, Bertell. 2003. *Dance of the Dialectic*. Urbana: University of Illinois Press.

Osserman, Robert. 1995. *The Poetry of the Universe*. New York: Doubleday.

Rancière, Jacques. 1989. *The Nights of Labor: The Workers' Dream in Nineteenth Century France*. Philadelphia: University of Pennsylvania Press.

Sheppard, E. 2005. 'Dialectical Space-Time: Harvey on Space'. In Castree, N. and Gregory, D. (eds), *David Harvey: A Critical Reader*. Oxford: Basil Blackwell.

Smith, Neil. 1984. *Uneven Development: Nature, Capital and the Production of Space*. Oxford: Basil Blackwell.

Soja, Edward. 1989. *Postmodern Geographies: The Reassertion of Space in Critical Social Theory*. London: Verso.

Third Berlin Biennial for Contemporary Art. 2004. *Catalogue: Judith Barry, Voice Off*. Berlin: Biennale.

Thompson, E. P. 1967. 'Time, Work Discipline and Industrial Capitalism', *Past and Present*, 38.

Whitehead, Alfred North. 1964. *The Concept of Nature*. Cambridge: Cambridge University Press.

Williams, Raymond. 1989. *People of the Black Mountains: The Beginnings*. London: Chatto and Windus.

8
Persistencies of the Dialectic: Three Sites

Fredric Jameson

I have the feeling that for many people the dialectic (insofar as it means anything at all) means an adjunct or supplementary kind of thinking: a method, or mode of interpretation, which is only intermittently appealed to, and somehow only occasionally added on to our normal thought processes. This means that not many people are capable of thinking dialectically all the time, and it may also mean that the dialectic is not a form of thought generated by this particular kind of society, for which positivism, empiricism, and various other anti-theoretical traditions seem more congenial and appropriate. (It is of course a dialectical thought as such to suppose that the various social formations – or more precisely, modes of production – secrete forms of thinking and abstraction that are specific to them and functional within their own particular structures: a presupposition that does something to the 'truth' of those various kinds of thinking that it would be best not to call relativistic, even though this dialectical or 'absolute' relativism certainly has its kinship with other progressive contemporary relativisms.)

In that case, perhaps it would be plausible to conjecture that, despite ample pioneering exploration in the works of Hegel and Marx (and intermittently of many others), the dialectic is not a thing of the past, not some chapter in the history of philosophy, but rather a speculative account of some thinking of the future which has not yet been realized: an unfinished project, as Habermas might put it; a way of grasping situations and events that does not yet exist as a collective habit because the concrete form of social life to which it corresponds has not yet come into being. Perhaps we might try to imagine a society in which the antinomies of individual versus collective being, the indivisibility of the negative and the positive, the inevitable alienation of our productive acts, and the peculiar 'Heisenberg principle' presented by the ideology of our point of view are all commonplaces, as widely understood as the old-time religions or the current Western forms of scientific common sense. It is for a society like that that the rhetoric of 'transparency' has often been deployed – not because everything in it would be immediately meaningful, and no longer obscured by the structures required to legitimate capitalism (or precapitalist forms of power), as rather because of the paradoxes of the collective and the social will, which have long since been identified as such. Perhaps one should add that in a society of this kind, a henceforth dialectical society, what we call Marxism today, namely the science of capitalism, will also have disappeared in that form, giving way to the dialectical philosophy or ontology latent in it, but unable to be developed or codified in the present world: both Lukács and Gramsci have written suggestive pages on this 'historicist' proposition, which should probably be taken as a warning not to try to work out anything like a Marxian philosophical system or ontology in our own time.[1]

Such a historicist view of the dialectical also demands that we account for the privileged positions of Hegel and Marx as moments in which anticipations of the dialectic were possible: both were indeed social-revolutionary periods of history, in which the window onto a radically different future was, however slightly, pushed open. Sympathy with the French Revolution allowed Hegel to form a very different concept of actuality and of history than the ones he inherited from the theology and philosophy of his own time; while for Marx, the universal commodification of labor power, or the universalization of wage labor, accompanied by the first forms of labor organization and militancy (from the 1848 revolutions all the way to the First International and the Paris Commune), enable a structural theorization of what would necessarily, until that time, have remained a visionary anticipation of a radically different society. But these 'conditions of possibility' are what you work your way back to, after the fact: we cannot deduce in advance what new kinds of dialectical conceptions the current cybernetic revolution, along with the capitalist 'end of history', may or may not have put us in a position to produce and to think.

I have found it useful to characterize the dialectic in three different ways, which surely do not exhaust the possibilities, but may at least clarify the discussion and also alert us to possible confusions or category mistakes, to interferences between them. The first of these directions involves reflexivity, or thinking itself: perhaps it can be described as a relatively synchronic form of the dialectic. The second raises problems of causality and historical narrative and explanation (and is thus more diachronic). Hegel and Marx are the obvious places in which these first two aspects of the dialectic are the most richly exercised, respectively.

The third feature or aspect of dialectical thinking does not seem to offer a model (as these first two might seem to do), as rather to isolate the fundamental feature of the operation itself: this is, indeed, the emphasis on contradiction as such, and we may honor Brecht for his insistence on this requirement, and for his lesson, in a great variety of contexts and forms, that dialectical thinking begins with the contradiction, that it means finding the inevitable contradiction at the heart of things and seeing and reconstructing them in terms of contradictions, or (if you prefer) that the various forms of non-dialectical thinking can always be identified as so many strategies for containing, repressing, or naturalizing contradictions as such. This is a less exclusive formula than the first two, and (while not exactly a method) perhaps offers the most practical hints for the application and identification of the dialectic alike.

Turning first to reflexivity – to the originality of the dialectic as a recognition of the way in which we are mired in concepts of all kinds and a strategy for lifting ourselves above that situation, not for changing the concepts exactly but for getting a little distance from them – it is certain that today self-consciousness (as this is also sometimes called) has a bad press; and that if we are tired enough of philosophies of consciousness, we are even more fatigued by their logical completion in reflexivities, self-knowing and self-aware lucidities, and ironies of all kinds. The current period has been a reconquest of the superficial over the obligatory depths; while all of modern philosophy and thought (Freud included) has been in therapeutic flight before older moralizing notions of the subjective and its cultivation. Perhaps consciousness and self-consciousness have been too closely allied with various forms of repression, with various class-bound notions of the self or the ego. Those were, Adorno might have said, fruits of the entrepreneurial period of bourgeois subjectivity; now that we are in full transition from the older entrepreneurs and patriarchal robber barons to the age of transnational monopolies and the new anonymous global collectivities, the glorification of the self comes to seem a historical curiosity and an outworn, impossibly expensive luxury of the past, like a private railroad car. But perhaps the reading of Hegel in such terms was itself a projection of that bygone modernist historical period; and just as Freud has come to be rewritten without the stoicism and without the mirage of the cure (in that sense, indeed, the supreme moment of self-consciousness or reflexivity as such), so also Absolute Spirit might perhaps be readapted to the more modest and schizophrenic tastes of the present age, as sheer historical overlaying and simultaneity.

The more serious question, however, turns on the use we may or may not still have for self-knowledge: for the deeper reason why this value seems to have been first reduced in price and put on sale, and then consigned to the ash can of history outright is that the self has also lived its time, and that multiple selves, multiple subject-positions, no longer seem to offer anything very interesting or tangible to know. Not much knowledge there any longer, let alone much wisdom.

Let me anticipate a little here and suggest that we may be looking in the wrong place: if subject-positions are not optional changes of clothing, whose possibilities finally depend on your pocketbook, then perhaps they ought to be seen as responses to situations. That means that their multiplicity and coexistence today correspond to the way in which postmodern people live within several coexisting situations all at once: the past seems to have been simpler in this respect, pre-urban and ordered by religious repression, but then one never knows about the past and it may well be, as the Nietzscheans among us are fond of asserting, that multiple subject-positions were always with us and that the village was no less complicated than California at its most feverish. The point is, however, that in that case what has been called self-knowledge is not really a knowledge of the self, but rather a consciousness of its situations, a way of gaining and keeping awareness of precisely that multiplicity of situations in which the 'self' finds and invents itself. That kind of knowledge need not have any of the old subjectivist, bourgeois-introspective connotations we used to endow it with (and you could reread Hegel, for that matter, as a series or sequence of situations, rather than of essentialist forms). I don't want to dwell on any of this any longer, but would like very rapidly to associate these first remarks on the dialectic with some of Derrida's early thoughts about cancellation or 'rature' in the *Grammatology*, which warned us that we could scarcely modify the concepts in our head in some Utopian fashion and leap ahead to a wholly new philosophical outlook, without utterly changing the world in the first place, and producing new situations (not his formulation) in which the new concepts might somehow find some currency or use.

But this turn in the discussion of self-consciousness now reminds us to name its other, more Marxian variant, which is to be sure the concept of ideology itself, the last and most important conceptual achievement of the enlightenment drive to banish the idols and the superstitions. It is above all in this that deconstruction, for example, is related to

Marxism, as cross cousins in some extended kinship system; and that the best way to undertake the comparison would be to begin with an analysis of deconstruction as a form of *Ideologiekritik*, as they used to call Marxism in Germany now so many years ago. Here we must return, in a new way, to imagery from the previous version, that is, to the formulation in terms of reflexivity. For the point is the same: we are submerged in our ideologies (indeed, the 'self' itself is just such an ideology, as the dialectician Lacan has shown us) and becoming aware of our own ideologies is rigorously the same as what was then called 'self-consciousness'. For ideology-critique begins at home, with the so-called self and its baggage and furnishings, and can only thereafter be trained with some accuracy and precision on the doings of the outside world. In this respect, Hegel once said an instructive thing about his own period: our situation as philosophers, he observed, is radically different from that of the Greeks, in that they had first of all to generate usable abstractions out of the immanence of empirical daily life; we, however – the historical situation is clearly that of the first modernity of Hegel's day – are drowning in abstractions, we have to find a way of getting out of them without precisely sinking back into the sheer instinctive traditional life of the pre-philosophical.[2] That way, clearly enough, he called the dialectic; but it is further illuminated by Marx's wonderful comment, which one is tempted to take as a gloss on this one of Hegel. Bourgeois philosophy, said Marx, rises from the particular to the general; we must now rise – note the persistence of the verb – from the general to the concrete (Marx, 1986, vol. 28, 38). The concrete is no longer a tissue of generalities and abstractions, of universalities; but it is also no longer a mindless anti-theoretical empiricism; it is something else which we have yet to describe in any satisfactory way here, all the more so since this once so fashionable word 'concrete' seems also to have run its course.

The link between Hegelian analysis and the 'materialism' of *Ideologiekritik*, however, lies in the space and schematism of the philosophical 'category': or in other words, the mental forms that have from Aristotle to Kant been identified as intervening between us and the objects of our thought. In Aristotle and in Kant, the categories are inventoried and sorted out according to various classification schemes,[3] but they cannot be said to have been interpreted, exactly, since they do not have meanings in and of themselves but rather govern and organize meanings and to that degree stand outside of meaning as such. The originality of Hegel was to have enabled an approach to some intrinsic meaning of the categories themselves by way of a sequence of forms (through which the 'concept', the use of Hegelian language, gradually and historically becomes 'equal to itself'). We are today rather far from the picking and choosing implied by Croce's famous title ('what is living and what is dead in the philosophy of Hegel'); still, if Hegel and his works have an actuality and a practical value for us today, it cannot but lie in just this dialectic of the categories, which incites us to invent a distance from our own thoughts in which their failures and insufficiencies can be diagnosed and identified in terms of those of the mental categories we have been able to deploy. Already in Hegel, the conditions of possibility of specific mental categories (and not other, more adequate ones, for example) were the object of a properly historical diagnosis: the dialectical flaws in a given category (the way in which, for example, it might impose a false dualism upon us) are already indices of our historical situation; and with that, the way toward a certain Marxism is thrown open.

The return to Hegel today, in a variety of forms, is thereby justified: less as a scholarly and antiquarian project (although such research into the documents themselves and the history of philosophy is invaluable), than rather as a renewed effort to think through and elaborate the multiple and suggestive connections between a Hegelian analysis of categories and a Marxian analysis of ideology. I remain convinced that one of the most fruitful efforts to stage those connections lay in the ill-fated *Capitallogik* movement, in which the categories of Hegel's logic were experimentally juxtaposed with those of Marx's analysis of capital itself (see Ollman, 1993, esp. pts I, II; Smith, 1990).

The more frequent moves in this direction, however, lay in the attempt to bypass or neutralize a kind of form-content stereotype operative in the standard comparisons of Hegel and Marx: that is, provisionally to ignore the idea (probably encouraged by the preceding remarks) that in Hegel it is a question of the form of thoughts and attitudes, whereas in Marx we have to do with their concrete or empirical class content. *Capitallogik*, indeed, may be seen as attempting to give a concrete class content to Hegel's 'forms', while in other Marxian developments – most notably in Lukács' *History and Class Consciousness* – the strategy has been to reveal the categorical forms implicit in seemingly empirical class and political positions and opinions. This remains a rich area for work today, and it may also be observed to take place within our philosophical terminologies: I think, for example, of the suggestive and exciting results of the elaboration by Slavoj Zizek and his associates of the dialectics of Lacanian psychoanalysis, which are deployed very specifically in the force field opened up between Marxism and German objective idealism.

Thus, it is not so much the incompatibility of some Hegelian idealism and this or that Marxian materialism which vitiates the development of the dialectic today: on the contrary, as I hope to have suggested, such 'incompatibilities' are the space in which genuine philosophical innovation can take place. The more urgent problem today is a historical and a social one, and, if it strikes at the Hegelian dialectic by way of an omnipresent positivism and revulsion against theory itself, its consequences for the Marxian theory of ideology itself are no less momentous. For there is a question whether, today, in postmodernity and globalization, in the universal reign of the market and of a cynical reason that knows and accepts everything about itself, ideology still takes on its once classical form, and ideology-critique serves any purpose any longer. For that was once a cultural-revolutionary purpose and a collective pedagogy: not merely and not even foremost to discredit and unmask the enemies, but rather to transform the intellectual and practical habits of the collectivity itself, formed in and still poisoned by this social system. Today, and for the moment, we need more modestly to ask ourselves how ideology functions in the new moment, how the market achieves its unquestioned sway. What is paradoxical is that the crudest forms of ideology seem to have returned, and that in our public life an older vulgar Marxism would have no need of the hypersubtleties of the Frankfurt School and of negative dialectics, let alone of deconstruction, to identify and unmask the simplest and most class-conscious motives and interests at work, from Reaganism and Thatcherism down to our own politicians: to lower taxes so rich people can keep more of their money, a simple principle about which what is surprising is that so few people find it surprising any more, and what is scandalous, in the universality of market values, is the way it goes without saying and scarcely scandalizes anyone. Why did we need in the first place to invent the elaborate Geiger counters of ideology-critique developed on the left during the modernist period if it was all so simple all along? The implication is that the Cold War shamed the various Western bourgeoisies into complicated intellectual disguises for these motivations, which had to be deconstructed in equally complicated ways, but which no longer need the cloak of altruism or of higher philosophical justifications, now that they have no enemies any longer.

Perhaps, however, we need to entertain the idea that ideology today takes rather different forms than in the past, and in particular that our two great dominant ideologies – that of the market; that of consumption or of consumerism – are not exactly ideas in the older sense. Adorno wondered somewhere very pertinently whether today the commodity might not be its own ideology: thereby seeming independently to confirm the general conceptual movement away from an overt theory of ideology to one of practices (as in Bourdieu' s work, for example). That such an 'end of ideology' could never mean an end of class struggle seems obvious enough, but it would certainly entail a dilemma in the articulations of class struggle and in the opening up of new discursive spaces in which to fight it out. Perhaps this sense of the becoming immanent of ideology in late capitalism explains the renewed significance, on the left, of the theory of commodity fetishism, which was for Marx the undeveloped secret of any analysis of daily life in our social system. The renewal of a theoretical interest in religion may also have its relevance here as well (and not only in the empirical social world around us), since Marx's brief analysis is staged in religious terms. At any rate, contributions from psychoanalysis and colonial philology alike (Zizek, 1989; Pietz, 1985) have converged on this interesting matter, which also surely holds a key to practical politics in the current scheme of things.

But now it is time to move to the second way in which the dialectic has often been understood and misunderstood, and that has to do with telos, narrative, and history: with the story of change, or in other words, with the diachronic, rather than with the structures of consciousness as such. Marx has often, along with Hegel, been accused of having a 'philosophy of history' (which is evidently supposed to be a bad thing; and also of being somehow religious, replicating Christian historicism unconsciously, and projecting a salvational narrative of a movement of history toward some end of time – in short, of perpetuating the noxious doctrine of a telos); and in a lesser accusation, of being not only teleological but also a proponent of historical inevitability, whatever that may mean. No reader of *The Eighteenth Brumaire of Louis Bonaparte* can believe any of these things, to which I can only reply in abbreviated form. I certainly hope that Marxism projects a salvational history; why it should be Christian I cannot particularly understand, since Christian salvation remains essentially individual, and the day of judgment is a figure for the end of history altogether, rather than, as in Marx's own words, the end of 'prehistory'. This is perhaps also the moment to deal with the much stigmatized concept of totality: it is capitalism which totalizes, which constitutes a total system, not its critics. We have to think, however, in terms of a totalizing transformation of the social system precisely because this system is itself a total one (something Foucault teaches even better than Marx, by the way and which is also implicit in Derrida's ideas of the closure of conceptuality in the *Grammatology*). Salvational is then that kind of transformation: that it is inevitable we are, chastened by the lessons of the last few years, no longer supposed to say. But here too it was never socialism that was inevitable, but the implosion of the contradictions of capitalism. Marx allows as much when he pointedly observes that some world-historical conflicts end 'not with the reconstruction of society as a whole, but rather with the mutual ruin of contending classes' (Marx and Engels, 1976, 484). Indeed, the two things are not 'on all fours' as the philosophers like to say: capitalism is a system and a machine with irresolvable internal contradictions; socialism is a human and a collective act, a collective project. The fate of the former does not depend on us; that of the latter is at one with our collective praxis.

But these perspectives – sometimes supposed to be 'grand narratives' – are not really narratives at all; they are axiology and Utopian vision. They enable the construction of this or that historical narrative, but are not themselves narrative as such. If we look for a moment at those texts in which we can speak of some genuinely dialectical narrative – I mentioned *The Eighteenth Brumaire* a moment ago – what we observe is indeed the very opposite of this allegedly pious rehearsal for longed-for truths, of history written as wish-fulfillment and as the simple-minded interaction of a few abstractions. Rather *The Eighteenth Brumaire* gives us to witness a narrative which is at every point a perpetual and dazzling, sometimes bewildering, cancellation of previously dominant narrative paradigms. Here the dialectic is a constant reversal of older stereotypes of causality, of historical or narrative efficacy, and of efficiency: it constantly underscores the absolutely unforeseeable consequence, the bitterly ironic reversal, the inversion of human (individual) intention, and the progress inherent in the worst rather than the best, in failure rather than victory. History puts its worst foot forward, as Henri Lefebvre liked to say, and not its best, as bourgeois or Whig, progress-oriented historiographies claim and try to demonstrate by their own narratives. To be sure, the great forefather of this historiographic practice was again Hegel (he had his own precursors in Adam Smith and Mandeville), and in particular his notion of 'the ruse of reason' or the 'ruse of history', the way in which a collective history uses the passions and intentions of individuals, and even of individual nations, behind their backs in order to produce some utterly unexpected result. But in that programmatic form, the dialectic is still too simple and itself becomes predictable: the dialectic of history in Marx wishes to escape just that predictability. But here we now draw closer to an understanding of the dialectic as a set of operations, in situation, rather than as some static 'view' or even 'philosophy' – in this case of history itself. Among our inner ideologies, in other words, are notions of what an event is, how things happen, what effective causes are, how change can best be influenced: the dialectic wishes ceaselessly to interrogate and undermine those narrative and historical ideologies, by allowing us to see and grasp historical change in a new and more complex way. But that's the difference with postmodern historiography in general: the dialectical one still does wish to give a provisional picture of historical change, a provisional narrative, with provisional interpretation of the events, and therefore still implies that those events are not altogether meaningless, and that historical narration is not an altogether ideological process.

Now at a certain point along the way, it seems to me that such dialectical narratives froze over and became codified; so that new narrative procedures had to be invented to undermine them in their turn. The two I would above all wish to single out for twentieth century historiography are Freud's *Nachträglichkeit*, his so-called 'retroactive effect', whereby the arrival of puberty, for example, triggers events that have in some sense already happened at the age of three, but in another sense have not yet happened at all; and alongside that, Derrida's notion of 'supplementarity', in which, following Jakobson's notion of the synchronic, a new moment in the system comes complete with its own brand-new past and (as in Husserl) reorders our perception around itself as a center (whose permanency is then projected back endlessly into time). I believe that both these historiographic forms have occasionally been understood as critiques of the dialectic, and I understand why; but I hope it will also be clear why I now perversely consider both as contributions to a dialectical rewriting of history rather than as some newfangled post-dialectical inventions.

It all depends, you will say, on how we define the dialectic in the first place. No doubt; and the first Derrida we know, the Derrida of the recently published master's thesis of 1953, the dialectical (rather than anti-dialectical) Derrida (1994), grasped dialectics as essentially a matter of mediation. The dialectic is what lets us think the unity of opposites, and (in that particular case, which was the critique of Husserl's philosophy), the identity of activity and passivity, of constituting and constituted, even subject and object, and so forth. What of that particular version of the dialectic? This is the point at which we must touch on the third of our topics, namely contradiction; and in which we must bring in other, less philosophical names, and in particular that of Brecht, supposed to be the student, in dialectics, of Karl Korsch.

I will omit that obligatory digression, however, and simply repeat Brecht's stress that what defines the dialectic above all is the observation – everywhere and always – of contradictions as such. Wherever you find them, you can be said to be thinking dialectically; whenever you fail to see them, you can be sure that you have stopped doing so.

My reason for drawing Brecht into the discussion in so seemingly arbitrary a fashion (besides implicitly shedding a little cross-light on his adversary, Lukács) is to restore some of the forgotten prehistory of contemporary anti-dialectical positions, which we mostly lump under the designation post-structuralist. I have come to believe, indeed, that much in the arsenal of attacks on the dialectic actually derives from the dialectical tradition itself, and specifically from Brecht, whose plays exploded like a thunderbolt in summer 1954, in a Parisian intellectual atmosphere dominated absolutely by so-called existential Marxism.

The body of critical writing that most vigilantly and intelligently transmitted the Brechtian ethos to France and to the French intellectual and political climate of those years, which is to say to the nascent French sixties and nascent post-structuralism, is the work of Roland Barthes, whose *Mythologies* constitutes a splendid series of Brechtian estrangement-effects, including a theory of estrangement rewritten for French usages. I am, however, more interested in Barthes' attacks on identity, which seem to me faithfully yet creatively and imaginatively to transmit the Brechtian positions on this particular theme. In particular, what seems to be Barthes' semiological undoing of the individual 'subject' (Barthes, 1970) – its fragmentation into multiple semes, its x-raying into overlapping *actants*, the death of the author-subject as well, and finally the dissolution of the writing subject into the unselfsufficient moments of textual production – this actually can be seen to derive from Brecht's dramaturgy; not only the reconstruction of the individual subject in *Mann ist Mann*, or the positive and negative personae of *The Good Person* (but of many other plays as well), but above all, the sense that subjectivity itself is in reality *gestus*, that we do wrong to try to empathize this or that inner feeling of the character, and indeed that in any given gesture a multiplicity of motivations overlap. Barthes' further dismantling of the event, in his so-called proairetic code, is very reminiscent of the Brechtian staging of the gestus, and the insistence on showing the audience that any number of other versions of these gestures and reactions might have been possible in other frames and other situations. The practice of multiple subject-positions, therefore, is already present in Brecht (despite his lack of interest in what is still simply Freudian psychoanalysis); and the persistent undermining of the whole range of forms taken by an illusory identity in his most inveterate critical posture.

In Barthes as well (who however benefited from a double lesson on the subject, having also learned it from his other master, Sartre), we find the fundamental Brechtian insistence on the primacy of the situation, whether this has to do with political choices, subject-positions, or literary theories and forms. This insistence on the situation as such is what makes it so difficult to codify this dialectic, about which it becomes evident that its terms and emphases must vary according to the demands of circumstance and of strategy. Brecht is not the only modem thinker to have insisted on the relationship between strategy and thought, between strategy and dialectics: but his lesson has been enormously influential.[4]

Where, finally, do we find contradiction in all this? In the structure of the situation itself, first of all; but also in the relationship of the gesture or *gestus* to the situation it tries to change; and finally within the *gestus* and the subject-position itself, where the sheer multiplicity of elements itself constitutes a contradiction. The misunderstanding would lie in imagining that Brecht desired this multiplicity and these contradictions to be done away with; that with him, as in those caricatures of the Hegel alongside whom he now lies buried, some 'synthesis' must necessarily follow on the proverbial thesis and antithesis; or else, at the outside limit, we will find ourselves forced to evoke a 'dialectic without a synthesis', as though that were not simply the nature of the dialectic *tout court*. Where, however, this distinction has been drawn in a programmatic way, and a perpetual movement back and forth between opposites or within a dualism contrasted with some alleged dialectical 'totalization' in which the opposites and the contradictions are supposed to be laid to rest, then I think one can contrast the notion of the contradiction and that of the antinomy, which is the form taken by contradictors in so much anti-dialectical post-structuralist thought, and on which I have commented elsewhere (Jameson, 1994).

I want to add, returning to the beginning of this discussion, that I think notions of the mediation as a solution or bridge between contradictories are also something of a misunderstanding, and attribute to the dialectic philosophical and ontological ambitions it must not have: this notion of the mediation is redolent of the old Hegelian and dialectical-materialist notion of a 'dialectics of nature', for example, while the Brechtian position I have tried to outline here would I believe be more inclined to identify mediation and contradiction as such: where you can perceive a contradiction, there you already intuit the union of opposites, or the identity of identity and non-identity. Mediation is thus not some strange and fluid event in the world: it characterizes the way our spectatorship and our praxis alike construct portions of the world with a view toward changing them.

Notes

1. See Georg Lukács, 'What is Orthodox Marxism?', in Lukács, 1971, 1–26; and Antonio Gramsci, 'The Revolution against *Das Kapital*', in Gramsci, 1949, 39–42.
2. 'The manner of study in ancient times differed from that of the modern age in that the former was the proper and complete formation of the natural consciousness. Putting itself to the test at every point of its existence, and philosophizing about everything it came across, it made itself into a universality that was active through and through. In modern times, however, the individual finds the abstract form ready-made; the effort to grasp and appropriate it is more the direct driving-forth of what is within and the truncated generation of the universal than it is the emergence of the latter from the concrete variety of existence'. (Hegel, 1977, 19)
3. 'The 'what', quality, quantity, place, time and any similar meanings which 'being' may have; and again besides all these there is that which is potentially or actually' (Aristotle, 1985, Book VI, chapter 2).
4. See Jameson, 1998, for a fuller discussion.

References

Aristotle. 1985. *Metaphysics*. In *Complete Works*, Vol. II. Princeton, New Jersey: Princeton University Press.

Barthes, Roland. 1957. *Mythologies*. Paris: Seuil.

Barthes, Roland. 1970. *S/Z*. Paris: Seuil.

Derrida, Jacques. 1994. *Le Probleme de la genese dans la philosophie do Husserl*. Paris: PUF.

Gramsci, Antonio. 1949. *Pre-Prison Writings*, ed. R. Mellamy, trans. V. Cox. London: Cambridge University Press.

Hegel, G. W. F. 1977. *Phenomenology of Spirit*, trans. A. V. Miller. Oxford, England: Oxford University Press.

Jameson, Frederic. 1994. *The Seeds of Time*. New York: Columbia University Press.

Jameson, Frederic. 1998. *Brecht and Method*. London: Verso.

Lukács, Georg. 1971. *History and Class Consciousness*, trans. Rodney Livingston. Cambridge, Massachusetts: MIT Press.

Marx, Karl. 1986. *Grundrisse*. In Karl Marx and Friedrich Engels, *Collected Works*, Vols 28–29. New York: International Publishers.

Marx, Karl, and Friedrich Engels. 1976. *The Communist Manifesto*. MECW, Vol. VI. Moscow: Progress Publishers.

Ollman, Bertell. 1993. *Dialectical Investigations*. New York: Routledge.

Pietz, William. 1985. 'The Problem of the Fetish'. *RES*, 9 (Spring).

Smith, Tony. 1990. *The Logic of Marx's* Capital. New York: SUNY Press.

Zizek, Slavoj. 1989. *The Sublime Object of Ideology*. London: Verso.

9
The Dialectics of Walking on Two Legs

Bill Livant

What is dialectics? Dialectics is walking on two legs.

I start here for a particular reason. If our focus is to grasp the relation between the whole society and the individual, we should try to grasp the whole person. In short, if we want to start with everybody in society, we should try to make sure that we have all the parts of the individual there as well. Start with the whole. And then move to what Marx called the 'cell', the abstraction, where the forms of motion of the whole are gathered. Where they are concentrated, as are animals at a watering hole.

So my entry into dialectics is to compose the physical, human body. Is it really all there in our dialectics? Has something physical been left out? If so, the first step is to put it back.

I think something central has been missing from our philosophy.

So my abstraction, my 'cell', includes a form of motion that has been left out. Walking. Hence my starting point for dialectics: walking on two legs.

Legs! (And when I speak of legs, I mean both legs and feet.) There is a rich dialectical literature on the hands and, through them, on the mind. But who in our tradition speaks of legs? Why this neglect? Were legs considered too 'lowly'?

Yet, the legs of the human body show us something that is not obvious when we focus on our hands alone. When we put the legs back, we start our thinking about the human as someone *in* the world and not *outside* it. The human in the world should not be a goal to be derived theoretically, but a starting point that facilitates making dialectical connections with everything else. So start with the body, the *whole body in motion.* Start with the *walking* body.

Most people have great difficulty grasping the reality of change (movement, development, maturation, etc.). This is largely the result of operating with a conception of human nature that views people as fixed in space. Whatever movement occurs has to be imported from outside. It is something or someone outside us that makes us move. With this conception, matter (our substance, what we are) and motion (what we do) are split apart, with the latter reintroduced into the body as unidirectional and therefore undialectical, mechanical motion later on.

In so far as people are conceived as moving, when walking is viewed as an essential part of what we are, it becomes much easier to think of other things as moving as well. It also becomes easier to grasp the human's interaction with the world as a two-way street, with movement coming from both directions. If, as Marx says, movement is given and the *appearance* of stability is the problem to be explained, then humans have to be in movement. Motion has to be internal, and it can't be if the motion of the legs is absent.

But how does the body, the whole body, move on its legs? This is where the *two* legs are important for dialectics. Get up and try to walk. Feel the weight of your body when you move as you transfer the weight from one foot to the other. Can you feel the point at which the center of weight, the center of gravity, your whole body, moves? There is a momentary transfer of the whole body's weight in the continuous motion from the back foot to the front one. And now the body is at a different place in space. The simple act of walking, if we attend to it, shows us both separated and continuous motion (dialectical discontinuity within continuity) in the same act.

Once we have put motion back into the body where it belongs, we can also make an important abstraction that we couldn't make before. I'll call it the abstraction of walking and handling together as a differentiated unity. The history of handling the world is the history of abstracting pieces of it and shaping them to the needs of the human body. With handling, we reach for the world. With walking, we reach into it. Walking does not pluck pieces of the world and does not directly shape it. Rather, it puts the whole body in motion within the world, creating in the process innumerable new opportunities for handling.

In philosophy, virtually all the mental abstractions we make are handling abstractions. They are based on a static totality, and hence are divorced from what it really is to be in the world. Walking shows us the error of this exclusive focus on handling. It is the mental equivalent of walking on one leg. Walk on two! That's *materialist* dialectics, not all of it, but it's a good start. Now for home practice.

And when you walk you will have good company. Hear Rousseau,

> I can only meditate when I am walking. When I stop I cease to think; my mind only works with my legs … There is something about walking which stimulates and enlivens my thoughts. When I stay in one place I can hardly think at all; my body has to be on the move to set my mind going … It serves to free my spirit, to lend a greater boldness to my thinking, to throw me, so to speak, into the vastness of things, so that I can combine them, select them, and make them mine as I will, without fear or restraint. (1953, 382)

Also William Blake, that traveler through dialectical space. And Mao, that terrestrial walker on his march of ten thousand li.

Reference

Rousseau, Jean-Jacques. 1953. *Confessions*, trans. J. M. Cohen. London: Penguin.

10

Dialectical Transformations: Teleology, History and Social Consciousness

István Mészáros

Social interaction and uneven development

According to Marx, the potential impact of the interaction between the material base and the superstructure can be both positive and negative, from early stages of historical development right up to that point in history when human beings consciously take control over the conflicting social forces of their situation. Hence ideology, too, appears in his conception with diametrically opposed connotations. On the one hand, it is presented in its negativity as a mystifying and counterproductive force that greatly hinders development. Yet, on the other hand, it is also seen as a vital positive factor – bent on overcoming determinate social constraints and resistances – without whose active contribution the forward driving potentialities of the given historical situation quite simply could not unfold.

Some critics see an 'ambiguity' in this view and try to remove it by giving ideology a one-sidedly negative connotation. The trouble with such interpretations is that they end up with a circular definition of both science and ideology as self-referential opposites to one another. To quote one example,

> The comprehensive view [of the Marxian conception of ideology] holds that *all* philosophical, political, legal, etc., forms are ideological, though this is not said in so many words. The restrictive interpretation holds that only those philosophical, political, legal, etc., forms *which are ideological* can be opposed to science, without implying that they are always necessarily so. I think this interpretation is more

consistent with Marx's other tenets, but one has to accept that an ambiguity exists in Marx's text. (Larrain, 1983, 172)

Unfortunately, the evidence put forward by the people who argue on these lines in support of their curious approach is rather flimsy. Thus we read in the same book: 'In the 1859 Preface Marx referred to the "forms of social consciousness" which correspond to the economic structures, *but he does not equate them with ideology, nor does he use the term superstructure to refer to them*' (Larrain, 1983, 171).

This sounds very firm and conclusive indeed, establishing in the author's view the negative conception of ideology on Marx's authority. For if this is how Marx sees things, then it would appear to follow, as the author in fact later asserts, that 'the superstructure of ideas refers to a global societal level of consciousness, whereas ideology is only a restricted part of the superstructure which includes specific forms of *distorted consciousness*' (Larrain, 1983, 173).

Surprisingly, however, our quote from p. 171 continues like this: '*None the less, in a subsequent passage* Marx affirmed that' – and there follows a quotation (from the 1859 Preface) in which Marx clearly states the very *opposite* of what he was supposed to have said earlier in the same passage, namely he refers in general terms to: 'the legal, political, religious, aesthetic or philosophic – in short, *ideological forms* in which men become conscious of this conflict and fight it out'. Hence, one cannot quite understand the meaning of 'none the less', nor of the vagueness of 'in a subsequent passage' which implies some ambiguous second thought on Marx's part. For the fact is that the so-called 'subsequent passage' is part of the *same paragraph*, just a few lines from Marx's reference to the correspondence between the material/economic base and 'definite forms of social consciousness', written in the same breath and representing the logical continuation, not the ambiguous opposite of that thought.

Thus, the claimed ambiguity is not a feature of the Marxian conception. Rather, it is a requirement of the construct that wants to establish the one-sidedly negative characterization of ideology on Marx's authority, at the cost of oversimplifying his views by removing the alleged 'ambiguity' (in truth the *dialectical complexity*) from the Marxian approach. For the real dynamics and vitality of *multidimensional dialectical determinations* disappear without a trace if one opts for the tempting simplicity of an 'unambiguously' negative conception of ideology.

In truth, there can be no aprioristic predetermination as to how the historical dialectic will unfold on the basis of the original correlates of the social metabolism. Nor can one a priori prejudge the way in which new material and intellectual factors – emerging at subsequent stages of historical development – will affect the overall complex in its temporary synthesis of the interacting forces at a progressively higher plateau from which later advances may be attempted.

To say that the plateau is progressively higher – thanks to the cumulative and at times dramatic advancement of the social productive forces – does not mean that there is something even vaguely resembling a *linear* progression. It simply means that *if and when* (or inasmuch as) the conflicting 'moments' of the dynamic social interaction *resolve* their tensions – through devastations and revivals, relapses and qualitative improvements, the destruction of some forces and communities and the injection of new blood into others; in short, through the complicated trajectory of 'uneven development' – then humanity finds itself at a higher level of actual productive accomplishment, with new forces and potentialities of further advance at its disposal. However, there can be no guarantee of a positive resolution of the social antagonisms involved, as the suggestions that the struggle may end 'in the common ruin of the contending classes' (Marx and Engels, 1976, 484) and that the historical alternative is 'socialism *or* barbarism' clearly acknowledge.[1]

Problematical character of labor's spontaneous teleology

Looking back from a certain distance at actual historical development – a distance from which the *already consolidated* plateaus stand out as 'necessary stages' of the whole itinerary, while the manifold specific struggles and contradictions leading to them (which contain numerous pointers toward possible alternative configurations) fade into the background – one may have the illusion of a 'logically necessary' progression, corresponding to some hidden design. Viewed from such perspective, everything firmly established acquires its *positive* sense, and the consolidated stages by definition must appear to be positive/rational in virtue of their actual consolidation.

The historical images conceived in this way represent a rather problematical achievement, as manifest in the idealist conceptions of history. Understandably, therefore, there is an aversion to discussing teleology and a tendency to treat it in general as a form of theology. This is due to a large extent to the long prevailing conjunction of the two in an important current of the European philosophical tradition which formulated its explanations in terms of 'final causes' and identified the latter with the manifestation of the Divine purpose in the order of nature. However, the summary equation of teleology and theology is quite unjustifiable, since the objective teleology of labor is an essential part of any coherent materialistic historical explanation of social development. Such an explanation, dealing with actually unfolding causal factors and not with a priori preconceived schemes, has nothing whatsoever to do with *theological* assumptions, even though determinate *teleological* propositions are inseparable from it.

Indeed, human history is not intelligible without some kind of teleology. But the only teleology consistent with the materialist conception of history is the objective and dialectically open-ended teleology of labor itself. At the fundamental ontological level, such teleology is concerned with the way in which the human being – this unique 'self-mediating being of nature' – creates and develops itself through its purposeful productive activity.

In this process, labor fulfils the function of active mediation in the progressively changing metabolism between humankind and nature. All potentialities of socialized human being as well as all characteristics of social intercourse and social metabolism emerge from the objective teleology of this dialectical mediation. And since the labor involved in these processes and transformations is the producers' own labor, the active mediation between humankind and nature, too, cannot be considered other than *self-mediation*. The latter, as a framework of explanation, is radically opposed to a theological – that is, hypostatized as divinely predetermined – conception of teleology.

In this sense, history must be conceived as necessarily open-ended in virtue of the qualitative change that takes place in the natural order of determinations: the establishment of a unique framework of ontological necessity of which *dialectically self-mediating human teleology* itself is an integral, and indeed a vitally important, part. (This is why *biological determinism* is a non-starter.)

The *historically created* radical *openness* of history – human history – is, therefore, insurmountable in the sense that there can be no way of theoretically or practically *predetermining* the forms and modalities of human *self*-mediation. For the complex teleological conditions of this self-mediation through productive activity can only be satisfied – since they are constantly being created and recreated through this self-mediation itself. This is why all attempts at producing neatly self-contained and closed systems of historical explanation result either in some arbitrary reduction of the complexity of human actions to the crude simplicity of mechanical determinations, or in the idealistic superimposition of one kind or another of *a priori transcendentalism* on the *immanence* of human development.

However, the radical openness of the historical process – which is responsible for the simultaneously 'positive negativity' and 'negative positivity' of its results – is by no means fully characterized by emphasizing the *immanent* and *self-mediatory* nature of the teleology of labor. There are three further major considerations that must be taken into account:

1. In accord with the inherent characteristics of the labor process, the *purpose* envisaged in its immediacy can only be a *partial* one, directly related to the task at hand, even if the cumulative partial solutions are always inserted into an increasingly broader context. Hence the *positivity* of a successful solution is necessarily defective inasmuch as it cannot possibly control the *global* consequences and implications of its own success, which may in fact turn out to be utterly disastrous on a longer timescale, despite the positivity originally posited and implemented in the specific teleological activity in question.

   As the multiplicity of limited teleological designs is realized in the course of practical productive activity, interlinking and integrating the specific results in a more or less coherent overall complex, a 'totalization' of some kind in fact takes place. However, it is a 'totalization without a totalizer',[2] and therefore the conscious partial projects must suffer the (negative, unintended) consequences of being inserted into a 'blind' overall framework that seems to defy any attempt at being controlled. As a result, not only is the originally posited meaning of the partial projects deflected and distorted, but at the same time the unconscious totalization of the partial results – later rationalized as the benevolent 'hidden hand' of market society becomes the necessary foundation and structurally vitiated (i.e., from the very beginning distorting and alienating) presupposition and guiding principle of the partial teleological activities themselves.

   Undoubtedly, historical development – through the growing division of labor, coupled with the unfolding interconnectedness, indeed integration of the social organization of production – makes the particular purposes envisaged by the labor process increasingly more global even in their limited specificity. Thus at a highly advanced (e.g., capitalist) stage of the social division of labor not only the *solution* of partial tasks cannot be envisaged without bringing into play a whole network of scientific, technological and social processes. Indeed, for a start the *tasks themselves* cannot be conceptualized without keeping in mind an equally complex network of linkages, both to the immediacy of the given labor process from which the specific tasks arise and to the broader context of their *destination* as products and *commodities*.

Nevertheless, this circumstance *per se*, notwithstanding its potentially far-reaching positive implications, does not carry with it a greater effective control over the social metabolism as a whole. It does not even imply a more positive orientation toward the partial positing activities. For they remain in fact more than ever strictly subordinated to the irrationality of the prevailing global determinations.

The positive meaning of this objective tendency toward a global integration of the labor process is that it opens up the possibility of consciously controlling the social metabolism as a whole. For the latter is either controlled *in its integrality*, or, due to the contradictions among its constituent parts on a global scale, it continues to elude human control, no matter how devastating the consequences. At a primitive stage of social development – when the teleology of labor is hopelessly constrained by the crude immediacy of its positing activity as sternly confronted, and to a large extent directly dominated by nature – the question of conscious control over the social metabolism cannot conceivably arise. The removal of such constraints through the full development of the forces of production creates the potentiality of making the partial tasks and processes homogeneous with the overall structures, thereby producing the possibility of conscious action, both at the level of the immediate/limited tasks and at that of an overall social plan and coordination. But, of course, the historical unfolding of labor's objective teleology creates only the *potentiality* of a successful control of the conditions of human self-mediation and self-realization. This potentiality can only be translated into *actuality* through a radical *break* with the prevailing system of determinations as a result of a *conscious human enterprise* that envisages itself as its own end, in contrast to the present modality of labor's teleology in which the positing activity is dominated by alien ends, from the fetishism of the commodity and extraneous political domination over labor – in the service of enforced surplus-labor extraction – to antagonistic contradictions among states.

2. Another inescapable condition that reinforces the radical openness of the historical process, with all its positive/negative as well as negative/positive implications, concerns the *permanent*

structural presence of basic material determinations in the changing social metabolism. For no matter to what degree the direct material determinations are displaced in the course of historical development, they always remain *latent* under the surface of the displacing mechanisms; and they may massively re-emerge on the horizon of even the most advanced society, including a genuinely socialist one. The jungle may be cleared with great effectiveness; nevertheless it is bound to reassert with even greater effectiveness, its original claim if the necessary conditions for its successful banishment are not constantly recreated and adequately renewed.

Nor could one consider the expansion of historically created needs some sort of a priori guarantee in this respect. Quite the opposite. For the development of complex needs – the 'luxury' of erstwhile political economy – may indeed displace the realm of bare necessity. But it can do so only at the cost of activating a new, and far more extensive, order of necessity whose mastery becomes increasingly more difficult within the framework of capital's perverse logic. As a result, we have to reckon not only with the permanent *latency* of the most fundamental material determinations but also with the increasing *fragility* (or vulnerability) of the globally more and more intertwined social metabolism. This is why, at the present juncture of history, the 'positive negativity' and 'negative positivity' of open-ended social development can only be pictured in the image of Janus, with one of his two faces pointing in the direction of human triumph, the other confronting in anguish the hell of self-destruction.

But even if we envisage the successful mastery of capital's perverse logic, the latency of basic material determinations remains the implicit premise of all future social interaction, notwithstanding its qualitatively changed meaning. For 'real history' is not the *end* of history but, on the contrary, a full *awareness* of its radical openness. Such awareness, however, by its very nature cannot wish out of existence the paradoxical ambivalence of objective determinations, including the permanent structural vulnerability of a globally intertwined and managed – or, for that matter, perilously mismanaged – social metabolism. In view of the necessary reproduction of this latency as the natural foundation of human existence even at the highest conceivable level of social development, the path between success and failure is bound to remain extremely narrow, even if not threatened at every turn by capital's inherent irrationality. One may envisage successfully threading such a narrow path only *on condition* that the required full awareness of the positive/negative meaning of history's radical openness asserts itself as the *permanent orienting force* of all social enterprise.

3. The third major point to stress is closely connected with the previous two. It concerns a characteristic that happens to be totally ignored by all kinds of utopianisms – irrespective of their political/ideological orientation – including the capitalistically inspired technological idealizations of the 'third industrial revolution'. The point is that any increase in the powers of *production* is simultaneously also an increase in the powers of *destruction*. Indeed, a careful examination of the balance sheet of history in this respect reveals the sobering fact that the underlying trend is the worst kind of *uneven development*. 'For while it is not only unrealistic but totally inconceivable to envisage a technology that solves all of humanity's problems with one clean swoop and on a permanent basis, notwithstanding the wishful postulates of 'post-industrial' ideology, we have *already* reached the stage where the existing destructive devices of technology – fully deployed in fact to spring into action at the push of a button – could right here and now put an end to human life on this planet. [3]

Thus technology, as constituted throughout history – far from being 'neutral' – is inherently *problematical* in itself. Nor is its connection with natural science (in the name of which the ideologies of technological manipulation legitimate themselves) such a blessing as many people try to make us believe. In fact natural science itself, as we know it, also has a gravely problematical side that is ignored by all those who counterpose their positivistically idealized 'science' to 'ideology' *tout court.*

What needs to be stressed in the present context is that the inescapable material reality of the powers of destruction *necessarily* arises from all advances in productivity known to us. Evidently, the metabolism between humankind and nature has to subdue nature with nature's own might. Hence, the more extensive and multiform society's needs *vis-a-vis* nature (necessarily implying an equivalent and ever-growing resistance on nature's side too), the greater – and also potentially more destructive – the forces that must be constantly activated in order to secure their satisfaction. The irony inherent in this relationship is that it is a matter of total indifference to nature whether its explosive forces move mountains and dig navigable canals in the service of human beings, or, on the contrary, irreversibly destroy the elementary conditions of human existence itself.

However, the problems are further aggravated by the way in which the fundamental metabolic relationship between socially produced needs and nature is articulated and reproduced in the course of historical development, with regard to the instruments and productive forces as well as the social organization of production. The teleology of both technology and natural science is ultimately rooted in the primitive technology of labor. The original limitations of the latter – the constraining results of the necessary *partiality* of its positing activity earlier referred to – are reproduced even at the most advanced phase of capital's development. This partiality, which tends to render technology totally blind to the destructive implications of its own mode of operation, is greatly aggravated by three additional conditions:

a) technological teleology is necessarily linked to determinate instruments and material structures, with a limited life span and a corresponding 'economic imperative' (cycle of amortization, etc.) of their own; under the rule of capital such limited material objectivations inevitably impose their logic – the problematical logic of their material and economic dictates – on the labor process as a whole, tending to intensify the original partiality and fragmentariness of labor's teleological positing, instead of pushing it in the opposite direction;

b) technology fights the *latency* of basic material determinations in accordance with its own material *inertia*: by pursuing 'the line of least resistance' that best suits its direct material/ economic dictates, even if it means producing 'artificial appetites', indeed a tendency toward the destruction of non-renewable resources, and so on, rather than real solutions;

c) the inherently limiting and problematical characteristics of technology *per se* are devastatingly enhanced and multiplied by its *embeddedness in class society*, articulated in the service of the rulers so as to secure the permanent subjugation of the dominated; the development of technology in the course of history up to the present is inseparable [4] from this structure of domination and subordination: the *technological* division of labor is a subordinate moment of the *hierarchical social* division of labor, rather than the other way round, as it is usually misrepresented in the 'camera obscura' that produces the upside-down images of ruling class–inspired mystification; [5] the destructive sides and implications of technological developments, which otherwise would be easily visible on strictly technical and scientific ground, are systematically camouflaged and rationalized as a result of this lopsided social embeddedness of technology in the ruling order.

Naturally, technological utopianism – which refuses to see the negative side of technological/scientific developments – has nothing whatever to do with the Marxian approach, even if it has penetrated the working-class movement quite a long time ago. As Walter Benjamin rightly observed,

> The conformism which has been part and parcel of Social Democracy from the beginning attaches not only to its political tactics but to its economic views as well. It is one reason for its later breakdown. Nothing has corrupted the German working class so much as the notion that it was moving with the current. It regarded technological development as the fall of the stream with which it thought it was moving. From there it was but a step to the illusion that the factory work which was supposed to tend toward technological progress constituted a political achievement...Josef Dietzgen proclaimed: "The saviour of modern times is called work. The improvement...of labor constitutes the wealth which is now able to accomplish what no redeemer has ever been able to do." This vulgar-Marxist conception of the nature of labor bypasses the question of how its products might benefit the workers while still not being at their disposal. It recognizes only the progress in the mastery of nature, not the retrogression of society. (1970, 260–1)

Under the disorienting impact of capital's postwar success, and influenced by the technologically oriented idealizations of this success by 'scientific' neopositivism, structuralist vulgar Marxism pursued the direction first embarked upon by early Social Democracy, even if the crudeness of its message – linked for a while to a pseudoradical political rhetoric – was carefully wrapped in several layers of hermetic jargon. The 'self-critical' conversions and intellectual collapses that later followed merely brought the verbal radicalism of the original political posturing in line with the right from the beginning thoroughly conformist theoretical substance.

Nor should it be surprising to witness the ideological manifestations of capital's technological rationalization under so many different – and apparently even contradictory – forms. For the practical field in which such anti-dialectical ideologies are formulated is dominated by capital's mighty material structures, many of which are explicitly or implicitly taken for granted, as unquestionable premises, by these rationalizing conceptualizations of the 'scientifically' sound and feasible mode of action. And they are taken for granted whether they positively identify themselves with capital's practical domain, or try to devise within its framework strategies of limited opposition that remain structurally constrained and effectively contained by the criticized material structures. It is by no means accidental that by far the most durable form of ideology in the age of globally articulated and technologically legitimized capital is *positivism*, from its early nineteenth-century manifestations (Comte, Taine, neo-Kantianism, etc.) to 'socialogism', 'pragmatism', 'relativistic positivism', 'instrumentalism', 'juridical positivism', 'logical positivism', 'linguistic analysis', 'structural functionalism', 'relationalism', 'structuralism', etc., and to many fashionable neopositivistic 'philosophies of science'.

Interdependence and global control

All this takes us back to the problem raised at the beginning of this article, concerning the ambivalent position of social consciousness in the dialectical interrelationship between base and superstructure. For while all three fundamental structural constraints discussed above – namely the *partial* character of labor's original teleology, the *permanent latency* of the most fundamental material determinations in the ontology of social being, and the inseparable *destructive* dimension of all productive advance – are only amenable to a *conscious* solution, there seems to be no way out of the dilemma which this solution presents us with. For social consciousness itself, as manifest in all history known to us, is severely affected and vitiated by the overbearing determinations of its own ground: the material base of society.

It is not difficult to see that the partial character of labor's teleological positing is a constitutive determination of the labor process itself, inasmuch as the latter cannot help being directed at specific tasks. Hence the comprehensive dimension can only be a later acquisition, coupled with conscious coordination at the highest level, provided that the material prerequisites of structural coordination are successfully produced and reproduced – with a high degree of homogeneity and on a global scale – by an advanced stage of social/economic development. Furthermore, the material conditions themselves, no matter how advanced, cannot amount to more than *mere prerequisites* to a conscious control of the social metabolism in all its dimensions, and *never* to some a priori guarantee of its continued success. The conditions of a successful global control of the social interchange by consciousness must be constantly *reproduced*, just as much as those directly required for the trouble-free functioning of the material infrastructure, and *none* of the constituents involved in this complex dialectical relationship can be taken for granted. This is the real magnitude of the task facing consciousness with regard to labor's spontaneous teleology and its necessary – indeed qualitatively different and higher – completion by social consciousness itself.

As regards the permanent *latency* of basic material determinations in the social ontology of the natural/human being, the role of consciousness in preventing its re-emergence with a vengeance is, obviously, of paramount importance. For natural necessity can never be *abolished*: only *displaced* by socially mediated material determinations of increasingly higher complexity. The dialectical tension between socially created needs and the conditions of their gratification means that – since the production process, through the challenge to meet the demand inherent in a given set of needs, must raise itself above its immediate object in order to succeed, and thus must itself generate new needs while satisfying old ones – the mode of reproduction of human needs cannot help being a constantly *enlarged* one. This implies not only the growing mobilization of the available material resources, but simultaneously also an ever-increasing sophistication in 'working them up', both as directly consumable goods and as instruments/skills/technology, and institutional/organizational framework required by the appropriate processes of production and distribution. To expect a *material mechanism* to deal with the growing complexities of this situation would be, of course, an absurd suggestion. As to whether or not consciousness itself will be able to do so remains at this stage of historical development a completely open question. What is clear, nevertheless, is that *if* consciousness is to cope with the situation which it is called upon to confront, it must be an adequately 'totalizing' social consciousness: namely, one free from the structurally vitiating dimensions of antagonistic material determinations.

Equally, since the destructive side of productive advance is not attached simply to isolated objects and processes, but to the social complex as a whole in which the negative partial features become cumulative and reciprocally intensify one another, an adequate control over the growing threat is conceivable only as the work of globally coordinated social consciousness. Thus, in view of the measure and severity of the issues at stake, advocating their solution by 'piecemeal social engineering' is as rational as expecting to defeat Hitler's armies by firing shots in the dark with blank cartridges.[6]

The structural constraints of social consciousness

The problems surveyed so far lead to the uncomfortable conclusion that the necessary precondition for finding a real solution to them – in place of rationalizations and manipulative diversions is the ability (if it is feasible to have one) to successfully challenge the existing mode of inter-action between the base and superstructure, with the aim of minimizing the structurally vitiating determinations that emanate from the material base of social life. The practical relevance of understanding the *dialectic of base and superstructure* consists in its help to identify the mechan-isms and distorting constituents of this relationship without which the question of their corrigibility (or otherwise) cannot be seriously raised.

Are the distortions of social consciousness that we can pinpoint throughout history corrigible or not? Are the objective structural constraints that result in ruses of rationalization and 'false conscious-ness' contingent to antagonistic forms of social interaction, hence in prin-ciple removable, or, on the contrary, are they inherent 'in the structure of consciousness itself' and in the necessary failure of consciousness in its attempt to reach any object not immanent to its individualistic self-constitution? For if the latter is the case, as many philosophers argue,[7] then the fundamental problems and challenges which we encounter cannot be really tackled, except in the form of struggling against *symptoms* but not *causes*, producing thereby necessarily inconclusive results in accordance with the very nature of such a priori derailed confrontations.

As we have seen, the problems discussed earlier (which seem to escape human control) all involve the necessity of 'totalization'. For the funda-mental contradictions inherent in the growing structural dysfunctions of the social metabolism are amenable to a solution only in the event of a conscious control of the *totality* of the relevant processes, and not merely the more or less successful temporary management of *partial complexes*. However, while teleological positing in relation to specific, limited objectives can point to *individual* consciousness as its carrier, the controller of a *totality* of social processes is an intensely problematical concept.

Thus, we find ourselves in a truly paradoxical situation. On the one hand, the limited teleology of individual consciousness is constitutionally incapable of dealing with the global challenges that must be faced. At the same time, on the other hand, the seat of 'true collective consciousness' – as contrasted with antagonistically determined collective conceptualizations that manifest more or less pronounced characteristics of 'false consciousness' – cannot be readily identified. Furthermore, the existing material order seems to provide an 'irrefutable proof' for the soundness of the prevailing ideological conceptions. For the dominant individualistic ideologies have their institutional counterpart – including the practical teleology of the market and the 'hidden hand' of its 'parallelogrammatic'[8] interactional instrumentality – which effectively operate in accordance with the well-established structures of material inertia. At the same time, the conditions for the successful functioning of a collective 'true consciousness' – which, in order to be able to successfully engage in a lasting global control of its tasks, would require as its material ground a *non-inertial* institutional framework – are as yet nowhere in sight today, even in an embryonic form. Hence arose the triumphalist mythology of unsurpassable 'market society' and the complete disorientation – indeed the unhappy self-disarming – of the forces of the much-needed radical negation which we have witnessed in the recent past.

All this raises a number of important questions that help to define the scope of ideology and dialectically draw the necessary line of demarcation between modalities of true and false consciousness:

(1) In view of the growing failure of 'unconscious social interaction', fittingly described as 'totalization without a totalizer', Is it possible to constitute a 'collective totalizer' in a sense that is completely free from the idealistic connotations of theological teleology? Or, to put it more precisely, How is it possible to envisage the conditions of a *conscious collective totalization* and the material articulation of its necessary *non-inertial institutional framework and corresponding instrumentality*?

(2) How is it possible to regulate the interaction between the material base and the superstructure in such a way that social consciousness should be able to actively and positively intervene in the operation and dialectical transformation of the fundamental social metabolism?

(3) What are the salient characteristics of ideology, in its positive and negative senses, and how is it possible to differentiate between various forms of true and false consciousness?

(4) How does it come about that consciousness becomes structurally vitiated by its own material ground? Or, to put it in a different way, What are the contradictory social determinations through which social consciousness acquires a perversely dependent/independent existence and, through its self-oriented alienation, becomes a predominantly negative force of domination, instead of emancipation?

(5) How is it possible to minimize the negative dimension of social consciousness on the ground of a radically open history? That is to say, How is it possible to envisage extricating social consciousness from its structural vitiation by its material ground without being trapped by the contradictions of postulating, however unwittingly, a 'closure' of and an end to history?

These and some related questions are discussed in four earlier published books (Mészáros, 1972; 1986; 1989; 1996) and are also pursued in the longer study of which the present article is an integral part (Mészáros, forthcoming). The aim has been to situate our problems within the overall social framework in which they inescapably arise, and to underline their importance for understanding the dialectical nature of historical transformations.

Notes

1. Rosa Luxemburg's expression. Marx asserts much the same in *The German Ideology*.
2. See Sartre, 1978, a greatly neglected work. For even if Sartre's solutions are rather problematical, the questions he raises in the *Critique* are of the greatest importance.
3. It is worth remembering in this context the alarm recently raised by Nobel Prize winner Professor Joseph Rotblat, concerning the profit-driven research activities pursued in the field of biotechnology and 'cloning'. As we know, under the rule of capital such activities – entrapped by the system's expansionary imperatives, whatever the human and environmental consequences – represent a new dimension of humanity's potential self-destruction. This new dimension is now being added to the already existing arsenal of nuclear, chemical and biological weapons: each capable of inflicting on us a universal holocaust many times over.
4. See in this respect Stephen Marglin's excellent study (Marglin, 1974). See also the well-documented book by Stewart Clegg and David Dunkerley (1980).
5. One must resist the temptation of *personifying* technology as an autonomous evil; a temptation to which even some major figures of 20th-century 'critical theory' succumbed. Underestimating the social embeddedness of technology inevitably carries with it a shift of perspective in that direction.
6. The gratuitous postulate of solving our problems by 'piecemeal social engineering' and nothing but 'piecemeal social engineering' rests on three arbitrary assumptions: (1) that the contemptuous rejection of the concept of the 'whole' as 'holism' – whether in its Hegelian variety (summed up as 'the truth is the whole'), or in its Marxian formulations – represents a superior, rationally unchallengeable form of wisdom; (2) that the overall context within which the concept of 'piecemeal' remedial intervention must be situated in order to make *any sense* at all is not some kind of a 'whole', even if a bastardized and ideologically camouflaged one; and (3) that such interventions in the social transformatory process, in the form of 'piecemeal social engineering', which

programmatically oppose the idea of any *comprehensive* strategy – and thus can only be considered 'shots in the dark', even if in the case of the naive well intended, not to speak of their apologetic connotations as the general rule – are, none the less, *capable* of producing the desired positive overall impact, rather than utter disaster, sooner or later. For without an overall frame of reference within which the likely impact of the particular interventions can be properly assessed – rather than uncritically and self-servingly glorified as the only legitimate rational procedure – absolutely *nothing* can be said about their suitability to produce the anticipated results.

Naturally, a deeper layer of arbitrary assumption which 'supports' the three implicit projections mentioned above, like the cosmic turtle of Indian mythology supports the elephant that carries the world on its back, is that the only rationally conceivable whole to which there can be *no alternative* – is the established social order, no matter how much riddled with contradictions and antagonisms.

7. Following in Husserl's footsteps, Sartre, for instance. Indeed he does so not only in *Being and Nothingness*, where he stipulates the 'ontological solitude of consciousness', but even in his 'marxisant' (Sartre's expression) *Critique of Dialectical Reason*. It must be emphasized, however, that this is by no means some special characteristic of a French existentialist approach. On the contrary, it seems to be the rule, rather than the exception, in the last two centuries of philosophical development, dominated by atomistic conceptions of the relationship between individual and society.

8. A term used by Engels, although in a broader sense, intended by him to identify the 'unwanted outcome' of individual interactions in general.

References

Benjamin, Walter. 1970. 'Theses on the Philosophy of History'. In Hannah Arendt, ed., *Illuminations*. London: Jonathan Cape.

Clegg, Stewart and David Dunkerley. 1980. *Organization, Class and Control*. London: Routledge and Kegan Paul.

Larrain, J. 1983. *Marxism and Ideology*. London: Macmillan.

Marglin, Stephen. 1974. 'What Do Bosses Do? – The Origins and Functions of Hierarchy in Capitalist Production'. *Review of Radical Political Economics*, No.6, 60–112.

Marx, Karl, and Friedrich Engels. 1976. *The Communist Manifesto*. MECW, Vol. VI. Moscow: Progress Publishers.

Mészáros, István. 1972. *Lukács's Concept of Dialectic*. London: The Merlin Press.

Mészáros, István. 1986. *Philosophy, Ideology and Social Science*. New York: St. Martin's Press.

Mészáros, István. 1989. *The Power of Ideology*. New York: New York University Press.

Mészáros, István. 1996. *Beyond Capital*. New York: Monthly Review Press.

Mészáros, István. Forthcoming. *Social Structure and Forms of Consciousness: The Dialectic of Structure and History*.

Sartre, Jean-Paul. 1978. *Critique of Dialectical Reason*. London: New Left Books.

11
Dialectics and Revolution: Trotsky, Lenin, Lukács

Michael Löwy

There seems to exist an intimate link between the dialectical method and the revolutionary theory: not by chance, the high period of revolutionary thinking in the twentieth century, the years 1905–1925, are also those of some of the most interesting attempts to use the Hegelo–Marxist dialectics as an instrument of knowledge and action. Let me try to illustrate the connection between dialectics and revolution in the thought of three distinct Marxist figures: Leon D. Trotsky, Vladimir I. Lenin and Georg Lukács.

Trotsky's theory of permanent revolution, as sketched for the first time in his essay *Results and Prospects* (1906), was one of the most astonishing political breakthroughs in Marxist thinking at the beginning of the twentieth century. By rejecting the idea of separate historical stages – the first one being a 'bourgeois democratic' one – in the future Russian Revolution, and raising the possibility of transforming the democratic into a proletarian/socialist revolution in a 'permanent' (i.e. uninterrupted) process, it not only predicted the general strategy of the October Revolution, but also provided key insights into the other revolutionary processes which would take place later on, in China, Indochina, Cuba and so on. Of course, it is not without its problems and shortcomings, but it was incomparably more relevant to the real revolutionary processes in the peripheries of the capitalist system than anything produced by 'orthodox Marxism' from the death of Engels until 1917.

Now, a careful study of the roots of Trotsky's political boldness and of the whole theory of permanent revolution reveals that his views were informed by a specific understanding of Marxism, an interpretation of the dialectical materialist method, distinct from the dominant orthodoxy of the Second International, and of Russian Marxism. The

151

young Trotsky did not read Hegel, but his understanding of Marxist theory owes much to his first lectures in historical materialism, namely, the works of Antonio Labriola. In his autobiography he recalled the 'delight' with which he first devoured Labriola's essays during his imprisonment in Odessa in 1893 (1960, 119). His initiation into dialectics thus took place through an encounter with perhaps the least orthodox of the major figures of the Second International. Formed in the Hegelian school, Labriola fought relentlessly against the neo-positivist and vulgar-materialist trends that proliferated in Italian Marxism (Turati). He was one of the first to reject the economistic interpretations of Marxism by attempting to restore the dialectical concepts of *totality* and *historical process*. Labriola defended historical materialism as a self-sufficient and independent theoretical system, irreducible to other currents; he also rejected scholastic dogmatism and the cult of the textbook, insisting on the need of a *critical* development of Marxism (1970, 115, 243).

Trotsky's starting point, therefore, was this critical, dialectical and anti-dogmatic understanding that Labriola had inspired. 'Marxism', he wrote in 1906, 'is above all a method of analysis – not analysis of texts, but analysis of social relations'. Let us focus on *five* of the most important and distinctive features of the methodology that underlies the Trotsky's theory of permanent revolution, in his distinction from the other Russian Marxists, from Plekhanov to Lenin and from the Mensheviks to the Bolsheviks (before 1917).

1. From the vantage point of the dialectical comprehension of the unity of the opposites, Trotsky criticized the Bolsheviks' rigid division between the socialist power of the proletariat and the 'democratic dictatorship of workers and peasants', as a 'logical, purely formal operation'. This abstract logic is even more sharply attacked in his polemic against Plekhanov, whose whole reasoning can be reduced to an 'empty syllogism': our revolution is bourgeois, therefore we should support the Kadets, the constitutionalist bourgeois party. Moreover, in an astonishing passage from a critique against the Menshevik Tcherevanin, he explicitly condemned the *analytical* – i.e. abstract-formal, pre-dialectical – character of Menshevik politics: 'Tcherevanin constructs his tactics as Spinoza did his ethics, that is to say, geometrically' (Trotsky, 1971, 289, 306–12). Of course, Trotsky was not a philosopher and almost never wrote specific philosophical texts, but this makes his clear-sighted grasp of the methodological dimension of his controversy with stagist conceptions all the more remarkable.

2. In *History and Class consciousness* (1923), Lukács insisted that the dialectical category of totality was the essence of Marx's method, indeed the very principle of revolution within the domain of know-ledge (1971, chapter 1). Trotsky's theory, written 20 years earlier, is an exceptionally significant illustration of this Lukácsian thesis. Indeed, one of the essential sources of the superiority of Trotsky's revolu-tionary thought is the fact that he adopted *the viewpoint of totality*, perceiving capitalism and the class struggle as a world process. In the Preface to a Russian edition (1905) of Lassalle's articles about the revolution of 1848, he argues,

> Binding all countries together with its mode of production and its commerce, capitalism has converted the whole world into a single economic and political organism...This immediately gives the events now unfolding and international character, and opens up a wide horizon. The political emancipation of Russia led by the working class...will make it the initiator of the liquidation of world capitalism, for which history has created the objective condition. (quoted in Trotsky, 1962, 240)

Only by posing the problem in these terms – at the level of 'maturity' of the capitalist system in its *totality* – was it possible to transcend the traditional perspective of the Russian Marxists, who defined the socialist-revolutionary 'unripeness' of Russia exclusively in terms of a *national* economic determinism.

3. Trotsky explicitly rejected the un-dialectical economism – the tendency to reduce, in a non-mediated and one-sided way, all social, political and ideological contradictions to the economic infra-structure – which was one of the hallmarks of Plekhanov's vulgar-materialist interpretation of Marxism. Indeed, Trotsky's break with economism was one of the decisive steps toward the theory of permanent revolution. A key paragraph in *Results and Prospects* defined with precision the political stakes implied in this rupture: 'To imagine that the dictatorship of the proletariat is in some way auto-matically dependent on the technical development and resources of a country is a prejudice of 'economic' materialism simplified to absurdity. This point of view has nothing in common with Marxism' (Trotsky 1962, 195).

4. Trotsky's method refused the un-dialectical conception of history as a pre-determined evolution, typical of Menshevik arguments. He

had a rich and dialectical understanding of historical development as a contradictory process, where at every moment alternatives are posed. The task of Marxism, he wrote, was precisely to 'discover the 'possibilities' of the developing revolution' (1962, 168). In *Results and Prospects*, as well as in later essays – for instance, his polemic against the Mensheviks, 'The proletariat and the Russian revolution' (1908), he analyzes the process of permanent revolution toward socialist transformation through the dialectical concept of *objective possibility*, whose outcome depended on innumerable subjective factors as well as unforeseeable events – and not as an inevitable necessity whose triumph (or defeat) was already assured. It was this recognition of the open character of social historicity that gave revolutionary praxis its decisive place in the architecture of Trotsky's theoretical-political ideas from 1905 on.

5. While the Populists insisted on the peculiarities of Russia and the Mensheviks believed that their country would necessarily follow the 'general laws' of capitalist development, Trotsky was able to achieve a dialectical synthesis between the universal and the particular, the specificity of the Russian social formation and the world capitalist process. In a remarkable passage from the *History of the Russian Revolution* (1930), he explicitly formulated the viewpoint that was already implicit in his 1906 essays:

> In the essence of the matter the Slavophile conception, with all its reactionary fantasticness, and also Narodnikism, with all its democratic illusions, were by no means mere speculations, but rested upon indubitable and moreover deep peculiarities of Russia's development, understood one-sidedly however and incorrectly evaluated. In its struggle with Narodnikism, Russian Marxism, demonstrating the identity of the laws of development for all countries, not infrequently fell into a dogmatic mechaniz-ation discovering a tendency to pour out the baby with the bath (Trotsky, 1965, 427).

Trotsky's historical perspective was, therefore, a dialectical *Aufhebung*, able to simultaneously negate-preserve-transcend the contradiction between the Populists and the Russian Marxists.

It was the combination of all these methodological innovations that made *Results and Prospects* so unique in the landscape of Russian Marxism before 1917; dialectics was at the heart of the theory of permanent revolution. As Isaac Deutscher wrote in his biography, if one reads again this pamphlet from 1906, 'one cannot but be impressed by the sweep and boldness of this vision. He reconnoited the future as one who surveys from a towering mountain top a new and immense horizon and point to vast, uncharted landmarks in the distance' (1954, 161).

Until 1914, Lenin used to consider himself, on the theoretical and philosophical level, as a faithful follower of the orthodox Marxism of the Second International, as represented by figures such as Karl Kautsky and G. V. Plekhanov. His main philosophical work from the early years, *Materialism and Empiriocriticism*, is much influenced by the kind of Marxism represented by the leader of the Menshevik faction.

His philosophical thinking began to change radically after 1914, when he saw – and at first could not believe – that German Social Democracy (including Kautsky) voted the war credits for the Kaiser's government in August 4, 1914 – a choice reproduced in Russia by Plekhanov and several of his comrades. The catastrophe of the Second International at the outbreak of World War I was, for Lenin, striking evidence that something was rotten in the state of Denmark of official 'orthodox' Marxism. The political bankruptcy of that orthodoxy led him, therefore, to a profound revision of the philosophical premises of the Kautsky–Plekhanov sort of historical materialism. It will be necessary one day to retrace the precise track that led Lenin from the trauma of August 1914 to the *Logic* of Hegel scarcely a month after. The simple desire to return to the sources of Marxist thinking? Or a clear intuition that the methodological Achilles' heel of Second International Marxism was the absence of dialectics?

Whatever the reason, there is no doubt that his vision of Marxist philosophy was profoundly changed by it. Evidence of this is the text itself of the *Philosophical Notebooks*, but also the letter he sent on January 4, 1915, shortly after having finished reading Hegel's *The Science of Logic* (December 17, 1914) to the editorial secretary of Granat Publishers to ask if 'there was still time to make some corrections [to his *Karl Marx* entry] in the section of dialectics' (quoted in Garaudy, 1969, 40). And it was by no means a 'passing enthusiasm': seven years later, in one of his last writings, *On the Significance of Militant Marxism* (1922), he called on 'the editors and contributors' of the party's theoretical journal (*Under the Banner of Marxism*) to 'be a kind of Society of Materialist Friends of Hegelian Dialectics'. He insists on the need for a 'systematic study of Hegelian Dialectics from a materialist standpoint', and proposes even to 'print in the journal excerpts from Hegel's principal works, interpret them materialistically and comment on them with the help of examples of the way Marx applied dialectics' (Lenin, 1970, 667–68, 672).

What were the tendencies of Second International Marxism which gave it a *predialectic* character?

1. Primarily, the tendency to ignore the distinction between Marx's dialectical materialism and the 'ancient', 'vulgar', 'metaphysical' materialism of Helvetius, Feuerbach, and so on. Plekhanov, for instance, could write these astonishing lines: 'In Marx's *Theses on Feuerbach*...none of the fundamental ideas of Feuerbach's philosophy are refuted; they are merely amended...Marx and Engels' materialist views were elaborated in the direction indicated by the inner logic of Feuerbach's philosophy' (Plekhanov, n.d., 30–31)!

2. The tendency, that flows from the first, to reduce historical materialism to mechanical economic determinism in which the 'objective' is always the cause of the 'subjective'. For example, Kautsky untiringly insists on the idea that 'the domination of the proletariat and the social revolution cannot come about before the preliminary conditions, as much economic as psychological, of a socialist society are sufficiently realised.' What are these 'psychological conditions'? According to Kautsky, intelligence, discipline and an organizational talent. How will these conditions be created? 'It is the historical task of capitalism' to realize them. The moral of history: 'It is only where the capitalist system of production has attained a high degree of development that economic conditions permit the transformation, by the power of the people, of capitalist property in the means of production into social ownership' (Kautsky, 1903, 185–87, translation modified).

3. The attempt to reduce the dialectic to Darwinian evolutionism, where the different stages of human history (slavery, feudalism, capitalism, socialism) follow a sequence rigorously determined by the 'laws of history'. Kautsky, for example, defines Marxism as 'the scientific study of the evolution of the social organism'. Kautsky had, in fact, been a Darwinian before becoming a Marxist, and it is not without reason that his disciple Brill defined his method as 'bio-historical materialism'.

4. An abstract and naturalistic conception of the 'laws of history', strikingly illustrated by the marvelous pronouncement of Plekhanov

when he heard the news of the October Revolution: 'But it's a violation of all the laws of history!'

5. A tendency to relapse into the analytical method, grasping only 'distinct and separate' objects, fixed in their differences: Russia – Germany; bourgeois revolution – socialist revolution; party – masses; minimum program – maximum program, and so on.

There is no doubt that Kautsky and Plekhanov had carefully read and studied Hegel; but they had not, so to speak, 'absorbed' and 'digested' him into their theoretical systems, grounded on evolutionism and historical determinism.

How far did Lenin's notes on (or about) Hegel's *Logic* constitute a challenge to predialectical Marxism?

1. First, Lenin insists on the philosophical abyss separating 'stupid', that is, 'metaphysical, undeveloped, dead, crude' materialism from Marxist materialism, which, on the contrary, is nearer to 'intelligent', that is, dialectical idealism. Consequently, he criticizes Plekhanov severely for having written nothing on Hegel's *Great Logic*, 'that is to say, basically on the dialectic as philosophical knowledge', and for having criticized Kant from the standpoint of vulgar materialism rather than in the manner of Hegel (Lenin, 1981b, 179, 276, 277).

2. He fully grasps the dialectical conception of causality: 'Cause and effect, ergo, are merely moments of universal reciprocal dependence, of (universal) connection, of the reciprocal connection of events.' At the same time, he praises the dialectical process by which Hegel dissolves the 'opposition of solid and abstract', of subjective and objective, by destroying their one-sidedness (Lenin, 1981b, 159, 187, 260).

3. He emphasizes the major difference between the vulgar evolutionist conception of development and the dialectical one: 'the first, [development as decrease and increase, as repetition] is lifeless, pale and dry; the second [development as a unity of opposites] alone furnishes the key to the 'leaps', to the 'break in continuity', to the 'transformation into the opposite', to the destruction of the old and emergence of the new' (Lenin, 1981a, 358).

4. With Hegel, he struggles 'against making the concept of law absolute, against simplifying it, against making a fetish of it' (and adds, 'NB for modern physics!!!'). He writes likewise that 'laws, all laws, are narrow, incomplete, approximate' (Lenin, 1981b, 151).

5. He sees in the category of *totality*, in the development of the entire ensemble of the moments of reality, the essence of dialectical cognition (Lenin, 1981b, 157–8, 171, 196, 218). We can see the use Lenin made immediately of this methodological principle in the pamphlet he wrote at the time, *The Collapse of the Second International* (1915): he submits to severe criticism the apologists of 'national defense' – who attempt to deny the imperialist character of the Great War because of the 'national factor' of the war of the Serbs against Austria – by underlining that Marx's dialectic 'correctly excludes any isolated examination of an object, that is, one that is one-sided and monstrously distorted' (Lenin, 1981a, 235).

Against the isolation, fixation, separation and abstract opposition of different moments of reality, Lenin insists in dissolving them through the category of totality, arguing also that the dialectic is the theory which shows why human understanding should not take contraries as dead and petrified but as living, conditioned, mobile, interpenetrating each other.

What interests us here most is less the discussion of the philosophical content of Lenin's *Notebooks* of 1914–1915 'in itself' than that of its political consequences: the socialist-revolutionary conception developed by the Bolshevik leader in his 'April Thesis' from 1917. It is not difficult to find the red thread leading from the category of totality to the theory of the weakest link in the imperialist chain; from the interpenetration of opposites to the transformation of the democratic into the socialist revolution; from the dialectical conception of causality to the refusal to define the character of the Russian Revolution solely by Russia's 'economically backward base'; from the critique of vulgar evolutionism to the 'break in continuity' in 1917; and so on. But the most important is quite simply that the critical reading, the materialist reading of Hegel had freed Lenin from the straitjacket of the pseudo-orthodox Marxism of the Second International, from the theoretical limitation it imposed on his thinking. The study of Hegelian logic was the instrument by means of which Lenin cleared the theoretical road leading to the Finland Station of Petrograd, where he first announced 'All the power to the soviets.' In March–April 1917, liberated from the obstacle represented by predialectical Marxism, Lenin could, under the pressure of events, rid himself in good time of its political corollary: the abstract and rigid principle according to which 'The Russian revolution could only be bourgeois, since Russia was not economically ripe for a socialist revolution.' Once he crossed the Rubicon, he applied himself to studying the problem from a practical, concrete and realistic angle: What are the measures, constituting in fact the transition toward socialism, that could be made acceptable to the majority of the people, that is, the masses of the workers and peasants? This is the road which led to the October Revolution.

The philosophical work that best gave expression to the dialectics of revolution after October 1917 was probably Georg Lukács's *History and Class consciousness* (1923). By dissolving the reified moments in the contradictory process of the historical totality, and by emphasizing the unity between the subjective and the objective in the revolutionary praxis, Lukács was able to dialectically supersede (*Aufhebung*) the traditional oppositions between 'ought' and 'being', values and reality, ethics and politics, final goal and immediate circumstances, human will and material conditions. Since this *opus magnum* of Marxist dialectics in the twentieth century is well known, I would like to add a few comments on another piece by Lukács, only recently discovered, *Chvostismus und Dialektik*.

For many years scholars and readers wondered why Lukács never answered to the intense fire of criticism directed against *History and Class Consciousness* (HCC) soon after its publication, particularly from Communist quarters. The recent discovery of *Chvostismus und Dialektik* – probably written around 1925 – in the former archives of the Lenin Institute shows that this 'missing link' existed: Lukács *did reply*, in a most explicit and vigorous way, to these attacks, and defended the main ideas of his Hegelo–Marxist masterpiece from 1923. One may consider this answer as the last revolutionary/Marxist writing of the Hungarian philosopher, just before a major turn in his theoretical and political orientation – the philosophical 'reconciliation with reality' proposed by his essay on Moses Hess from 1926.[1]

Chvostismus und Dialektik – English translation: *Tailism and the Dialectics* (T&D) – may be considered as a powerful exercise in revolutionary dialectics, against the crypto-positivist brand of 'Marxism' that was soon to become the official ideology of the Soviet bureaucracy. The key element in this polemical battle is Lukács' emphasis on the *decisive revolutionary importance of the subjective moment in the subject/object historical dialectics*. If one had to summarize the value and the significance of *Tailism and the Dialectics*, I would argue that it is *a powerful Hegelian/Marxist apology of revolutionary subjectivity*. This motive runs like a red thread throughout the whole piece, particularly in its first part, but even, to some extent, in the second one too. Let us try to bring into evidence the main moments of this argument.

One could begin with the mysterious term *Chvostismus* of the book's title – Lukács never bothered to explain it, supposing that its – German? Russian? – readers were familiar with it. The word was used by Lenin in his polemics – for instance in *What is to be done?* – against those 'economistic Marxists' who 'tail-end' the spontaneous labor movement. Lukács, however, uses it in a much broader historiosophical sense: *Chvostismus* means passively following – 'tailing'– the 'objective' course of events, while ignoring the subjective/revolutionary moments of the historical process.

Lukács denounces the attempt by Rudas and Deborin to transform Marxism into a 'science' in the positivist, bourgeois sense. Deborin – an ex-Menshevik – tries, in a regressive move, to bring back historical materialism 'into the fold of Comte or Herbert Spencer' (*auf Comte oder Herbert Spencer zurückrevidiert*), a sort of bourgeois sociology studying transhistorical laws that exclude all human activity. And Rudas places himself as a 'scientific' observer of the objective, law-bound course of history, whereby he can 'anticipate' revolutionary developments. Both regard as worthy of scientific investigation only what is free of any participation on the part of the historical subject, and both reject, in the name of this 'Marxist' (in fact, positivist) science any attempt to accord 'an *active and positive* role to a subjective moment in history' (Lukács, 2000, 50, 135, 137; see Lukács, 1996, 9).

The war against subjectivism, argues Lukács, is the banner under which opportunism justifies its rejection of revolutionary dialectics: it was used by Bernstein against Marx and by Kautsky against Lenin. In the name of anti-subjectivism, Rudas develops a fatalist conception of history, which includes only 'the objective conditions', but leaves no room for the decision of the historical agents. In an article in *Inprekor* against Trotsky – criticized by Lukács in *T&D* – Rudas claims that the defeat of the Hungarian revolution of 1919 was due only to 'objective conditions' and not to any mistakes of the Communist leadership; he mentions both Trotsky and Lukács as examples of a one-sided conception of politics which overemphasizes the importance of proletarian class consciousness.[2]

While rejecting the accusation of 'subjective idealism', Lukács does not retract from his voluntarist viewpoint: in the decisive moments of the struggle 'everything depends on class consciousness, on the conscious will of the proletariat'– the subjective component. Of course, there is a dialectical interaction between subject and object in the historical process, but in the crucial moment (*Augenblick*) of crisis, it gives the direction of the events, in the form of revolutionary consciousness and praxis. By his fatalist attitude, Rudas ignores praxis and develops a theory of passive 'tail-ending', considering that history is a process that 'takes place independently of human consciousness'.

What is Leninism, argues Lukács, if not the permanent insistence on the *'active and conscious* role of the subjective moment'? How could one imagine, 'without this function of the subjective moment', Lenin's conception of insurrection as an art? Insurrection is precisely the *Augenblick*, the instant of the revolutionary process where *'the subjective moment has a decisive predominance (ein entscheidendes Übergewicht)'*. In that instant, the fate of the revolution, and therefore of humanity 'depends on the subjective moment'. This does not mean that revolutionaries should 'wait' for the arrival of this *Augenblick*: there is no moment in the historical process where the possibility of an active role of the subjective moments is completely lacking (Lukács, 2000, 48, 54–8, 62; see Lukács, 1996, 16).[3]

In this context, Lukács turns his critical weapons against one of the main expressions of this positivist, 'sociological', contemplative, fatalist – *chvostistisch* in his terminology – and objectivist conception of history: the *ideology of progress*. Rudas and Deborin believe that the historical process is an evolution mechanistically and fatally leading to the next stage. History is conceived, according to the dogmas of evolutionism, as permanent advance, endless progress: the temporally later stage is necessarily the higher one in every respect. From a dialectical viewpoint, however, the historical process is 'not an evolutionary nor an organic one', but contradictory, jerkily unfolding in advances and retreats (Lukács, 2000, 55, 78, 105). Unfortunately Lukács does not develop this insight, that points toward a radical break with the ideology of inevitable progress common to Second and – after 1924 – Third International Marxism.

Another important aspect related to this battle against the positivist degradation of Marxism is Lukács critique, in the second part of the essay, against the views expressed by Rudas on technology and industry as an 'objective' and neutral system of 'exchange between humans and nature'. This would mean, objects Lukács, that there is an essential identity between the capitalist and the socialist society! In his viewpoint, revolution has to change not only the relations of production but also revolutionize to a large extent the concrete forms of technology and industry existing in capitalism, since they are intimately linked to the capitalist division of labor. In this issue too Lukács was well ahead of his time, but the suggestion remains undeveloped in his essay (Lukács, 2000, 134–5).

Notes

1. On the meaning of this work in Lukács's intellectual evolution, I refer to the last chapter of my book *Georg Lukacs. From Romanticism to Bolshevism* (Löwy, 1980).

2. As John Ree very aptly comments, Rudas and Deborin stand in direct continuity with Second International positivist/determinist Marxism:

> In Rudas' mind, Trotsky and Lukács are linked because they both stress the importance of the subjective factor in the revolution. Rudas steps forth as a defender of the 'objective conditions' which guaranteed that the revolution was bound to fail. The striking similarity with Karl Kautsky's review of Korsch's *Marxism and Philosophy*, in which he attributes the failure of the German revolution to just such objective conditions, is striking testimony to the persistence of vulgar Marxism among the emerging Stalinist bureaucracy. ('Introduction' to Lukács 2000, 24–5)

3. Of course, this argument is mainly developed in the first chapter of the first part of the essay, which has the explicit title 'Subjectivism'. But one can find it also in other parts of the document.

References

Deutscher, Isaac. 1954. *The Prophet Armed*. London: Oxford University Press.

Garaudy, Roger. 1969. *Lenine*. Paris: PUF.

Labriola, Antonio. 1970. *La concepcion materialista de la historia (1897)*. La Habana.

Lenin, V. I. 1970. *Selected Works*, Volume 3. Moscow: Progress Publishers.

Lenin, V. I. 1981a. *The Collapse of the Second International* in *Collected Works*, Volume 21. Moscow: Progress Press.

Lenin, V. I. 1981b. *Philosophical Notebooks, Completed Works*, Volume 38. Moscow: Progress Press.

Löwy, Michael. 1980. *Georg Lukacs. From Romanticism to Bolshevism*. London: New Left Books, 1980.

Lukács, Georg. 1923. *History and Class Consciousness*. London: New Left Books.

Lukács, Georg. 1996. *Chvostismus und Dialektik*. Budapest: Aron Verlag.

Lukács, Georg. 2000. *Tailism and the Dialectics*. London: Verso.

Kautsky, Karl. 1903. *The Social Revolution*. Chicago: Charles Kerr.

Plekhanov, George V. n.d. *Fundamental Problems of Marxism*. London: Martin Lawrence.

Trotsky, Leon. 1960. *My Life*. New York: C. Scribner's Sons.

Trotsky, Leon. 1962. *Results and Prospects*. London: Simon and Schuster.

Trotsky, Leon. 1965. *History of the Russian Revolution*, Volume 1. London: Simon and Schuster.

Trotsky, Leon. 1971. *1905*. London: Random House.

12
Dialectics and Revolution, Now

Savas Michael-Matsas

'Why dialectics? Why now?'

Recently reformulated by Bertell Ollman (2003), in this direct and urgent manner, the question about the actuality of dialectics includes the paradox of its terms and their mutual relationship – 'dialectics' and 'now':

- How does dialectics stand in front of the challenge posed by 'Now', the present moment in history?
- How does the 'Now-Moment' in history appear in front of the challenge posed by dialectics?

It is well known that dialectics, both Hegel's idealist version – 'the basis of all dialectic' according to Marx (Marx and Engels, 1983, 166) – and Marx's materialist dialectics, has supposedly fallen into disrepute following the (mis)use of dialectical materialism as *state philosophy* (the accurate description is by Georges Labica) by the Stalinist bureaucracy in the Soviet Union. With the collapse of the Soviet state and of other 'Soviet' type states in Eastern Europe, it is often argued that dialectics has been buried, once and for all, under their ruins.

It would be a fatal error, however, to equate communist emancipation with Stalinism and materialist dialectics with 'dia-mat', this monstrosity that was used as an apologetic defense of bureaucratic rule, a technology of pseudo-knowledge adapted to a technology of power. What relation can possibly exist between dialectics as 'the study of contradictions in the essence of the objects' (Lenin, 1981, 252), and the empiricist methods of a bureaucracy frightened by the very idea of contradictions and desperately trying to escape from their influence by mismanaging them? This is the same bureaucracy, which, while using dia-mat as state philosophy, found it necessary to abolish the law of negation of negation by Stalin's diktat!

The question of whether or not dialectics has survived the historical tragedy of the October Revolution cannot be judged by its false identification with its antithesis, the bureaucratic construct of dia-mat. In a different historical framework, Marx had already made a sharp distinction between mystified, apologetic forms of the dialectic and its rational, critical and revolutionary form: 'In its mystified form, dialectic became the fashion in Germany, because it seemed to transfigure and to glorify the existing state of things. In its rational form it is a scandal and abomination to bourgeoisdom and its doctrinaire professors...' (Marx, 1986a, 29). Mystified 'dialectical materialism' as the ideological transfiguration and glorification of the bureaucratic state of things in so-called 'actually existing Socialism' is definitely dead and buried. But materialist dialectics still remains a living scandal and abomination to the bourgeoisie and its ideological defenders. The judgment of Now, of the present as History, should not be confounded with the bourgeois prejudices prevailing now and spread globally by the assumed 'victors' of the Cold War.

A method which is critical and unapologetic toward the existing state of things has not only to be self-critical but also critical of the concept of time, particularly of the concept of 'now' itself. When we pose the question 'Why dialectics? Why now?', we should not forget that just as dia-mat is not dialectics, so the 'Now' of the question is not the now considered as a point in an infinite series on a line of gradual progress of 'empty, homogeneous, historical time'. As Walter Benjamin rightly warned, 'In the now the truth is charged with time to the point of explosion' (1989, 479). The Now-Moment, Benjamin's *Jetztzeit*, is not an indifferent point on a homogeneous continuum but the edge of a heterogeneous time, the point of the rupture of the continuity, the opening of History to possibility, what the ancient Greeks called Kairos/Καιρός, the right Moment, Νυν Καιρός, the Now-Moment, or Καιρού ακμή, the edge of Time as Moment.

Time is central in all considerations of dialectics. Bertell Ollman, in asking the question 'Why dialectics? Why now?', has himself suggested an answer by exploring the future (communism) as the potential within the (capitalist) present.

Following the path opened by Benjamin, these temporal relations can be approached by the formation of *a new constellation of dialectics with Now*, where (to continue in Benjaminian language), dialectics 'flashes its lightning image in the Now of its recognizability' (1989, 479). In other words, we need to search for the dialectic in the Now of a present world in crisis, as the moment of its recognizability at the edge of time. And vice versa, the Now-Moment has to be grasped by a dialectic that challenges it by uncovering its inner contradictions that drive it to its negation.

Crisis as a school of dialectics

In the famous 1873 'Afterword' in the second German edition of *Capital*, Marx sums up, in a way that is superb in its density, the main elements of the dialectical method that made it a scandal and an abomination to the ruling class and the ruling ideology. Inseparably connected with the materialist reversal and re-working of Hegel's Logic, Marxist dialectics 'includes in its *comprehension and affirmative recognition of the existing states of things*, at the same time also, the recognition of the *negation* of that state, of its inevitable breaking up', discovering the *work of the negative* within the positive, the *'contradictions* inherent in the movement of capitalist society'. On this basis it grasps the link between movement and change, *transition*, for it regards 'every historically developed social form as in fluid movement, and therefore takes into account its *transient* nature no less than its *momentary existence*.' Last but not least, 'it lets *nothing impose* upon it' rejecting all pre-established dogmas and all intrusions external to the process of discovering the truth. Composing all previously mentioned elements into one integral whole, materialist dialectics 'is in its essence *critical* and *revolutionary*' (Marx 1986a, 29, emphasis added).

It is understandable that in this post-1989/1991 age of 'obscure disaster' (Badiou, 1991), our rulers' 'common sense' should feel such outrage when confronted with dialectical reasoning. Amidst the celebrations for the 'final and complete triumph' of liberal capitalism – and, supposedly, the 'end' of communism, revolution, classes, class struggle, ideologies, philosophy, art, History, etc. – to demand the 'comprehension and affirmative recognition of the existing state of things' in the post–Cold War chaotic world, to explore the 'work of the negative within the positive' can only appear 'scandalous' in their eyes. For what is demanded here is to grasp the dialectic of negativity of globalized capitalism, its 'momentary existence' and, above all, its 'transient nature', letting nothing impose itself upon the theoretical and practical struggle for emancipation, not the prevailing conservative, philistine prejudice from the Right nor the skepticism of a defeatist Left. What is so scandalous to our ruling class is defying the status quo by a critical and revolutionary approach to the Now-Moment, grasping it as the edge of time and an opening in history, an unexplored landscape of possibilities, an unknown horizon for a historical praxis to change the world.

In the conclusion of his remarks on method in the 1873 'Afterword', Marx forewarned his enemies of the lesson that the approaching capitalist crisis would teach them about dialectics: 'By the universality of its theater and the intensity of its action [the crisis] will drum dialectics even into the heads of the mushroom-upstarts of the new, holy Prusso-German Empire' (Marx, 1986a, 29).

Empires, their rulers and their docile servants are bad students. Usually they learn nothing and forgive nothing. This applies both to the old, 'holy' Prusso-German Empire as well as to the new, unholy North American global Empire about which the neoconservatives in Washington fantasize. Even in the hour of doom, when the proverbial writing is on the wall, the new Balthasars and their imperial guards are unable to understand the logic of their own doom, namely dialectics.

No one can doubt that the lesson, or rather the 'revenge' of dialectics that Marx predicted is already upon us: the capitalist crisis is here, the universality of its theater covers the entire planet, and the intensity of its action is already strongly felt both in the metropolitan centers and in the countries of the periphery. The transformation into the opposite is being taught not by textbooks but by the devastating experiences of the last 15 years.

The initial euphoria and the triumphalism of capitalists following the implosion of the Soviet Union have dissipated. The pipedream of the establishment of an eternal and peaceful kingdom of liberal capitalism on earth has been transformed into a nightmare of perpetual wars, from the Balkans to Central Asia, from the dismemberment of former Yugoslavia to Afghanistan and the Iraqi inferno. The declarations about universal peace after the end of Cold War were replaced by the terror of a permanent 'war on terror', where, to paraphrase Brecht, peace itself is reduced into an unconventional 'extreme case' of war. The rhetoric on human rights has been transformed into the horror of Abou Ghraib and Guantanamo. 'Exporting democracy' has become synonymous with brutal occupation abroad and importing police state techniques at home, abolishing the State of Law by law, and establishing in the metropolitan centers in Europe and the U.S. a 'State of Emergency', which, as Benjamin predicted, gets transformed from the exception into a rule. And civil peace itself becomes civil strife with continuous attacks on civil liberties and preparatory steps taken for the possibility of civil war clashes in the big urban centers.

The material basis for all these violent manifestations is the crisis of capitalist globalization itself. 'Globalization', as the dominant myth of the last two decades, was originally presented as the 'final and complete victory' of capitalism on the planet, as the free movement of capital beyond the recurrent threat of systemic crises, but also as the driving force for enrichment for all, both in the countries of the privileged center and of the poor periphery.

Obviously, over the last two decades, finance globalization has become the driving force for exactly the opposite: for mass impoverishment on an unprecedented scale, for the decline of 'Third World' continents like Africa into the limbo of a 'Fourth World' and for the creation of vast 'Third World' zones inside the 'First World' metropolitan centers. There are concentrated masses of working poor, of 'new poor', of wageless workers, of new and old kinds of socially excluded, as well as the victims of gigantic waves of mass immigration that 'globalization' has driven from the social catastrophe of their home countries in the South and East to the social misery and over-exploitation in the West and North. Capitalist globalization has become the most powerful driving force for global pauperization, and for the over-concentration of the wealth of the world in the hands of a tiny minority of finance speculators and corporate brigands. The monstrous exacerbation of social inequalities on a global scale, *this dialectic of poverty is the indictment for the poverty of all anti-dialectics.*

Finance globalization was itself a product of crisis and a generator of an even greater one. The liberalization of the movement of capital and the globalization of financial markets emerged as a temporary way out of the unprecedented crisis of over-production of capital, once the equally unprecedented post–World War II capitalist expansion had reached its limits in the early 1970s. The global domination of this 'consummate automatic fetish, the self expanding value, the money-making money … a Moloch demanding the whole world as a sacrifice', as Marx prophetically predicted, produced across the length and breadth of the globe the most wild fetishist illusions in capitalist history (Marx, 1975b, 455–6). The implications on mass consciousness and ideology should not be underestimated. Among other things, this is the powerful source of anti-dialectics and of the idolatry of the simulacrum in our days.

But the flight to the international skies of speculation, the tremendous expansion of fictitious capital as a way out of stagnating surplus capital, in the long run exacerbated the crisis of over-accumulation. Globalization of capital has reproduced on an extended scale, and globalized all its contradictions, bringing them to the point of explosion. A series of financial shocks followed by social upheavals erupted in the late 1990s. From the international crash of 1997 centered in the Asian–Pacific region to Russia's default in 1998, to the burst of the financial bubble of the 'dot.com' economy on Wall Street in 2000 and from the Enron and Parmalat scandals to the state bankruptcy of countries once lauded as 'success stories' of so-called neo-liberalism (like Argentina in 2001), the universality of the theater and the intensity of action of the world systemic crisis of capitalism has become clear for all to see. Furthermore, these financial earthquakes were internally related to a generalized destabilization that produces internationally social unrest and popular revolts, anti-imperialist mobilizations and class battles with revolutionary potential, from Latin America (Argentina, Ecuador, Bolivia, Peru, Venezuela) to Europe (the mass social movements culminating in the NO vote to the EU constitution in France) and the Middle East (the Palestinian Intifada, the Iraqi Resistance). The emergence of the powerful movement against capitalist globalization in the battles that took place in Seattle and Genoa, as well as the biggest anti-war demonstrations in history in February 2003 on the eve of the imperialist war against Iraq, are unmistakably the manifestation of the social forces unleashed in the battlefield by the crisis of capitalist globalization.

The world crisis, as Marx explained, 'must be regarded as the concentration and forcible adjustment of *all* the contradictions of bourgeois economy' (Marx, 1975a, 510, emphasis added). The logic of contradictions in their totality is precisely dialectics.

Lenin made the remark that 'if Marx did not leave behind him a *"Logic"* (with a capital letter), he did leave the logic of *"Capital"* and this ought to be utilized to the full in this question' (Lenin, 1981, 317). The study of this dialectical logic is now more than ever urgent: *contradictions* exploding into crisis, the *transformation into their opposite* of all the features of a previous period, a post–Cold War world in an extremely painful *transition*... the list could go on. Avoiding dialectics now is an expression of the fear of contradictions, a turning away from the demands of an epoch of transition, a refusal to transform the present hell into its opposite; one which clings to the forlorn hope of an afterlife of a liberal parliamentary capitalism with a 'human face'.

Under the star of a catastrophe

An epochal turn, marked by historical upheavals, wars, revolutionary upsurges of the oppressed masses or retreats and counterrevolutions, is always the moment of recognizability of dialectics. It is the moment that makes possible the recognition of a void in History – the Real in Lacanian terms; an apparent impossibility demanding and simultaneously preventing its penetration by cognition. On the border of this void in History dialectics can be found, leaning and hovering over the void like the Rouah Elohim (the Spirit of God) over the waters of the abyss in the beginning of the Torah. Out of this encounter with impossibility, which is also a period of historical crisis and transition, arises the need to form a new constellation between dialectics and the demands of the Now-Moment.

Dialectics, as Hölderlin wrote in 1805, (in a very dense poetical/philosophical commentary on Pindar's fragments that he had translated anew, closely interconnected with his profoundly dialectical *Remarks* on Sophocles's tragedies *Oedipus* and *Antigone*, see Hölderlin, 1965), is 'the art of being sure in one's understanding in the midst of positive errors' (2004, 704–5). At crucial turning points, when everything appears estranged, alien (*Fremde*), an intense training in dialectics is particularly demanded: 'If our understanding has been exercised intensely, it retains its strength, even in diffusion; inasmuch as it easily recognizes the Alien (*das Fremde*) by its own honed sharpness, and so is not easily confused in unknown situations' (p. 705).

The German poet, an unrepentant Jacobin writing in post-Thermidorian conditions of bourgeois reaction, 'in lean years' [*in dürftiger Zeit*] no less obscure than ours, turns to 'the art of remaining faithful in changing circumstances' (Hölderlin, 2004, 326–7). He remained faithful to the Revolution in permanence by refusing to fixate on what appeared unchangeable, devoting himself to a new re-working of the texts by Pindar and Sophocles, and in this way established a new understanding of the dialectic of modernity in relation to antiquity.

Dialectics in modern times always makes its appearance under the star of a catastrophe, when the old world is passing away and the new one has not yet fully arisen. The year 1789 produced the dialectical insights of Hölderlin and Hegel's *Phenomenology* and *Logic*. The European crisis and Revolution of 1848 became the first arena for Marxian dialectics. The first Russian Revolution of 1905 was the birth place for Trotsky's dialectical theory of Permanent Revolution. The outbreak of the First World War in 1914 and the collapse of the Second International led Lenin to turn to Hegel's *Logic* and to the entire dialectical tradition starting from the ancient Greeks as a necessary theoretical preparation for the first victorious proletarian revolution in 1917. The epic tragedy of the German Revolution in 1919 gave the impulse to the great dialectical contributions by Walter Benjamin and Ernst Bloch. The 1933 catastrophe, with the victory of Hitler's Nazism and the political death of a bureaucratized Comintern, pushed Trotsky to follow Lenin's path and make a fresh study of Hegel's Logic. Benjamin's 1940 *Theses on the Concept of History*, a major attack on the anti-dialectical gradualist conceptions of social democracy and Stalinism that led to such disastrous policies, was drafted when 'it was midnight in the century'...

And *Now*? The question remains open.

Metamorphosis

A dialectical materialist, Benjamin stresses, 'cannot consider history otherwise than as a constellation of dangers...' (1989, 487). And as a *materialist*, he or she recognizes that real dangers cannot be confronted solely with theoretical explanations or rationalizations. A historical *praxis* of transformation of the existing conditions is also required. Materialist dialectics is a theory permanently revolutionizing itself, as well as a method to revolutionize the historical practice of the revolutionary class that takes the lead in transforming social conditions; it is both a critical and a practical revolutionary activity, directed toward mobilizing the oppressed to deal with a real, 'actual state of emergency' (Benjamin, *Thesis* VIII) against the 'fictitious state of emergency' declared by the ruling classes and their terrorist 'Patriot' Acts.

In Marx's 1844 Introduction to the *Critique of Hegel's Philosophy of Right* (a founding Ur-text of Marxism), this dialectical method of revolutionary mobilization is presented in a condensed form: 'These petrified relations must be made to dance by singing to them their own melody!'[*man muss diese versteinerten Verhaeltnisse dadurch zum Tanzen zwingen, dass man ihnen ihre eigne Melodie vorsingt!*] (Marx, 1976, 381).

Bertell Ollman chose this phrase as a guiding principle and the motto for his book appropriately entitled *Dance of the Dialectic*.

Three elements are included in this Marxian sentence that summarize the entire dialectical project: (a) a critical recognition of the *petrifaction* of historical social relations; (b) the discovery and artful '*singing of their own melody*'; (c) the active transformation of their present petrifaction into its opposite by making use of their own laws of motion in a rhythmical movement, in a *dance* of liberation.

Let us look more closely at these three elements of historical materialist dialectics.

Petrifaction

The first step for a critical study of social relations is the recognition of their *historicity*, their conditional, transient nature; that is to say, the study of their transition, the discovery of their actual historical character, and the particular movement of their life-process. 'Petrifaction' refers to the epoch of historical *decline* of a social formation when it becomes an anachronism, because it can no longer meet the growing demands of nor take advantage of the expanding potential in its developing mode of production. In other words, this metaphor contains in nucleus the historical materialist conception that Marx develops later on.

Marx's metaphor referred in the first place to Germany on the eve of the 1848 Revolution, an *Ancien Régime* fossilised in modern capitalist society. Later the metaphor was extended to include all declining social formations, repeating as a farce what was primarily a tragedy in history.

Contemporary, 'globalized' capitalism, despite all its pretensions to be an ultra-modernizing force, is in reality 'our' *Ancien Régime*. Modernity was born under capitalist conditions but is not identical to them. There is not just unity but also a growing *contradiction* between modernity and capitalism that apologists always try to forget or hide, a contradiction that globalization has greatly exacerbated. Modernity is the tendency to universality, the ceaseless transgression of all previously established boundaries, an almost limitless force generated by capital in its character as self-expanding value, but which has come into sharper and sharper conflict with the limits inherent in the capital relation itself. As Marx emphasized in *Grundrisse*: ' ... the universality for which capital ceaselessly strives, comes up against barriers in capital's own nature, barriers which at a certain stage of its development will allow it to be recognized as being itself the greatest barrier in the way of this tendency and will therefore drive forward its transcendence through itself' (Marx 1986b, 337). The world socialist revolution is precisely the emancipation of this universalizing tendency of modernity, which has been blocked by the petrified conditions of a capitalism in decline and crisis, through the self-emancipation of a universal class, the modern proletariat.

One might object, of course, that contemporary finance globalization is characterized by an extreme 'fluidity' rather than by motionless petrifaction. But this fluidity, the extreme velocity of finance transactions on a planetary scale, represents the free movement of *abstract* capital (as Hilferding correctly called finance capital), that is capital separated from the conditions of its origins in the production of surplus value.

Finance globalization is the apotheosis of a social and economic system whose regulative principle is abstract labour, the exchange of 'masses of congealed labour time', frozen time or, if you like, of petrified time (Marx, 1986a, 47). World capitalism, a society where 'the individuals are now ruled by *abstractions*', as Marx pointedly wrote, despite or rather because of the extreme mobility of these abstractions in today's conditions, clashes sooner rather than later with its own barriers, its own rigidities, as every new financial shock makes clear (Marx, 1986b, 101). To repeat, then, it is now our *Ancien Régime*.

The petrifaction of relations of social *life* under capitalism means their *reification*, a reversal of the relations of life and death, a specific form of human alienation where, as is explained in the famous chapter on 'Fetishism' in *Capital I*, material relations between persons assume the fantastic form of social relations between things (Marx, 1986a, 78).

In Marx's theory of alienation and fetishism can be found not only the continuity but above all the *discontinuity* of his method with that of Hegel. While for the idealist Hegel, alienation is the same as objectification of the Idea and Nature is described as 'petrified intelligence', for the materialist Marx, alienation is based on the historical division of labour. Thus, the social powers of human beings are not always alienated. It is under capitalism, with its distinctive division of labor, that these powers become alienated and their accompanying social relations reified/petrified, in which form they come to dominate the entire life of society. In this society, all life becomes subjugated to the requirements of capital accumulation, giving to bourgeois power a character that Michel Foucault described as 'bio-power'. Petrified human life suffers, and every attempt to escape this situation can make the pain worse. As in Kafka's version of the Prometheus legend, the bound Prometheus' efforts to escape from the tearing beak of the eagle only succeeds in driving 'himself in his agony deeper and deeper into the rock until he became one with it' (Kafka, 2005, 49).

Petrified life, however, is still life. Petrifaction might be putrefaction, but, as Marx explained, in history, as in nature, putrefaction is the laboratory of life. It produces by negation of the old the elements of the new. Capital's globalization does not only represent its domination on a world scale but also, as Paresh Chattopadhyay (2002) has shown in an excellent paper, drives this 'dialectic of negativity' to its extreme limit and the point of explosion and revolutionary transformation. Even in his miserable petrified condition, Prometheus remains alive, defying all the oppressors and resisting tyranny. He continues listening for the song of freedom, a melody that reflects his own situation sung now by the forces of liberation.

The Song of Dialectics

How is the transition from petrified social conditions to a dance of life possible? This extraordinary metamorphosis cannot be arbitrary, or 'organic', or gradual, without a revolutionary break in continuity. First, Marx separates himself resolutely from reformism of all kinds, old and new: '...within bourgeois society, based as it is upon *exchange value*, [emphasis in the original] relationships of exchange and production are generated which are just so many mines to blow it to pieces. (A multitude of antagonistic forms of the social entity, whose antagonism, however, *can never be exploded by a quiet metamorphosis...*)' (Marx, 1986b, 96–7; emphasis added).

Capitalism as a minefield of contradictions will not explode automatically by itself, nor will it change peacefully in 'a quiet metamorphosis'. Capitalist globalization and its militarization have transformed the entire planet into a most dangerous minefield. Only those who try to reform, to 'humanize', globalized capitalist inhumanity can have the reactionary pipedream of 'a quiet metamorphosis' of the present inferno. The systemic 'mines', which are now blindly exploding all over the world in wars, mass impoverishment and unspeakable forms of barbarism, have to be activated by a revolutionary agency, the mobilization of the oppressed masses and their organized vanguard, in order 'to blow it to pieces'.

This mass activity should not be blind or arbitrary. It has to be 'the conscious expression of the unconscious process' of history, of the demands of historical development. Marx warns against any manifestation of historical idealism and blind voluntarism: '...if we did not find latent in society as it is, the material conditions of production and the corresponding relationships of exchange for a classless society, all attempts to explode it would be quixotic' (Marx, 1986b, 97).

In the discovery and exploration of these material conditions, the critique of the 'anatomy of civil society', of political economy, the method presented in the logic of Marx's *Capital* is vital. We have not yet finished re-reading this magnum opus. It is through such critical exploration that we uncover the distinctive logic of capitalism's evolving contradictions, that is hear the peculiar *melody* inherent in its petrified social relations that we have only to sing if these relations are to be made to dance. Hölderlin, again commenting on Pindar's fragment 140b, speaks in *Von Delphin* [Of the Dolphin] about the melody which can move and make appear forms hidden in the depths of nature and history:

> Which in the waveless sea's deep of flutes
> The song delightfully has moved

(2004, 711)

This is the Song of Nature itself, *der Gesang der Natur* in which ' each being utters its tone, its faithfulness, the way in which it relates itself within itself' (Hölderlin, 2004, 711; translations slightly altered). What is essentially hidden beneath the surface appears in response to a song sung in its own melody. Materialist dialectics is the ability to find the specific logic of each specific object, and the art to sing the song of nature, the real *das Lied von der Erde*. Dialectics, this 'most revolutionary element in Marxism', as Lenin put it, is also its Orphic principle. The question now becomes, How can the specific melody in something be discovered and then properly sung?

The melody, the specific logic, the inner connectedness of contradictions that moves an entity has to be abstracted from it, discovered within it, and not imposed upon it. Dialectics is not a pragmatic technology for acquiring knowledge, a set of rules to be applied from without on the object of cognition. The melody has to be found and learned in its inner source. How? Following explicitly Heraclitus, Lenin indicates the path: 'The splitting of a single whole and the cognition of its contradictory parts [...] is the *essence* (one of the "essentials", one of the principal, if not the principal, characteristics or features) of dialectics [...] the recognition (discovery) of the contradictory, *mutually exclusive*, opposite tendencies in *all* phenomena and processes of nature (including mind and society' (1981, 357–8). These are the 'mines to be exploded' that the 'destructive character' of Marxism has to find (Benjamin, 1999, 541–2). Or, to use our other metaphor, this is the 'melody' within the petrified condition with which – according the Orphic principle – we can make these conditions dance.

Hölderlin takes the same Heraclitean path in his commentary on Pindar's fragment 213 under the title *Das Unendliche* [The Infinite] (2004, 716–17). The poet poses the most acute *political* question of his (and our) times: when real human beings are involved in building on earth the City (or Plato's Utopian Republic, or the Jacobin revolutionary Republic, or a Workers Republic in the form of the dictatorship of the proletariat), how are Justice and the cunning of political Reason, its stratagems and deceptive tactics, related?

First of all, to avoid ideological distortions, we need to recognize the *contradiction* in the transition between justice in a realm of freedom and political reason in the Revolution itself. Hölderlin stresses that 'the wavering and the conflict between justice and cunning are resolved only in a relation of interpenetration [*in durchgängiger Beziehung*]', which includes the transformation of each into the other, its opposite. It is this relation of interpenetration between the historical *goal* and the actual *movement* which negates the existing state of things that is rejected both by reformists and by Utopians. From Bernstein to the present-day fetishists of the social movements, the goal of a universal human emancipation in a classless society has been dissolved into the everyday movement; conversely, all kinds of abstentionists and sectarians have isolated socialism from the actual class struggle.

To discover the interpenetration between justice and political reason, the connection, Hölderlin writes, should 'not to be ascribed to either of them but to a third by which they are connected infinitely (exactly), for that I have a divided mind' (2004, 717, translation slightly altered). In his final sentence, the German poet interprets the last verse in Pindar's fragment 213:

> Δίχα μοι νόος ατρέκειαν ειπείν
> Divided I have a mind to say it exactly

The Pindarian verse stands at the opposite pole from the conclusion of Wittgenstein's *Tractatus*. For Pindar, you can state the connection *exactly* only if the mind is *divided in contradictory parts*. An inner division in cognition – its movement through evolving and unfolding contradictions, its dialectical character – is necessary if it is to capture the inner splitting of a single whole into mutually exclusive and opposing tendencies.

This relation of interpenetration always involves the interpenetration of the object and the subject of cognition through practice. It is the union of dialectical cognition with revolutionary practice. From this standpoint, we have to pay attention to the word 'atrekeia'/ατρέκεια used deliberately by Pindar. Hölderlin translates it as *genau* (exactly) and interprets it as 'infinitely'. Ατρέκεια in ancient Greek in general and in Pindarian poetry in particular, however, has a dual meaning: it means 'unswerving accuracy', or exactitude, but at the same time it is also the name of the goddess of *Justice*, who was particularly venerated by the Locrians in south Italy, where the first Legal Code was said to be written. Consequently, Pindar's verse in fragment 213 can be taken as referring to the accuracy of statements made by a dialectical mind as well as to Justice itself. Dialectical cognition and justice in social relations exist here in a relation of interpenetration. It is not accidental that Hölderlin in his commentary on Pindar's famous fragment 169 on the law (which has been revisited today by Giorgio Agamben in his book *Homo Sacer*) stresses that 'the strictly mediate is the law' (2004, 713). Mediation as universal law, 'king of all both mortals and immortals', has to be grasped, according to Hölderlin, both as 'the highest ground for cognition' as well as that which stabilizes 'those living conditions in which, in time, a people has encountered itself' (2004, 713, translation slightly altered). It is, in other words, a relation of interpenetration of cognition with the material conditions of life. Finding this 'third', or mediating force, connecting the polar opposites in our moment of history is now more than ever the central problem of dialectics.

Hölderlin grasps mediation in a very different, actually opposite way from his old friend Hegel. It is on this critical terrain of the Hegelian conception of mediation and of negation of negation that Marx likewise meets Hölderlin. Mediation, in Hölderlin, is *not* reconciliation but involves a qualitative rupture, a 'caesura', an 'infinite separation', as he writes in his 'Remarks on Oedipus and Antigone'; it is a revolutionary upturn (*Umkehr*) (1965, 62–3). Philippe Lacoue-Labarthe rightly reminds us that in Hölderlin's historical milieu the word 'Umkehr' referred clearly to the Revolution that had just taken place in France.[1] *Revolution itself is the mediation*, the third force that connects the cunning of political Reason, or the strategy and tactics of the revolutionary movement, with Justice in an emancipated society.

Revolution is an ongoing process, full of contradictions and zig zags, leaps forward and regressions, encompassing an entire historical epoch of transition. During this time, the struggle for emancipation should not wait indefinitely in the antechamber of the revolution under the pretext that current conditions are too 'immature', nor should it exert all its energies in a chase after the gradual maturation of these conditions. Instead, adopting the standpoint of the final victory, it must consistently work to actualize the potential for a successful revolution that is inherent in the existing conditions. For the Song of Dialectics has always had as its refrain the melody of the *Internationale*: '*C'est la lutte finale!*'

The dance of revolution

The most crucial element in a revolution, as it is well known, is *time* itself. As Trotsky stressed, a dialectical analysis is always 'the highest qualitative and quantitative estimation of the objective reality from the standpoint of revolutionary action' (Trotsky, 1980, 58). In the concrete analysis of a concrete situation, being able to judge what is the right moment is crucial. As another Pindarian verse says,

> νοῆσαι δε καιρός ἄριστος
> to seize the right moment is the key aim of cognition.

But recognizing the 'Kairos' does not exhaust our task: we must also 'make the petrified conditions dance by singing to them their own melody', but the dance of the specific conditions in every country follows what the great Peruvian Marxist José Carlos Máriategui calls 'the rhythm of world history'. Today, this rhythm is determined by the world character of the economy, the politics, and the culture, and consequently by the world character of the revolution itself.

This last did not disappear with the lowering of the red flag in the Kremlin; on the contrary. The world historical circle opened in 1917 has not been closed as general opinion, that is bourgeois ideology, claims. All the tumultuous developments of the last 15 years, the non-stop wars from the Balkans to Iraq and Central Asia, the new rounds of the so-called 'orange (counter) revolutions' in the former Soviet space surrounding the Russian heartland etc., demonstrate that a confrontation is continuing on a world scale to determine the fate of our revolutionary heritage as well as the fate of the world in the twenty-first century. The dance of the revolution is before us, not behind us.

In elaborating the program of the revolutionary party of his time, Máriategui took account of the rhythm of world history as well as the conditions of his own country. We must do likewise. Then, if we are truly serious about 'dialectics' and 'revolution', we cannot avoid the crucial question of *revolutionary organization.* Lenin famously asked, 'What is to be done?' and the entire problematic on revolutionary organization must be part of any useful answer. To be sure, the subject needs to be re-considered dialectically on the basis of recent history, including the tragic experience of Stalinism and the struggle against it, but it can't be ignored.

Some radical thinkers have shown an interest recently in figures like St Paul and St Francis of Assisi, but, while they may be our remote precursors, it should be clear that they offer no model and are in no way a substitute for the revolutionary militant of the post-Bolshevik, post-1917 period. At this time when capitalist globalization is undergoing an insoluble crisis, we must be especially weary of historical amnesia, and strive instead to re-invent the *International* as an artful *Meistersinger* of the Song of Dialectics, as the new vanguard in the Dance of the World Revolution – the fiery Carmagnole of the twenty-first century.[2]

Notes

1. See the notes to Hölderlin, 1998, 246.
2. I want to thank Jeremy P. Lester (University of Reading, UK) for the editing of the English version of this essay.

References

Badiou, Alain. 1991. *D'un désastre obscur*. Paris: Edition de l'Aube.

Benjamin, Walter. 1989. *Paris Capitale du XIXe siècle – Le Livre des Passages*. Paris: Cerf.

Benjamin, Walter. 1999. 'The Destructive Character'. In *Selected Writings*, Volume 2, *1917–1934*. Cambridge: Harvard University Press.

Chattopadhyay, Paresh. 2002. 'Marx on Capital's Globalization – The Dialectic of Negativity', *Economic and Political Weekly*. Vol. XXXVII, No. 19, May 11.

Hölderlin, Friedrich. 1965. *Remarques sur Œdipe – Remarques sur Antigone*, French translation by F. Fédier, Paris: 10/18 Paris.

Hölderlin, Friedrich. 1998. *Œdipe le Tyran de Sophocle*, translated from the German by Philippe Lacoue Labarthe. Paris: Christian Bourgois.

Hölderlin, Friedrich. 2004. 'Pindar Fragments and Commentary'. In *Poems and Fragments*, translated by Michael Hamburger. Paris: Anvil.

Hölderlin, Friedrich. 2004. '*Brod und Wein*' [Bread and Wine]. In *Poems and Fragments*, translated by Michael Hamburger. Paris: Anvil.

Kafka, Franz. 2005. 'Prometheus'. In *The Great Wall of China and Other Short Stories*. New York: Pocket Penguin.

Lenin, V. I. 1981. *Philosophical Notebooks, Completed Works*, Volume *38*. Moscow: Progress Press.

Marx, Karl. 1975a. *Theories of Surplus Value Part II*. Moscow: Progress Press.

Marx, Karl. 1975b. *Theories of Surplus Value Part III*. Moscow: Progress Press.

Marx, Karl. 1976. 'Zur Kritik der Hegelschen Rechtsphilosophie. Einleitung' in *Marx- Engels Werke*. Berlin: Dietz Verlag.

Marx, Karl. 1986a. *Capital*, Volume I. Moscow: Progress Press.

Marx, Karl. 1986b. *Grundrisse*, in *Marx- Engels Collected Works*, Volume 28. Moscow: Progress Press.

Marx, Karl, and Friedrich Engels. 1983. *Letters on 'Capital'*. London: New Park Publications.

Ollman, Bertell. 2003. *Dance of the Dialectic-Steps in Marx's Method*. Champaign, IL: University of Illinois Press.

Trotsky, Leon. 1980. *The New Course*. Allagi- Greek edition by the EEK (Workers Revolutionary Party).

13
Towards a Systematic Dialectic of Globalization

Tony Smith

A great number of theorists have discussed from a great variety of perspectives a great number of issues associated with 'globalization'.[1] Some contributions to these debates share sufficient 'family resemblances' to justify speaking of a shared position, defined by a specific model of globalization purporting to describe the main features of the contemporary global order and a set of claims regarding this model, especially normative claims.

Here, as elsewhere, it is always possible to criticize a position from an external standpoint. Suppose, however, that a particular model of globalization implicitly includes elements contradicting the main claims made by its leading proponents. Establishing this would constitute a criticism of the framework internal to the framework itself, an *immanent critique*. Suppose further that some other position explicitly addressed these immanent contradictions. There would then be a systematic relationship between the two, justifying a theoretical progression from one to the other. If this second position in its turn were implicitly beset by immanent contradictions explicitly addressed in a third theoretical framework, the systematic progression could be continued. Such an ordering may be termed 'dialectical' since it is constructed by means of 'determinate negation', the central principle of dialectical methodology.[2] In so far as this sort of ordering does not reconstruct a historical progression, it is an example of 'systematic' rather than historical dialectics.[3] In the present chapter, I shall attempt to sketch a systematic dialectic of positions in the globalization debate.[4]

In any systematic dialectic, the first position to be considered must be the simplest and least complex. In the present context the *social state*

179

model of globalization meets these criteria, and so forms an appropriate beginning. Its essential features include the following:

- *national economies*, more specifically, capitalist national economies;
- *social states*;
- *foreign trade and investment between and among national economies*; and
- *an interstate system*, formed by relations among states and codified in treaties establishing a 'law of peoples'.

Defenders of this model accept the normative claim that capitalist markets in principle can attain a level of efficiency and liberty unsurpassed by any feasible alternative. But they can do so only if the proper background conditions are in place. Markets left to themselves, for example, necessarily tend to generate significant involuntary unemployment, high levels of poverty, and severe inequality, all of which block access to the material and cultural resources required for effective exercises of freedom. It is the responsibility of the social state to establish strong regulatory and redistributive programs to maintain full employment, alleviate poverty, and keep inequalities within bounds consistent with the fair value of political liberties and substantive equality of opportunity.[5]

This framework provides an appropriate starting point for a systematic dialectic of globalization in that the global order is conceptualized in the simplest possible manner, as a mere aggregate of distinct national economies and states bound together through external relations (trade; treaties). It is thus a minimalist account of the global order.[6]

There are two main immanent contradictions in this model. Foreign trade necessarily tends to lead to specialization in national economies. But the more specialization occurs, the less plausible it is to conceive the global economy as a mere aggregate of distinct national economies, and the more it must be conceptualized as a distinct totality ('the world market') with higher-order emergent properties. This conclusion is reinforced when we consider the technological dynamism of capitalism, which tends to lower the costs associated with cross-border flows of trade and investment. Declining costs encourage these flows to increase past the point at which 'quantity becomes quality', and national economies must be categorized as moments within a larger whole, the world market. Structural tendencies implicit within the social state model of globalization thus do not cohere with the manner in which the global economy is conceptualized in this model.

A second difficulty arises from the limits on state capacities imposed by the world market. In a world of extensive cross-border flows of commodities, policies designed to bring about full employment through stimulating the market may merely increase imports, leaving domestic employment levels unaffected. Further, whenever the regulatory and redistributive agenda of the social state exceeds what is compatible with the perceived self-interest of investors and corporations, they will tend to exercise the exit options granted to them by capitalist property rights.[7] The extensive regulatory and redistributive agenda called for by Rawls and other advocates of social democracy necessarily tends to exceed what investors and firms regard as compatible with their self-interest. The more these agents escape the national economy, the fewer tax revenues are available to meet the social state's essential tasks. In other words, the more adequately the social state fulfills the tasks assigned by its leading defenders, the sooner it is unable to fulfill these tasks. This is an immanent contradiction.

In the methodological framework of systematic dialectics, a transition to a new position is justified when immanent contradictions are shown to be implicit in a given position. The contradictions of the social state model of globalization provide a warrant for moving to the *neoliberal model of globalization*, which explicitly incorporates two essential features of the global order merely implicit in the social state model. First, national economies are conceptualized as moments of a single world market, rather than as externally related separate entities. Second, the incompatibility of the capitalist world market and the strong regulatory and redistributive agenda of the social state is explicitly recognized. This is not equivalent to affirming 'the death of the state'. But neoliberals do assert that any state wishing to prosper in the age of globalization must protect the rights of investors and corporations, foster the free flow of trade and investment, minimize burdensome regulations, and avoid excessively generous social programs (Wolf 2004).

For neoliberals, the restrictions imposed on states by the world market further the central normative principles of liberty and efficiency. Freely undertaken market agreements provide mutual benefits; otherwise they would not be freely undertaken. This point holds for economic transactions across borders no less than for activities within borders, and so government restrictions on cross-border flows of commodities and investment capital should be kept to a minimum. Any (relatively minor) social costs that may result are simply the price that must be paid for freedom and generalized prosperity (Hayek, 1976).

Perhaps the most important normative argument for neoliberalism concerns the so-called developing world. Throughout history poverty has prevented most people from developing their essential human capacities, fulfilling their essential human needs, or exercising their autonomy effectively. With neoliberal globalization this tragic dimension of world history is finally overcome. In principle, any region on the planet is able to tap into global capital markets and attract foreign direct investment, thereby gaining access to the investment funds required to export and grow. Economic growth through participation in global markets is the single most effective way to lift living standards, as the success stories of globalization prove. And so, neoliberals conclude, if global justice demands the overcoming of material deprivation, as it surely does, *they* have the best claim to speak in its name, not their opponents.[8]

Neoliberals cannot make this last argument without falling at once into an immanent contradiction. For the supposed success stories of the global economy to which they appeal were based on a state form that neoliberalism is designed to *dismantle*, the so-called 'developmental state'. The developmental state intervenes in the national economy far more extensively than neoliberal doctrine allows (see note 15).

Further, the deregulation of cross-border flows of trade and investment does not in fact tend to generate the material prosperity claimed by advocates of the neoliberal model of globalization. Neoliberal theorists avoid this conclusion by making various assumptions that are illegitimate from their own standpoint. Equilibrium models in support of free trade, for example, presuppose that small producers and wage laborers displaced by imports instantaneously shift to expanding sectors in the national economy. It is not difficult to show gains from free trade with this assumption. But the essential determinations of the neoliberal model do not justify the assumption that all displaced workers are immediately absorbed by expanding sectors. Given those determinations, it is far more plausible to expect massive unemployment and the erosion of the material foundations of entire communities to result, followed by migrations to areas that cannot absorb the displaced workers in new employment (Weisbrot and Baker, 2002).

Similarly, neoliberal theorists simply assume that financial markets allocate capital in the most rationally efficient manner. It is not difficult to establish gains from capital liberalization with this premise. But, once again, the logic of the neoliberal position does not justify the crucial assumption. That logic only suggests that financial investments will flow to sectors with the highest foreseeable returns. If I purchase a capital asset at a price that I know to be foolish, but believe that a bigger fool will come along to purchase it at a yet higher price, participating in a speculative bubble becomes eminently 'rational' by neoliberal criteria (Shiller,

2000). Capital liberalization can thus lead to stampedes of capital inflows and outflows, the funding and bursting of speculative bubbles in capital asset markets, and volatility in currency markets, all of which discourage long-term investments. Further, in order to attract foreign investments governments will be wary of instituting any policies that 'market sentiment' associates with inflation, including policies designed to reduce unemployment and raise wages. This exacerbates the depressionary bias in the neoliberal global order (Eatwell, 1996).[9]

Another feature of the neoliberal model, competition in the world market, warrants separate attention. Technological innovation is a crucial weapon in this competition. Private investment funds will generally be forthcoming for research and development projects with foreseeable commercial applications in the short-to-medium term. Most neoliberals recognize the need for government support of basic research, conceding that private funding for basic research necessarily tends to be significantly less than what is socially optimal. Even moderate neoliberals, however, minimize government support for R&D in the so-called 'valley of death' between basic research and short-to-medium term commercial development. As a result, units of capital in regions where more extensive state support is provided for R&D will tend to enjoy greater capacities for innovation. The more the neoliberal state is institutionalized in a given region, the greater the danger that units of capital in that region will suffer in international competition (Wessner, 2001). The more the neoliberal state has been institutionalized, then, the more likely it is that leading units of capital operating within its territory will organize effectively to replace it with a state form more compatible with their essential interests. The more thoroughly the neoliberal model is institutionalized, the sooner its demise; a sure sign that neoliberalism is beset by immanent contradictions.

The principle of determinant negation once again demands a transition to a new position explicitly addressing these immanent contradictions. The *catalytic state model of globalization* fulfills this imperative.[10] Its proponents grant that the strong regulatory and redistributive agenda of the social state is incompatible with globalization.[11] But they also insist that successful participation in the global economy requires more extensive government action than neoliberals recognize, including the establishment of:

- a *national innovation system* designed to help local firms compete successfully in global markets, with extensive government expenditures on research and development, infrastructure, and training of the workforce;

• significant *social safety nets* effectively addressing the disruptions imposed on individuals and communities by rapidly changing markets; and

• *regulations of the financial sector* minimizing the dangers of speculative bubbles and stampedes of capital inflows and outflows.

Neoliberalism does not exclude all such measures in principle. But, once again, at some point 'quantity becomes quality'. In the catalytic state these sorts of policies are pursued with a consistency, aggressiveness, and scope exceeding the bounds of the neoliberal state.

Leading advocates of the catalytic state model of globalization claim that it furthers efficiency in the global economy to a greater extent than any feasible alternative, while fostering the development of essential human capacities, the satisfaction of essential human needs, and the exercise of autonomy. The most distinguishing feature of their position is an emphasis on communitarian values, in contrast to the liberal individualism characteristic of most proponents of both the social state and neoliberalism (Miller, 2000). Within this framework, duties to fellow citizens are asserted to be more extensive than (and to generally have priority over) duties to people who are not members of our political community. The mutual obligations of citizens to each other, however, must be fulfilled in a manner that does not harm other political communities.

Are the normative principles of catalytic state theorists in fact institutionalized in the model of globalization they advocate? A first problem, which I shall not discuss here, is that the main measure proposed by catalytic state theorists to protect against the ravages of global capital markets is unlikely to attain its objectives.[12] Before addressing a second difficulty we need to investigate a systematic tendency on the level of the world market, the tendency to uneven development.

A number of factors underlie uneven development. In the present context, I shall concentrate on those most directly connected to the dynamic of technological change, an issue of crucial concern to advocates of the catalytic state. First, technological change demands fixed capital investment in plants, machinery, infrastructure, and so on. Once an extensive technological apparatus is in place, there are considerable advantages to replacing damaged or obsolete elements, as opposed to building another complex from scratch. There is also a strong incentive to invest in new types of technological artifacts complementing the fixed assets already in place. For these and other reasons most fixed capital formation remains within national borders; even in our age of globalization 'about 95% of all fixed capital formation is national, as opposed to overseas' (Moody, 1998, 57). In this manner regions that for one reason or another presently enjoy a higher level of capitalist development are generally able to reproduce their advantages over time.[13]

Foreign direct investment reinforces uneven development as well. Investments in productive facilities tend to flow towards regions where consumer markets are the biggest, labor and managerial skills are the most advanced, infrastructure is in place minimizing transportation, communications, and other transactions costs, advanced research and development is performed, and so on. Wealthy regions tend to enjoy these benefits the most. And so flows of foreign direct investment tend to reproduce the advantages of these regions over time. In recent decades over two-thirds of FDI has flowed into wealthy regions of the global economy, where a mere one-fifth of the world's population is found (UNDP, 1999).

A third consideration rests on the drive to appropriate surplus profits through product or process innovations (Mandel, 1975, Chapter 3; Smith, 2002). Units of capital with access to advanced (publicly or privately funded) R&D are best positioned to win temporary monopolies from innovations. And they are in the best position to establish a virtuous circle in which the surplus profits appropriated as a result of these monopolies enable a high level of R&D funding in the future, granting access to the next generation of innovations. In contrast, units of capital without initial access to advanced R&D tend to be trapped in a vicious circle. Their inability to introduce significant innovations prevents the appropriation of surplus profits, which tends to limit their ability to participate in advanced R&D in the succeeding period, restricting future innovations and future profit opportunities.

Units of capital with the greatest access to advanced R&D are clustered in wealthy regions of the global economy; units without such access are clustered in poorer regions. The former are thus in a far better position to establish and maintain the virtuous circle described above, while the latter have immense difficulty avoiding the vicious circle.[14] As a result, when units of capital in poorer regions engage in economic transactions with units of capital enjoying temporary monopolies due to innovations, the former necessarily tend to suffer disadvantageous terms of trade, while the latter tend to appropriate a disproportionate share of the value produced in production and distribution chains. This generates unrelenting pressure on work conditions, wage levels, and worker communities in poorer regions, pressure that is eventually transferred to working men and women and their communities in the so-called North. In this manner the drive to appropriate surplus profits through technological innovation – an essential feature of capitalist property relations – systematically tends to reproduce uneven development in the world market over time.[15]

Essential determinations of the catalytic state model of globalization necessarily generate tendencies to uneven development, which undermines the central claim of its proponents that the catalytic state effectively fosters the development of essential human capacities, the satisfaction of essential human needs, and the exercise of autonomy within the given political community. In regions suffering from the vicious circle described above, states necessarily tend to be 'weak states', unable to effectively protect their citizens from the profound social disruptions and social pathologies the catalytic state is supposed to eliminate. 'Strong states', clustered in regions where virtuous circles of innovation and profits are reproduced, have more resources of course. But uneven development transfers intense and unrelenting competitive pressures on work conditions, wage levels, and worker communities to wealthier regions as well. And the case for devoting just a bit more of the state's budget to providing the preconditions for successful competition in the global economy – and just a little less to the institutionalization of communitarian values – can be made again and again and again. The catalytic state is supposed to simultaneously be a competitive state and a communitarian state, but the dominate tendency is for the former to grow at the expense of the latter. Finally, maintaining virtuous circles of innovations and surplus profits simultaneously furthers the reproduction of vicious circles elsewhere. This implies that successful catalytic states systematically harm other political communities, whether intentionally or not. This too is inconsistent with the claim that the catalytic state model of globalization enables communitarian values to be instituted throughout the global order.

Once again, the dialectical methodology of 'determinate negation' demands a transition to a new position, explicitly addressing the immanent contradictions implicit in the previous framework. The root of the contradictions of the catalytic state model of globalization lies in the fact that states, even catalytic states, are unable to ensure an efficient and normatively attractive global order, given the essential determinations of the world market. Problems that arise on the level of the world market must ultimately be addressed on that level. A regime of global governance is required to attain what individual catalytic states cannot attain by themselves, a global order in which individuals and communities have access to material preconditions required to develop vital human capacities, meet essential human needs, exercise autonomy, and maintain flourishing human communities. *The democratic cosmopolitan model of globalization* is explicitly designed to fulfill this goal.

This fourth model, like the earlier three, is formed from a variety of viewpoints sharing strong family resemblances. All versions include some form of the 'moral equality principle', the most basic normative principle of democratic cosmopolitan theorists: 'Justice requires respect for the inherent dignity of all persons... this notion of dignity includes the idea that all persons are equal, so far as the importance of their basic interests are concerned' (Buchanan, 2004, 42).[16] And all versions hold that the institutionalization of this principle demands that extreme material deprivation and severe inequality in the capitalist global order be addressed on the global level. Examples of specific proposals include

- a global progressive tax redistributing income to the poorest states in the global economy (Barry, 1998);
- a 'global resources dividend' based on the idea that natural resources are the common property of all humanity, and so all individuals are owed a 'dividend' from those who use them (Beitz, 1979; Pogge, 2002); and
- a new international agency charged with ensuring high levels of basic income, full employment in the global economy, rights to access to decision-making power in industrial and financial sectors, the oversight of social investment funds targeted to the poorest regions in the global economy, global regulations regarding capital inflows and outflows, and so on (Held, 1995).

A closer examination of cosmopolitan democratic proposals uncovers a number of immanent contradictions within this framework. The first regards the set of proposals addressing uneven development. A global redistribution tax, a global resources dividend, or a pool of social investment funds targeted at poor regions would certainly improve matters at the margin considerably, eliminating many of the worst forms of material deprivation in the global economy. But they do not address the mechanisms in the global economy generating extreme inequality and poverty in the first place. The virtuous circle whereby privileged agents and regions are able to maintain their advantages for entire historical epochs through the dynamics of fixed capital formation, foreign direct investment, and the appropriation of surplus profits through innovation, would remain in place. The vicious circle reproducing the disadvantages of the poorest agents and regions of the global economy would remain in place as well. It is simply impossible to argue that in such a world 'all persons are equal, so far as the importance of their basic interests are concerned'. A model that fails to reverse this state of affairs thus contradicts essential claims of democratic cosmopolitan theorists regarding what is required for a normatively acceptable global order.[17] Another sort of contradiction arises when cosmopolitan theorists call for proposals that are effectively ruled out by the social relations defining the model they defend. Measures designed to provide high levels of basic income and meaningful 'access avenues' to industrial and financial decision-making throughout the global economy are ultimately incompatible with the capital/wage labor relation that remains an essential feature of the democratic cosmopolitan model (see Smith 2003b, 2005, Chapter 4). The reproduction of this relation requires that those who do not have access to capital continue to see entering into wage contracts as their best available option. This implies that social assistance must be quite limited, since few will choose to sell their labor power for the low wages most workers in the global economy are offered if acceptable alternatives were available. The limited level of basic income compatible with capitalist property relations is unlikely to provide the material conditions for effective exercises of autonomy to anything approaching the extent required by the precepts of cosmopolitan democratic theory. Similarly, the proposal to democratize exercises of economic power through 'access avenues' flounders in the face of the ineluctable fact that the capital/wage labor relation is *defined* by property rights granting the owners and controllers of capital economic powers all other 'stakeholders' lack. Consider Martha Nussbaum's formulation of the moral equality principle:

> If we agree that citizens are all worthy of concern and respect ... then we ought to conclude that policies should not treat people as agents or supporters of other people, whose mission in the world is to execute someone else's plan of life. It should treat each of them as ends, as sources of agency and worth in their own right, with their own plans to make and their own lives to live, therefore as deserving of all necessary support for the equal opportunity to be such agents (2001, 58).

As long as the capital/wage labor relation is at the core of social life, however, most people will spend most of their adult waking life 'executing someone else's plan of life' in the workplace (Smith, 2000a, Chapter 3). And what sense does it make to talk of an 'equal opportunity' to execute one's life plan in a world of uneven development, where the richest 1 percent of adults in the world own 40 percent of global assets, the richest 10 percent own 85 percent of the world total, and the bottom half own a mere 1 percent of global wealth (UNU-WIDER, 2007)? None at all.

The principle of moral equality is also fundamentally incompatible with another dominant tendency on the level of the world market, the tendency to overaccumulation crises (Brenner, 1998, 2002; Reuten, 1991; Smith, 2000b). The drive to appropriate surplus profits necessarily tends to lead to the entry of more efficient plants and firms in a given sector. But established firms and plants do not all automatically withdraw when this occurs. Their fixed capital costs are already 'sunk', and so they may be happy to receive the average rate of profit on their circulating capital. They also may have established relations with suppliers and customers impossible (or prohibitively expensive) to duplicate elsewhere in any relevant time frame. Further, their management and labor force may have industry-specific skills. And governments may provide subsidies for training, infrastructure, or R&D that would not be available if they were to shift sectors. When a sufficient number of firms and plants do not withdraw from a sector when more efficient competitors enter, the result is an overaccumulation of capital, manifested in excess capacity and declining rates of profit. When this dynamic unfolds simultaneously in leading sectors, an economy-wide fall in profit rates results for an extended historical period.

When overaccumulation crises break out, previous investments in fixed capital must be devalued. At this point, the entire system becomes convulsed in endeavors to shift the costs of devaluation elsewhere. Each unit, network, and region of capital attempts to shift the costs of devaluation onto other units, networks, and regions. And those who control capital mobilize their vast economic, political, and ideological weapons in the attempt to shift as many of the costs of devaluation as possible onto wage laborers, through increased unemployment, lower wages, and worsened work conditions. As the concentration and centralization of capital proceeds in the course of capitalist development, both overaccumulation and the resulting need for devaluation necessarily tend to occur on an ever-more massive scale. Global turbulence and generalized economic insecurity increasingly become the normal state of affairs.

Strictly speaking, it may not be logically impossible for a high level of basic income guarantees, rights to employment, democratic access to economic decision-making, and other democratic cosmopolitan imperatives to be maintained across the global economy in such circumstances. But this will surely necessarily tend to *not* be the case.[18] The democratic cosmopolitan model still retains capitalist property relations at its heart, and these relations necessarily tend to generate both overaccumulation crises and attempts to shift the burdens of overaccumulation crises to already disadvantaged agents in the global economy. No global order with these features can adequately institutionalize democratic cosmopolitan values. And so essential determinations of the democratic cosmopolitan model rule out the fundamental normative claims made by its leading proponents.

A position defined by a model of globalization that necessarily tends to function in a manner inconsistent with its proponents most fundamental normative principle suffers from an irresolvable immanent contradiction. The principle of determinate negation requires that such a position be left behind in a systematic dialectic. A transition must be made to a position explicitly acknowledging how capitalist property relations undermine the claims of efficiency and normative attractiveness made on behalf of the social state, neoliberal, catalytic state, and cosmopolitan models of globalization. Such a position may be termed a *Marxian model of globalization*, since Marx's concept of capital is an indispensable aid to its articulation. Three dimensions of this concept can be briefly sketched.

In all models considered previously, money is conceived as essentially a generalized means, allowing individuals and groups to pursue their particular ends. For neoliberals like Hayek, money naturally tends to function in this manner (Hayek, 1976, 8–9). For proponents of the three other positions, political regulations on the national and/or global level are required to ensure that money plays its proper role as a generalized means, subordinate to the ends of human flourishing and autonomy. From a Marxian standpoint, however, none of these views adequately grasps the bizarre and perverse ontological inversion introduced by capital. Once the property and production relations of capital are in place, 'capital' emerges as a totalizing force, a bizarre pseudo-subject that takes on various forms – investment capital (M), commodity capital (C), capital in production (P), inventory capital (C') – with the goal of attaining a form of existence adequate to its essence: M', or realized capital (with M'$>$M). The activities of human agents are thus subsumed under a non-human imperative, the accumulation of capital ('the self-valorization of value') as an end in itself. The satisfaction of human wants and needs and the development of human capacities occur only in so far as is compatible with the valorization imperative, 'Money must beget money!' (Marx, 1976, 255–6). As long as this is the case, human flourishing and human autonomy are systematically subordinated to the flourishing and autonomy of capital.

A second dimension of Marx's concept of capital emerges when we note how each moment of the M-C-P-C'-M' circuit expresses a dimension of capital/wage labor relation, in specific, the relation between a class that owns and controls investment funds (M), and one that does not; a class that purchases labor power as a commodity (C) alongside other commodity inputs, and one that is forced to sell its capacities; a class that has the power to inaugurate technological and organizational changes within the production process (P), and one whose labor process is an object of control; and, finally, a class that after the sale of newly produced commodities (C') retains its monopoly of investment funds (M'), and one that once again is forced to sell its labor power, having spent its wages to gain access to means of subsistence. Advocates of the social state, the neoliberal world market, the catalytic state, and a democratic cosmopolitan regime of global governance all presuppose that capitalist markets are equally in the interests of all, whether 'naturally' (neoliberalism) or with the proper political regulation. But in a capitalist order surplus value, the difference between the money capital initially invested (M) and that realized at the conclusion of a capital circuit (M'), is a function of the difference between the time workers spend producing an amount of value equivalent to what they receive in wages, and the time they spend engaged in surplus labor, producing a value beyond what they receive back. Any global economy in which exploitative class relations of this sort are systematically reproduced must be fundamentally at odds with the normative claims asserted at earlier stages in the systematic dialectic of globalization.

Finally, Marx's concept of capital also explores how the valorization imperative defines inter-capital relations, as well as the capital/wage labor relation. In specific, this imperative underlies inter-capital competition, expressed in the drive to appropriate surplus profits through innovation. As we have seen, this drive lies at the heart of the systematic tendencies to both uneven development and overaccumulation crises in the capitalist world market.

As long as the social relations defining capitalism are in place, the accumulation of capital will remain an end in itself on the level of society as a whole. The reproduction of the capital/wage labor relation will remain the reproduction of class exploitation. And the insane drive for surplus profits will continue to generate tendencies to uneven development and overaccumulation crises.[19] As long as advocates of the social state, neoliberal, catalytic state, and democratic cosmopolitan models of globalization accommodate, rather than reject, the capitalist world system, there will be profound immanent contradictions between their normative claims and the models of globalization they defend.[20] In contrast to the other positions in the systematic dialectic of globalization, leading defenders of the Marxian model of globalization do not make normative claims regarding the capitalist global order that are inconsistent with the essential determinations and tendencies of the model. Whatever errors and omissions may characterize Marxian accounts, this position is not beset by the same sort of fundamental immanent contradictions. From this perspective we can say that the systematic dialectic of globalization has reached closure.

Crucial questions remain, however. What might an alternative model of globalization that would be efficient and normatively attractive look like? Does the immanent development of the dialectic traced thus far provide any clues?

I believe that the systematic reconstruction of the globalization debate traced in this chapter implies that an efficient and normatively acceptable model of globalization must include five essential features: (a) decisions regarding the level of overall new investment in the global economy must be democratized, (b) the priorities of new investment must also be a matter for democratic discussion, (c) new investment funds must be allocated to different regions of the global economy on a per capita basis (at least this should be the presumption in the absence of compelling reasons to do otherwise), (d) scientific-technological knowledge must be treated as a free global public good, and (e) socially necessary labor must not be predominantly organised in the social form of wage labor (see Schweickart, 1993, 2002; Smith 2000a, Chapter 7, 2005, Chapter 8).

The first two features are necessary to break the domination of capital over social life. These proposals do not imply the immediate abolition of all markets. It is not the mere presence of markets *per se* that establishes the alien power of capital, but the institutionalization of the drive to accumulate surplus value to the greatest possible extent, whatever the social costs. These first two proposals also do not imply bureaucratic central planning on a global level. We can imagine democratically accountable decision-making bodies operating on global, regional, national, and local levels along the lines sketched by Held and other cosmopolitan democratic theorists, with these bodies now replacing, rather than merely complementing, private capital markets. After decisions have been made regarding the general level of new investment and social priorities, the actual allocation of investment funds to enterprises could then be undertaken by community banks, whose boards would include representatives of a broad range of social groups affected by the banks' decisions.

The drive to accumulation as an end in itself, overriding all other social ends, is put out of play when decisions regarding the rate and direction of new investment are a matter for democratic debate and decision. Democratizing these decisions would also allow for greater coordination of investments, eliminating the systematic tendency to overaccumulation crises.

The third and fourth measures are designed to overcome the systematic tendency to uneven development in the present global order. If the principle of the equal moral worth of all individuals is to be adequately institutionalized, all individuals must be granted an equal right to the material preconditions for the effective exercise of autonomy. Democratic cosmopolitan thinkers fully acknowledge the force of this argument, and insist that all regions have access to the preconditions for a flourishing economy. But they fail to recognize that this implies the (*prima facie*) equal right of all regions to its fair share of new investment funds, something capitalism can never provide. It also implies that scientific-technological knowledge not be a weapon of economic warfare, monopolizable by the economically powerful.[21]

With the fifth and final measure the class relationship upon which the law of value is based, the capital/wage labor relation is abolished. We may imagine community-owned enterprises organised as worker co-operatives, with those exercising authority in the workplace democratically elected by and accountable to those over whom the authority is exercised. In such circumstances, adequate basic income guarantees and rights to employment could be established, two structural changes that are not compatible with the global reproduction of the capital/wage labor relation. Any earnings above and beyond the basic guarantee would then depend upon the shares individuals received as members of their co-operative.

These proposals may well require significant revision.[22] Be that as it may, the two main conclusions of this chapter remain in force. First, the social state, neoliberal, catalytic state, democratic cosmopolitan, and Marxian models of (capitalist) globalization are internally related in ways that can be made explicit in a systematic dialectic of globalization. Second, this systematic dialectic points to the need for a radical break from the social forms of global capitalism. At this point, systematic dialectical theory gives way to the vastly more important dialectic of theory and practice.

Notes

1. I am using the term 'globalization' in a broad and neutral sense in which, for example, 'imperialism' counts as a particular form. Other usages, of course, are possible (see Petras and Veltmeyer, 2001).
2. There is 'negation' in that the position suffering from immanent contradictions is left behind in the ordering. The negation is 'determinate' in that the position which follows is determined by the requirement that it explicitly address the implicit shortcomings of the previous stage.
3. For further discussion of the distinction between systematic and historical dialectics see Smith, 1990, 2003a and Arthur, this volume. A comprehensive and very useful survey of dialectical theories is found in Ollman, 1993. It should be stressed that a systematic dialectic can only complement, and never replace, historical investigations.
4. The account presented here is extremely compressed. For a fuller presentation, see Smith 2005b.
5. In contemporary political philosophy, the social state model of globalization is most associated with John Rawls (1971; 1999).
6. 'Realists' in international relations theory also conceptualize globalization as a set of external relations among states and national economies. If 'realism' had been selected as the starting point, however, the subsequent course of the dialectic would have been unaffected. It too is subject to the first immanent contradiction discussed below.
7. The rise of the 'eurodollar' market in the 1960s is a classic illustration of this dynamic. See Guttmann, 1994. A more recent example is, 'A government report published in 2004 found that 61% of American companies paid no federal income tax during the boon years of 1996–2000. Much of this was thanks to moving profits – rather than actual business – to tax havens....' (*The Economist*, 2007, 10).
8. 'Indeed, for all the churning that global capitalism brings to a society, the spread of capitalism has raised living standards higher, faster and for more people than at any time in history. It has also brought more poor people into the middle classes more quickly that at any time in human history ... According to the 1997 United Nations Human development report, poverty has fallen more in the past fifty years than in the previous five hundred. Developing countries have progressed as fast in the past thirty years as the industrialized world did in the previous century. Since 1960, infant mortality rates, malnutrition and illiteracy are all significantly down, while access to safe water is way up.' (Friedman, 2000, 350. See also Wolf, 2004, 141, 160).
9. Empirical evidence corroborates the thesis that there is a depressionary bias in the neoliberal model of globalization. Between 1980 and 2000 – a period characterized by greater global integration along neoliberal lines – growth rates in all categories of countries declined in comparison to the previous 20- year period. For the poorest countries (based on per capita income) the decline was from 19 percent a year to –0.5. The second poorest quintile

declined from 2 percent to 0.75 percent, and the third from 3.5 percent to 0.9 percent. The rate fell in the second richest quintile from 3.4 percent to 1.1 percent, and in the top group from 2.5 percent to 1.75 percent (Weisbrot et al., 2002).

10. This term is taken from Weiss, 1998.

11. In the words of one of this model's leading defenders: 'Social democracy belongs to a world that cannot be revived' (Gray, 1998, 80).

12. I refer to the taxing of short-term speculative inflows of portfolio capital – the 'Tobin tax', in honor of James Tobin, the economist who first suggested it. This tax is the major substantive proposal for minimizing the dangers of financial instability suggested by John Gray and other advocates of the catalytic state (Gray 1998, 200). It is a transaction tax, and transactions continue even when such a tax is in place as long as anticipated profits are sufficiently high. The potential rewards from participating in speculative bubbles in financial assets are such that a transaction tax at the levels discussed by Tobin and others would prove ineffectual in precisely the cases that matter most (Davidson 2002, 207).

13. There are countertendencies at work too, of course. When profit rates decline in a particular region, capitalists will seek a 'spatial fix' and shift their investments elsewhere (Harvey, 1999). Hegemonic firms and regions in the 'center' may lose their leading position over time, and under certain conditions certain poor regions in the 'periphery' may enjoy high rates of growth and rising per capita income for extended periods. But fluidity within the general pattern of uneven development does not imply that this pattern does not persist. Consider the following ratios of per capita income of the fifth of the world's people living in the richest countries to the fifth in the poorest: 1820: 3 to 1; 1870: 7 to 1; 1913: 11 to 1; 1960: 30 to 1; 1990: 60 to 1; 1997: 74 to 1 (UNDP, 1999).

14. At present 95 percent of research and development is located in the so-called 'first world', and 97 percent of all patents today are granted to entities based in the first world (Friedman, 2000, 319). The push to extend the definition and enforcement of intellectual property rights – an absolutely central element of U.S. foreign policy under both Democratic and Republican administrations – is designed to reinforce the intertwining of virtuous and vicious circles in the global economy.

15. This does not imply that poor regions cannot enjoy rapid growth and improvements of living standards. The successes in East Asia of the 'developmental state', a variant of the catalytic state, show that the tendency to uneven development can be put of play. These successes, however, rested on contingent geopolitical considerations that do not generally hold. For example, the Cold War motivated the U.S. government to accept high levels of exports from East Asian countries, despite the fact that they greatly restricted both imports from U.S. manufacturers and portfolio capital investments from the U.S. With the end of the Cold War, this arrangement ceased being acceptable to U.S. political and economic elites. Another important issue concerns the fallacy of composition. From the fact that *some* regions are able to win a higher place in the hierarchy of the world market it does not follow that *all* can. For a comprehensive critical assessment of the so-called East Asian miracle, see Burkett and Hart-Landsberg, 2000.

16. Similar statements are found in Held, 1995, 147, Pogge, 2002, 92, and Habermas, 2001, 94, 103. Martha Nussbaum's version of this principle is given below.

17. Few political philosophers are more concerned with material deprivation in the global economy than Thomas Pogge. But for Pogge the problems in the global economy stem from a combination of aftereffects from colonialism and contemporary contingencies (ranging from first world agricultural subsidies to the international recognition granted to corrupt political elites). He goes so far as to write, 'Present radical inequality demonstrates the power of long-term compounding more than powerful centrifugal tendencies of our global market system' (Pogge, 2002, 205). For a full account of just how powerful these centrifugal tendencies are, see Shaikh 2007.

18. The systematic tendency to overaccumulation crises provides a further reason to reject the claim that the catalytic state model of globalization can attain its objectives. When overaccumulation crises break out and previous investments in fixed capital must be devalued on a massive scale, the generalized economic insecurity and social disruptions that tend to accompany the world market in the best of circumstances are greatly exacerbated. As long as the systematic tendency to overaccumulation crises is in place, catalytic states will not be able to protect communities from a level of social disruptions and pathologies inconsistent with the communitarian values professed by their proponents. Analogous arguments reinforce the case against the social state and neoliberal models of globalization.

19. This list of the irrationalities and antagonisms of capitalism here is hardly been complete. The systematic tendencies to environmental crises in capitalism, and the social-psychological effects of the most intensive, extensive, and scientifically rational system of propaganda in the history of the human species (corporate advertising) are just two of the many additional topics that would need to be considered in a more comprehensive account (see Burkett, 1999; Klein, 2000, respectively).

20. This conclusion does not imply that social movements struggling for reforms of the global economy do not warrant support. Reforms that only improve matters on the margin can still alleviate human suffering to a profound extent. And the attempt to bring about reforms can contribute to a transformation of political consciousness in which it gradually – or, perhaps, not so gradually – comes to be recognized that an adequate institutionalization of acceptable normative values eventually requires a profound rupture with capitalist property relations.

21. See Perelman, 1998.

22. See Ollman, 1998.

References

Barry, Brian. 1998. 'International Society from a Cosmopolitan Perspective'. In D. Mapel and T. Nardin (eds.) *International Society: Diverse Ethical Perspectives*. Princeton: Princeton University Press, 144–63.

Beitz, Charles. 1979. *Political Theory and International Relations*. Princeton: Princeton University Press.

Buchanan, Alan. 2004. *Justice, Legitimacy, and Self-Determination,* New York: Oxford University Press.

Burkett, Paul. 1999. *Marx and Nature: A Red and Green Perspective.* New York: St. Martin's Press.

Burkett, Paul, and Martin Hart-Landsberg. 2000. *Development, Crises and Class Struggle: Learning from Japan and East Asia.* New York: St. Martin's Press.

Brenner, Robert. 1998. 'The Economics of Global Turbulence'. *New Left Review* 229: 1–264.

Brenner, Robert. 2002. *The Boom and the Bust: The US in the World Economy.* New York: Verso.

Davidson, Paul. 2002. *Financial Markets, Money and the Real World.* Northhampton, MA: Edward Elgar.

The Economist. 2007. 'A Place in the Sun: A Special Report on Offshore Finance'. February 24.

Eatwell, John. 1996. *International Financial Liberalization: The Impact on World Development.* New York: United Nations Development Programme Discussion Paper Series.

Friedman, Thomas. 2000. *The Lexus and the Olive Tree: Understanding Globalization.* New York: Random House.

Gray, John. 1998. *False Dawn: The Delusions of Global Capitalism.* London: Granta.

Guttmann, Robert. 1994. *How Credit-Money Shapes the Economy: The United States in a Global System.* Armonk, New York: Sharpe.

Habermas, Jürgen. 2001. *The Postnational Constellation,* Cambridge: MIT Press.

Harvey, David. 1999. *The Limits to Capital.* London: Verso.

Hayek, Friedrich. 1976. *Law, Legislation, and Liberty, Volume 2: The Mirage of Social Justice.* Chicago: University of Chicago Press.

Held, David. 1995. *Democracy and the Global Order: From the Modern State to Cosmopolitan Governance.* Stanford: Stanford University Press.

Klein, Naomi. 2000. *No Logo: Taking Aim at the Brand Bullies.* New York: Harper Collins.

Mandel, Ernst. 1975. *Late Capitalism.* London: Verso

Marx, Karl. 1976. *Capital, Volume I.* New York: Penguin Books.

Miller, David. 2000. *Citizenship and National Identity.* Malden, MA: Blackwell Publishers.

Moody, Kim. 1998. *Workers in a Lean World.* New York: Verso Press.

Nussbaum, Martha. 2001. *Women and Human Development,* New York: Cambridge University Press.

Ollman, Bertell. 1993. *Dialectical Investigations.* New York: Cambridge University Press.

Ollman, Bertell (ed.). 1998. *Market Socialism: The Debate Among Socialists.* New York: Routledge.

Perelman, Michael. 1998. *Class Warfare in the Information Age.* New York: St. Martin's Press.

Petras, James and Henry Veltmeyer. 2001. *Globalization Unmasked: Imperialism in the 21st Century.* New York: Zed Books.

Pogge, Thomas. 2002. *World Poverty and Human Rights,* Malden: Polity Press.

Rawls, John. 1971. *A Theory of Justice.* Cambridge, MA: Harvard University Press.

Rawls, John. 1999. *The Law of Peoples.* Cambridge MA: Harvard University Press.

Reuten, Geert. 1991. 'Accumulation of Capital and the Foundation of the Tendency of the Rate of Profit to Fall'. *Cambridge Journal of Economics* 15/1: 79–93.

Schweickart, David. 1993. *Against Capitalism*. Cambridge: Cambridge University Press.

Schweickart, David. 2002. *After Capitalism*. Lanham, MA: Rowman & Littlefield.

Shaikh, Anwar (ed.). 2007. *Globalization and the Myths of Free Trade*. Oxford: Taylor and Francis.

Shiller, Robert. 2000. *Irrational Exuberance*. Princeton: Princeton University Press.

Smith, Tony. 1990. *The Logic of Marx's Capital*. Albany: State University of New York Press.

Smith, Tony. 2000a. *Technology and Capital in the Age of Lean Production: A Marxian Critique of the 'New Economy'*. Albany: State University of New York Press.

Smith, Tony. 2000b. 'Brenner and Crisis Theory: Issues in Systematic and Historical Dialectics'. *Historical Materialism* 5: 145–78.

Smith, Tony. 2002. 'Surplus Profits from Innovation: A Missing Level in *Capital III*?' In M. Campbell and G. Reuten (eds.). *The Culmination of Capital: Essays on Volume III of Marx's Capital*. New York: Palgrave, 67–94.

Smith, Tony. 2003a. 'Systematic and Historical Dialectics: Towards a Marxian Theory of Globalization'. In R. Albritton, ed., *New Dialectics and Political Economy*. New York: Palgrave, 24–41.

Smith, Tony. 2003b. 'Globalisation and Capitalist Property Relations: A Critical Assessment of Held's Cosmopolitan Theory'. *Historical Materialism* 11/2: 3–35.

Smith, Tony. 2005. *Globalisation: A Systematic Marxian Account*. Leiden: Brill.

United Nations Development Programme (UNDP). 1999. *Human Development Report, 1999*. New York: Oxford University Press.

UNU-WIDER (United Nations University World Institute for Development Economics Research). 2007. *The World Distribution of Household Wealth*. Helsinki. www.wider.unu.edu.

Weisbrot, Mark, and Dean Baker. 2002. 'The Relative Impact of Trade Liberalization on Developing Countries'. *Center for Economic and Policy Research* (www.cepr.net/relative_impact_of_trade_liberal.htm).

Weisbrot, Mark, Dean Baker, Robert Naiman and Gila Neta 2002, 'Growth May be Good for the Poor – But are the IMF and World Bank Policies Good for Growth?', Center for Economic and Policy Research, www.cepr.net.

Weiss, Linda. 1998. *The Myth of the Powerless State*. Ithaca: Cornell University Press.

Wessner, Charles. 2001. 'The Advanced Technology Program'. *Issues in Science and Technology*. Fall (ww.issues.org/issues/18.1/p_wessner.html).

Wolf, Martin. 2004. *Why Globalization Works*. New Haven: Yale University Press.

14
The Hole in Hegel's Bagel

Bill Livant

1. Hegel's great insight is that the truth is the whole.
2. What about the hole? Is this hole part of the whole?
3. On first sight, it appears that it isn't, that in the hole there is nothing. But this is deceptive.
4. The etymology of the word 'hole' refers not to an empty place, but to a place where something is hidden.
5. Recall that Marx claimed that if everything were immediately perceptible, there would be no need for science. Finding what is hidden requires work.
6. For Marx, too, the hidden parts of anything are often what is most important for grasping both their systemic and dynamic character.
7. This is at the heart of the distinction he makes between appearance and essence, and explains the priority he gives to the latter in his studies.
8. How does one get to the hole in the center of the bagel? Only by eating your way through, by moving. But if your mind can't walk, can't move, you can't get there. And if you can't get there, there seems to be nothing there. Appearances seem to be all that there is.
9. Only by analyzing – getting into and then going beyond – appearances can we arrive at the essence of anything.
10. In sum, the whole without a hole is really a part in drag trying to pass itself off as everything, which, come to think of it, isn't a bad definition of ideology.

15
The Dialectic of Capital: An Unoist Interpretation

Thomas T. Sekine

Marxian economic theory constitutes a dialectical, not an axiomatic, system. Although some important features of the dialectic have already been discussed elsewhere, a more systematic treatment of the subject, specifically of the Hegelian–Marxian version of the dialectic, may be in order. Of course, many explanations of this type of dialectic are available in Marxist literature, but unfortunately not all of them are dependable. In fact, some of them are more misleading than informative. Part of the difficulty stems from the fact that a dialectic cannot be explained generally, or in the abstract, since it is not a strictly formal (abstract-general) logic but rather a formal-substantive (concrete-synthetic) one. It, in other words, constitutes a teleological rather than a tautological system. In a dialectical exposition we often talk of proceeding from abstract to concrete. This means that we advance from an emptier and less specified concept to a more 'enriched' and specified one. Here 'concrete' does not mean 'concrete-empirical' or 'concrete-historical'; it means 'concrete-synthetic' in the sense of 'containing more specifications of the subject'.

Perhaps it is useful to begin with the three fundamental characteristics of the Hegelian–Marxian dialectic: (1) it believes that 'the truth is the whole'; (2) it claims the identity of the subject and the object; (3) it proceeds by synthesizing 'contradictions' through the triad of thesis, antithesis and synthesis. The first two characteristics refer to the structure of the dialectic, and the third to its procedural aspect.

We know from our daily experience that a partial story is ultimately undependable. Only an unwise parent tries to settle a dispute between children on the basis of one party's tattle-taling. In order to be fair, he or she must listen to both parties concerned, and 'synthesize' the whole story. A law court operates on the same principle. It does not pronounce its verdict until it believes it has been informed of 'the whole truth' with regard to the case. Although human errors are unavoidable and the court oftentimes comes to a wrong decision on the basis of inconclusive evidence, it does not, in principle, accept tentative conjectures or refutable (falsifiable) hypotheses. The reason is simple. We know that for something to be really true, it must be absolutely or conclusively established to be true. A tentative hypothesis which we conventionally accept for the time being, 'relative to the present state of our knowledge', does not qualify as the real truth.

The dialectic takes the same view in its logical synthesis of an entire story. It does not accept a conclusion based on tentative assumptions, hypotheses or conjectures. The result of a dialectical investigation must, in other words, stand on its own without depending on any axiom or postulate. The subject matter, or the object of study, must be made 'self-explanatory' within the system in the sense that it leaves no unknowable or unexplainable 'thing-in-itself'. The logic of that system must, therefore, be inherent in it rather than imposed on it from the outside. That sort of self-explaining system is what Hegel called the 'concrete logical idea'. To bring out this character, I would say that the dialectic is 'auto-biographical'. An autobiographical story can be told only *from within*, and not from without.

Since the dialectic is autobiographical, it must have *a storyteller or a subject*. It is important to identify who is telling us the story. In the case of Hegel, the Absolute (God or the Christian logos) is the subject of the dialectic; in the case of Marx, it is capital. This important point is often overlooked by Marxian materialists. In their eagerness to 'abolish' Hegel's idealist concept of the Absolute, they do not stop to think what materialist subject they should put in its place. Engels, Lenin and the whole school of 'dialectical materialists' put Nature (or matter) in place of the Absolute without much reflection. But their project, as it turned out, was a complete non-starter. It had to fail because Nature (or matter) does not come forward to tell us its own story. Since it is not 'autobiographical', a dialectic of Nature (or of matter) is an impossibility. Nature passively sits out there and waits to be scrutinized, dissected, analyzed and described by us from the outside.

A dialectical subject must originate in human beings, yet it must also transcend us. Hegel's Absolute satisfies both conditions. For, as Feuerbach claimed, the Absolute is nothing but the 'infinitization (or absolutization)' of human virtues. We human beings are good, wise, powerful, and so on, only to some extent, and never infinitely or absolutely so. If, however, these desirable human characteristics are 'infinitized' or 'absolutized' in our mind, we can conceive of God, or the

Absolute. Thus instead of God creating us in his image, we, human beings, create God in our image. This is Feuerbach's well-known thesis of anthropomorphism. In this light, it is readily understandable why God privileges us, that is, human beings, as his agents. He must reveal himself through us. We, human beings, for our part, understand the nature (logic) of the Absolute (i.e., the divine wisdom or Reason) because it is nothing but the extrapolation of our own 'essence'. The religious teaching that God always gives us his grace and allows us to comprehend his intentions and designs is expressed 'philosophically', in the case of Hegel, by the thesis that the Absolute reveals itself completely to our finite reason.

We do not create Nature or matter by 'self-idealization', that is, by the process of infinitization of our own virtues. Nature, therefore, has no teleology to reveal to us. We can never know it completely. We can only gain partial knowledge of its behavior by constantly observing it from the outside. Nature does not privilege us by selecting us as its agent and letting us play out its logic. Although we belong to Nature, we have not created it. Consequently, we cannot see its logic from the inside, nor can we grasp it as a totality, that is, as a 'concrete logical idea'. The 'thing-in-itself' of Nature always remains beyond our reach. In other words, Nature or matter cannot be the subject of a materialist dialectic. If so, what else can the subject of a materialistic dialectic be? My answer is that it can be 'capital'.

Capital originates in our own 'economic motives', even though it transcends us because in it these human traits are already 'made infinite and absolute'. Through the creation of capital our economic motives are 'one-dimensionalized'. Since, however, capital is obtained by our own 'self-idealization', we comprehend it completely. All we have to do is to ask ourselves what we would do, if we pursued our own 'economic' goals single-mindedly at the expense of all other considerations, that is, if we behaved as mere 'bearers of economic categories'. In fact, that is how we learn the basics of economic theory. The present claim is equivalent to saying that capital, as the dialectical subject, reveals itself to us totally. Since capital is a product of our 'self-idealization', it contains nothing that we cannot really comprehend.

The identity of the subject and the object is the immediate consequence of this fact. In the dialectic, capital tells us its own story. Having transcended us and our limitations, capital now possesses its own identity separate from us. It has become the object, in the sense that it has gone beyond our finite subjectivity. Yet we can fully understand how capital 'thinks' because its 'logic' is only an extended version of our own thought. In other words, we are privy to the subjectivity of capital. Our finite subjectivity and capital's infinite subjectivity are different, and yet they are connected by what Marx called the 'force of abstraction' (1958, 8). By being 'subsumed' under capital and becoming its agent, we can think like capital.

It is interesting to recall that 'logic coincides with metaphysics' according to Hegel (Wallace, 1975, 36). All metaphysical categories represent characteristics of the Absolute, that is, purified human nature. The dialectic of the Absolute explains them in a logical order. We can similarly claim that 'logic coincides with economics', meaning that all economic categories represent characteristics of capital, that is, our economic motives 'made infinite'. In other words, the dialectic of capital is economic theory, and nothing else can be. Economic theory must, therefore, expose the logic or capital completely. The method of this complete exposition is the dialectic which proceeds by the triadic steps of thesis, antithesis and synthesis.

A dialectical system is a self-definition in the sense that the subject of the dialectic defines (specifies) itself completely. The definition, however, cannot be completed at one fell swoop. Instead the subject must be defined and redefined a great number of times, as we go through the many layers of its existence. As the level of discussion proceeds from abstract to concrete, the same concept returns many times, and each time it becomes more specified. The process ends only when it is fully synthesized or completely specified, all its layers being exposed.

The easiest way to understand the nature of this method is to think of how a painter works on a portrait. When he first begins with a few broad outlines, it is hard to recognize whose picture is being created. As he gradually adds details, however, the resemblance to the person who is sitting for him becomes increasingly clear. When the picture is completed, there is no longer any doubt as to whose portrait has been painted. Even in the first few of his bold brush strokes, however, the painter presupposes (has in his mind) the end result. He is aware that the spaces which he now leaves empty will be filled with elaborate detail in due course. In synthesizing something dialectically, we proceed in the same way. First we begin with broad contours, which pre-assign the spaces into which further details (or specifications) will be introduced later.

Let us, at this point, consider the famous Hegelian triad of 'being, naught and becoming'. The following illustration may clarify the dialectical meaning of 'contradiction' and its synthesis. Suppose that I ask a friend of mine the question: 'Have you got a child?' If the answer is

'Yes, I have one' (being) and 'No, I have none' (non-being) at the same time, it is contradictory in the formal-logical sense. Either my friend is mentally confused or he does not seriously want to answer my question. Obviously such a contradiction cannot be synthesized, overcome or resolved. For it is *not* a dialectical contradiction. Yet many self-appointed exponents of the dialectic come forward with the false exegesis that precisely this elusiveness illustrates what Hegel calls 'becoming'. That most decidedly is *not* the case.

When the friend answers my query with 'Yes, I have' (being), he has not yet specified his child at all. The child may, therefore, be a boy or a girl, a one-year old infant or an uncontrollable teenager, a whiz kid or mentally retarded, that is, anything that a child can be. It is this absence of any specification that is called 'nothing' or 'naught'. Indeed, without any further information other than merely that he exists, the child means absolutely 'nothing' to me. If I were to open his file, it would remain totally blank, except for a hypothetical name that I may decide to give him for convenience. Yet I cannot ignore the fact that there is a child in my friend's family. This constitutes the dialectical contradiction.

'Becoming' means, in the present case, that I may ask more questions and begin to complete a meaningful file of the child, or I may simply forget about it. I am formally free to let the child 'come to be' or 'pass away'. Since, from a formal point of view, there is no compelling reason for me to opt for either of the two alternatives, the state of 'becoming' is said to be fluid and unstable. However, so long as my original question was not asked frivolously, and was motivated by genuine curiosity, I will seek more information about that child.

If my friend responds to my further questioning, his child will not remain a pure being, but will become a determinate (or specified) being. At the same time my thought of the child moves from one level of abstraction to another, that is, it progresses one step forward in its dialectical journey from abstract to concrete. Soon I shall obtain a more synthetic idea of the child, insofar as that is possible from an external description. Once his file is thus complete, I may now wish to meet the child personally for an in-depth study of his character or inner motivation, subjecting him to further, more probing questioning. At that point, I seek his 'essence', having already confirmed his 'being'.

From the above example, it is apparent that dialectical 'contradiction' is quite different from 'contradiction' in the sense of formal logic. The dialectic clearly does not offend the so-called principle of non-contradiction in formal logic. A dialectical contradiction arises when a concept is posed without adequate specification. The concept itself demands more specification, which is not yet available. That constitutes a dialectical contradiction. To specify or determine something, however, is to relate it to something other than itself. For instance, a child can be a boy or a girl. To say that it is a boy means that it is not a girl. We thus determine the concept, in this case, by excluding its other possibility. This is in keeping with the well-known Spinozan contention that 'all determination is a negation'.

Unfortunately, an incorrect, and commonly encountered, explanation of the triad reverses this procedure and glorifies the mere truism that a boy (thesis) and a girl (antithesis) are both a child (synthesis). That, however, would be to move from the concrete (more specified) to the abstract (less specified). There is nothing dialectical in such a proposition. In the above illustration, by contrast. I first find out that there is a child. Next I ask a question to determine whether it is a boy or a girl. Once told that it is a boy, I then ask a further question to determine, for instance, what sort of age bracket he belongs to. Having received this information, I next try to determine whether he is an extrovert or an introvert, and so on. By proceeding in this fashion, I get to know what the child is like. I am in effect writing a 'biography' of the child. If, however, there exists a systematic questionnaire, or method of exhaustive questioning, ready for use by everyone, my task will be simplified. If the 'child' himself is mature enough, he can be his own interviewer and respondent with a help of this questionnaire. In other words, he can write his own 'autobiography'.

The greatness of Hegel lies in discovering such a systematic questionnaire for the first time. He was, according to Marx, 'the first to present the general forms of working of the dialectic in a comprehensive and conscious manner' (1958, 29). By simply responding to the questionnaire that Hegel designed, a dialectical subject is made to reveal its full 'autobiography'. That questionnaire consists of the three doctrines of Being, Essence and the Notion.

The doctrine of Being is further divided into quality, quantity and measure. Roughly speaking, the dialectical subject (say, my friend's child) is specified externally in this doctrine, by the method of 'becoming (transition)' or 'passing over from one form to another'. For instance, 'the child' becomes 'a boy', who becomes 'a teenager', who becomes 'an extrovert type', who becomes 'a talented musician', and so on. All items of information are put in the file of the child, which is in three parts. In the first part (quality), we find out what sort of a child he is (*Was für ein Kind ist es?*), that is, his being-for-self (*Fürsichsein*). Suppose that he is musically talented. Then, in the second part (quantity) of the file, we find out how his immanent talent is recognized, tested and measured externally by society. Finally, the last part of his file (measure) explains how the inner talent and its external recognition combine to enable the child to grow into a full-fledged musician.

At this point we enter the doctrine of Essence, which consists of the ground, appearance and actuality. This doctrine corresponds to the phase of internal specification of the subject. The dialectical method at work here is often called 'reflection (grounding)', which we may also call 'internalization'. In this case the dialectical subject does not simply delimit itself by excluding or circumventing what is other than itself, but rather 'internalizes' the opposing factors in a more positive and conciliatory fashion. For instance, the child may have inherited great musical talent from his forefathers, yet his family condition may not have been affluent enough to provide him with proper training in classical music. Under the circumstances he may have decided to adopt a simpler instrument and so developed into a popular musician. He thus preserves his talent (ground), but makes appropriate adaptations to the surrounding conditions (appearance) and establishes himself as a solid musician (actuality).

We then move to the last chapter of his autobiography, the doctrine of the Notion. We now look at the boy who has established himself as a popular musician. How does he fare and survive in this world? The doctrine is divided into the subjective notion, the object and the idea (*Idee*), and the dialectical method at work here is that of 'development or unfolding (*Entfaltung*)'. For example, our musician must regulate his life according to his own principles or self-imposed discipline (the subjective notion). The principles must be systematic and consistent; they must also serve his purpose. His life, however, cannot be completely regulated by his principles alone. There are other facts of life which go beyond the purview of his subjective principles. Since they (the object) cannot be ignored, he must find ways to reconcile himself with their requirements. For example, in planning a concert trip, he cannot ignore business considerations nor can he forget about how his parents and siblings feel about it. He may have to make certain necessary concessions. Only when he has learned the wisdom of harmonizing his subjective principles with the objective conditions that constrain them, do we get the real 'idea' of the person.

The present illustration is not meant to be a rigorous interpretation of Hegel's *Logic*. Far from that. However, what I wish above all to bring out with this exercise is that the Hegelian dialectic is not a mystical doctrine beyond the grasp of ordinary mortals. On the contrary, it is a very natural mode of thinking that we all practice in our daily life, whether we are conscious of it or not. For the dialectic is nothing but a system of our own 'thought-forms or thought determinations'. Our next task is to show how the same thought pattern is used to expose the concept of capital dialectically. In this case, we can afford to be a little more rigorous and precise in our interpretation of the dialectic. The dialectic of capital too consists of the three doctrines of circulation, production and distribution. The dialectical methods used in those doctrines are respectively, becoming, internalization, and unfolding. The guiding force of the dialectic of capital is the contradiction between value and use-values. Capital, the dialectical subject, reveals itself step by step by letting 'value', its most abstract specification, prevail over 'use-values' which represent everything 'other' than capital.

The doctrine of circulation. If you ask capital, 'What are you first of all, prior to all further specifications?' it will answer, 'I am abstract-general (i.e., commodity-economic or mercantile) wealth regardless of its concrete-specific or material property which satisfies you in one particular way or another.' That abstract-general side of wealth is called 'value' as opposed to the concrete-specific side, which is called 'use-value'. The simplest context in which the two 'contradictory' terms appear, co-existing side by side, is the 'commodity'. That is why Marx says, 'The wealth of bourgeois society, at first sight, presents itself as an immense accumulation of commodities, its unit being a single commodity' (1904, 19).

The value of a commodity cannot be seen. It is buried underneath the correlative use-value of the commodity. To overcome that restriction, value expresses itself in the form of a price, that is, in a definite quantity of the use-value of *another* commodity. By adopting the use-value of another commodity, it frees itself, as it were, from its own correlative use-value with which it has to co-habit in the same commodity. Thus it seeks solution outside that commodity. This kind of procedure illustrates the method of transition or becoming.

The expression of value in terms of commodities itself gives rise to money. Money is the commodity (such as gold) in the use-value of which all other commodities express their value. By virtue of this fact money purchases other commodities without qualitative restriction, and, in so doing, measures their value. It also takes the forms of active (transactions) money and idle money. The latter is money which stays outside the sphere of commodity circulation, awaiting the opportunity to become capital.

Capital is an operation that renders a sum of money into a greater sum of money by adopting the three forms. These are merchant, moneylending and industrial capital. The operation of the first is the most severely constrained by use-values, since the merchant is a middleman caught between producers and consumers. The last form can operate with the maximum of freedom from use-value restrictions, since an industrialist can, in principle, produce *any* use-value of his choice, provided that labor-power is available to him as a commodity.

The doctrine of production. Once the form of industrial capital is well established, a completely new type of 'contradiction between value and use-values' arises. This one is between capital as a form of 'chremat-istic' (value augmentation) and supra-historic 'real economic life', that is to say, the production of use-values in general, which it subsumes. This time the contradiction is solved by a more adequate and secure subsumption of the real economy under the form of value augmenta-tion. The real economic life common to all societies is 'internalized' by the chrematistic form of capital.

Use-values must be produced in all societies. Under capitalism, however, they are produced only as the reflection (or *Schattenseite*) of the production of surplus value. Commodities are produced for the surplus value that they contain, and not directly for their use-values. The production of surplus value requires a development of the specific-ally capitalist method of production, which is most typically repres-ented by factories equipped with machines. The use of machines entails the increasing perfection of labor-power as a commodity. The capitalist production of commodities, however, does not occur only inside the factory. What occurs inside it is controlled and regulated by what takes place outside it.

In this doctrine, the production of commodities as value, which contains surplus value, is studied in all its aspects, that is, inside the factory (as the production-process of capital), outside the factory (as the circulation-process of capital) and as the continuing activity of the aggregate-social capital (the reproduction-process of capital). The purpose of this doctrine is to establish the capitalist mode of production as a self-dependent system of commodity production, consistent with the supra-historic norms of real economic life. In other words, it is to show that capitalism constitutes a real historical society, rather than a mere toy model which we arbitrarily invent.

The doctrine of distribution. Once the viability and reproducibility of surplus value production is demonstrated, capital then proceeds to develop its own market, the capitalist market. Although every commodity is always produced as value, that is, indifferently to use-values, each commodity is nonetheless a distinct use-value, the production of which requires a specific technique. Sometimes, more than one technique is employed in the production of a particular use-value.

At this point the 'contradiction between value and use-values' arises in yet another form. This time it is a contradiction between the capitalist indifference to use-values and the unavoidability of technical variations in their production. Such a contradiction will be reconciled by the dialectic of unfolding or development, a method which is specific to the doctrine of distribution.

In the capitalist market, the surplus value that capital as a whole has produced is distributed to individual units of capital in proportion to the magnitude of its advance, and this involves the formation of the general rate of profit and production-prices (equilibrium prices) that deviate from values (the theory of profit). Industrial capital, however, is not the only partaker of surplus value. Although land does not directly participate in the production of value, it is nevertheless an indispensable factor in the production of use-values. Hence capital must cede part of surplus value to landed property, which collects various forms of rent (the theory of rent). The ownership of land entitles one to a stream of periodic revenues as rent.

The experience of sharing surplus value with landed property in this manner enables capital to reconceptualize itself as an asset or property. As a property, capital too is automatically entitled to a stream of interest revenues. Interest-bearing capital is the most synthetic and complete concept of capital (the theory of interest). This concept, however, can be reached only after industrial capital delegates its circulatory functions to loan-capital and commercial capital. These two forms of capital assist the surplus value production of industrial capital indirectly. By providing credit, loan-capital enables industrial capital to buy commodities which it would otherwise not be able to purchase. By taking over the difficult and time-consuming operation of selling commodities from industrial capital, commercial capital enables it to concentrate on the production of surplus value.

In all these cases, capital tries to distance itself from the production of use-values. The first principle of the distribution of surplus value as profit enables all units of industrial capital, regardless of the specific use-value they happen to be producing, to be equally rewarded in proportion to the magnitude of capital advanced. The second explains how surplus value may be shared between agriculture which is land-intensive and non-agriculture which is not. The last principle of distribution shows how all capitalists, whether engaged productively in industry (production of use-values) or unproductively in commerce and finance, may equally partake of the existing pool of surplus value in the form of interest, rather than of profit, in proportion to the magnitude of the ownership of capital.

The above explains the structure of the dialectic of capital in a very condensed form. An uncanny homomorphism between Hegel's *Logic* and the dialectic of capital may be noticed. That, however, is not strange to me. For the dialectical subject is always part of ourselves, though magnified and extended. There must be only one way to let such a subject expose itself totally and systematically, and that is the dialectical way.

References

Marx, Karl. 1904. *A Contribution to the Critique of Political Economy*. Chicago: Charles H. Kerr.
Marx, Karl. 1958. *Capital*, Vol. 1. Trans. Samuel Moore and Edward Aveling. Moscow: Foreign Languages Publishing House.
Wallace, W. 1975. *Hegel's Logic*. Oxford, England: Oxford University Press.

16
Systematic Dialectic

Christopher J. Arthur

In this paper I briefly establish the difference between historical dialectic and systematic dialectic; I go on to elucidate the latter.

The distinction between historical and systematic dialectic should be obvious enough, but unfortunately it is not often marked. Although most of Hegel's work (*Phenomenology of Spirit, Science of Logic, Encyclopedia*, and *Philosophy of Right*) was systematic, he frequently obscured this by using illustrations from different historical periods. As for Marx's great systematic work *Capital*, this has suffered from a virtually universal misreading, originally sponsored by Engels, according to which its method is 'logical-historical'; in other words, the two dialectics get conflated. But in this it is clear that the historical is taken to be precedent, the 'logical' part consisting merely in tidying up the history by disentangling pure forms from contingent accretions.

While it is true then that parts of these works of Hegel and Marx are often read in an historical key, I emphatically reject such readings. Elsewhere I have explicitly argued against such a reading of *Capital* (Arthur, 1996; 1997). It is worth noting that Engels not only misread Marx but also Hegel, in that the logical-historical method was supposed to be derived by Marx from Hegel. However, Hegel took care to explain in his lectures on the modern state that he was not developing the categories according to any historical ordering (1942, §32 and Addition; §182 Addition). Unknown to Engels, Marx also made the same point in the 'Introduction' to the *Grundrisse*, of course.

In discussions of dialectic generally it is most often taken to be a *historical* process; indeed it is frequently reduced to a type of efficient causality. A contradiction is said to 'produce' a resolution in much the same way as a cause 'produces' an effect. Now it is clear that if the paradigmatic works by Hegel and Marx mentioned above are not historical works any such interpretation is clearly irrelevant. What is characteristic of these works is that they treat a *given whole* and thus the ordering of the categories is in no way determined by historical matters, but is articulated on the basis of purely systematic considerations. Since all 'moments' of the whole exist synchronically all movement must pertain to their reciprocal support and development. While this motion implies that moments become effective *successively*, the movement winds back into itself to form a *circuit* of reproduction of these moments by each other (Arthur, 1998). Theory can trace a logic of mutual presupposition in the elements of the structure and hence of the *necessity* of certain forms and laws of motion of the whole under consideration.

In sum, the reason why, in these paradigmatic works, systematicity is of the essence is because the object of investigation is a totality. Dialectic grasps phenomena in their interconnectedness, something beyond the capacity of analytical reason and linear logic (Arthur, 1997). As Hegel argued, science in treating a totality must take the shape of system, 'since what is *concretely* true is so only as ... *totality*' (1991, § 14). The system comprises a set of categories expressing the forms and relations embedded within the totality, its 'moments'. The task of systematic dialectic is to organize such a system of categories in a definite sequence, deriving one from another logically. If such a systematic sequencing is to be undertaken, a method is required for making transitions from one category to another in such a way that the whole system has an architectonic. Now, if a whole is built up in this way, the systematic ordering of its categories may be understood both 'forwards', as a progression, and 'backwards', as a retrogression. After explaining this, I will lay special emphasis on the merits of the regressive aspect of the architectonic and hence the possibility of a 'pull' from the end of the line for motivating dialectical transitions within the development of the categories; and I will then illustrate the point with examples from Hegel and Marx.

Let us turn then to an account of the meaning of system. In doing so, I draw on the reading of Hegel provided by Klaus Hartmann (1972), and after him Terry Pinkard (1985), and (within Marxism) Tony Smith (1990), Geert Reuten and Michael Williams (1989). They are all concerned to rescue Hegel from any 'metaphysical' reading. Thus Hartmann adopts a 'non-metaphysical view' of Hegel, whose great merit is said to lie in his understanding of the necessity of categorial ordering, exhibited primarily in his *Logic*. Hegel's *Logic* shows how the categories may be systematically related to one another in such a manner that their exposition and 'reconstruction' (1969, 39) provides a theory whereby each category gains systematic meaning in virtue of its positioning with respect to the other categories and the whole. Taken in isolation, in abstraction, from its systematic placing a category is imperfectly grasped.

Although it is natural to read a linear exposition as one in which later categories are developed from their antecedents – at least in the sense that the latter must be analytically presupposed – in Hegel's view this cannot be the whole story, for he rejects any dogmatic founding category. The progressive development is therefore not securely established on a given presupposition. There is, however, another consideration. Since the linear progression cannot be validated as a deduction, it can only be *reconstruction*; as such what it is heading for must be granted.

But have we not merely duplicated the problem of the foundation? If the beginning cannot justify the end is it not also the case that the end cannot justify the beginning? The answer is that there is indeed an asymmetry here. The end, as the most concrete, complex, and complete reality, does adequately support and sustain all the elements that make it up, and thereby retrogressively justifies the logical sequencing from this viewpoint. Insofar as Hegel's dialectics finish with something 'absolute', its absolute character grants validity retrospectively to all the stages of its exposition and their dialectical relations through integrating them into its architectonic; if the truth is the whole, the moments of the whole gain their validity within it. Tony Smith explains this retrogressive character of systematic dialectic as follows: 'If the theory culminates in a stage that is true "for itself", i. e., concretely and actually, then this shows that an earlier stage leading up to it must have been true "in itself", that is, abstractly and potentially' (1990, 49). The method required, then, is to develop categorial items in a sequence that is to be considered as 'grounding' of categories regressively, and as disclosure, or presentation, of further categories, progressively.

The fact that the logical progression is at the same time 'a retrogression' means that the beginning may be shown to be 'not something merely arbitrarily assumed' but itself grounded as an abstract moment of the whole (Hegel, 1969, 70). The following key passage sums up Hegel's view:

> Each step of the *advance* in the process of further determination, while getting further away from the indeterminate beginning is also *getting back nearer* to it .... What at first sight may appear to be different, the retrogressive grounding of the beginning, and the progressive further determining of it, coincide and are the same. The method, which thus winds itself into a circle, cannot anticipate in a development in

time that the beginning is, as such, already something derived ... and there is no need to deprecate the fact that it may only be accepted *provisionally* and *hypothetically*. (1969, 841)

While every category depends on its antecedents for its constitutive moments, the problem of the beginning is resolved if the richness of the granted content presupposes analytically the simpler, more abstract, antecedent categories. To reiterate, the progressive introduction of new categories cannot be deduction (for the beginning is not to be taken as an axiom), it can only be a *reconstruction* of reality which takes for granted that what it is headed for is logically complete. So the sequence of categories has to be read in both directions, as a disclosure, or exposition, progressively, and as a grounding movement retrogressively (Hartmann, 1972, 104–7; Pinkard, 1985, 104–8). What constitutes progression is an arrangement of categories from abstract to concrete; successive categories are always richer and more concrete (Hegel, 1969, 840; Marx, 1973, 100). Indeed the basis of the advance is generally that each category is *deficient* in determinacy with respect to the next and the impulse for the transition is precisely the requirement that such deficiency must be overcome (Hegel, 1969, 828–9). It is important that the transition involves a 'leap' to a qualitatively new categorical level. A dialectical development has nothing in common with a vulgar evolutionism predicated on extrapolating an existent tendency.

All stages are deficient with respect to the final fulfillment of the dialectic in a systematically ordered totality. Indeed the progressive/regressive sequencing depends upon the presupposition that there is a whole from which a violent abstraction has been made so as to constitute a simple beginning which in virtue of this negation of its positioning in the whole has 'lost its footing', so to speak, and thus there arises a contradiction between the character of the element in isolation and its meaning as part of the whole. The treatment of this moment as inherently in contradiction with itself, on account of this, is given if it is assumed throughout the dialectical development that the whole remains immanent or implicit in it.

This provides the basis for the transitions in the development of the categorial ordering. There is an impulse to provide a solution to a contradiction – a 'push', one might say – and there is the need to overcome the deficiency of the category with respect to the posited end of the process – a 'pull', one might say. For the most part these elements exist in combination. Since dialectic is generally regarded in the former sense as the positing and resolving of contradictions, I want here to stress the importance of the final goal and the notion that any given stage is always deficient with respect to it.[1]

The impulse to move from one category to the next is the *insufficiency* of the existing stage to comprehend its presuppositions; while it is a necessary result of the previous stage it depends on conditions of existence that have yet to be developed; each stage 'takes care of', with the minimum of new elements, the problem perceived with the previous stage, but in turn is found insufficient. The presentation ends when all the conditions of existence needing to be addressed are comprehended by the entire system of categories developed. If it is presupposed that the whole system of categories is complete and internally self-sustaining, then it is possible to reconstruct its order precisely through moving sequentially from categories deficient in such respects (that is in being inclusive and self-sustaining) to ones less so, until the system as a totality is thereby exhibited as such. The method of presentation consists in exhibiting its categorial articulation in such a manner as to show how the logic of the system tendentially ensures its completeness through 'positing' all its presuppositions. Moreover a system is complete only when it returns to, and accounts for, its starting point; Marx was therefore correct in the first instance, having started with 'the commodity', to draft a final section entitled 'the commodity as product of capital' (1976, 949).

Hartmann, followed by Smith, gives an account of the relation of Hegel's *Logic* to the '*Realphilosophie*' (domains of nature, society, culture, etc.) as follows: 'The *Logic* contains all ontological distinctions of note on a comparatively abstract plane, discounting the difference externality might make categorially' (1972, 113). Then the more 'concrete' determinations of *Realphilosophie* are 'principled' by the body of logical categories; and the persuasiveness of the *Realphilosophie* provides a proof of the logic indirectly.

I believe that much of Hegel's and Marx's work can be interpreted in this way, as informed by Hegel's dialectical logic. In the remainder of this paper, then, I elucidate the points about dialectic made in its first half by treating some case studies, one from Hegel and two from Marx. These are: (1) the transition from right to morality in Hegel's *Philosophy of Right*; (2) the derivation of money in *Capital*; and (3) the resolution of the contradiction in the general formula of capital in *Capital*. The general aim in my interpretations of these examples will be to demonstrate that 'contradictions' in the strict sense may be predicated of a given stage only in virtue of the systematic placing of that stage with respect to the totality in question, whether of right (in the first example following) or of value (in the examples from *Capital*) purely personal actions are seen by the other party as themselves transgressive of their rights; hence a vendetta situation develops.

1. Hegel's overall objective in his political philosophy is to demonstrate that freedom is actualized in a system of 'right'. This system of right he articulates in a dialectical development from the supposedly basic right to property onwards to rights of citizenship and to the state organized so as comprehensively to underpin all the various spheres of right. At the end of the section on 'abstract right' he explains how right in the abstract is unable to maintain itself because, without morality, custom or law, everyone in defending their own property and honor against transgression may be 'asserting a right' but their purely personal actions are seen by the other party a themselves transgressive of their rights; hence a vendetta situation develops.

   Now many philosophers address this problem by arguing that to keep the peace a superior force must come on the scene. Hegel does not take this route at all. He wants the *concept* of right itself to become more developed, more comprehensive in its scope. This higher form of right at the next level is the concern for right as such, not simply one's own rights, a concern to do right even where this might not seem immediately in one's interests. How is this idea to be dialectically developed? In the basic vendetta situation there is no contradiction at all, only conflict, and there is nothing contradictory about supposing such vendettas interminable. The contradiction arises only if the concern for *right as such* is brought to bear.

   Clearly it is not possible for all parties to be 'in the right' all the time, so a situation in which everyone is left free to claim and defend their own rights contradicts the demand of a system of right that right be actualized in reality. There is clearly a 'pull' to the next higher category of right: 'morality', as Hegel calls it. However, there is more to it than this; for if this concern is imputed to the agents involved in a vendetta (that is, if the whole is taken to be *immanent* in the moments of each stage rather than merely an external benchmark of progress), then their own consciousness becomes contradictory. For if each claims to be avenging an infringement of right as such they are claiming that their cause is just, but justice is a universal that transcends the specific interest particular people have in prosecuting their own claims. Here, however, each is acting as judge and jury in their own case and their attempt to pursue the criminal cannot be distinguished from the subjective motive of revenge. This may be viewed as giving a 'push' to resolve this contradiction, to sort it out by casting around for a solution. Hegel concludes as follows:

> The demand that this contradiction…in the manner in which wrong is annulled be resolved…is the demand for a justice freed from subjective interest.…This' implies the demand for a will which, though particular and subjective, yet wills the universal as such. But this concept of *morality* is not simply something demanded, it has emerged in the course of this movement itself. (1942, §103)

The important thing to understand here is that, while dialectical development is *immanent* in the content under consideration, whether one thinks of the categorial structure as progressive or regressive in its architectonic the transitions are *conceptual* necessities. This is the sense here in which the concept of morality is *required*. As mentioned above such a move represents a qualitative leap. While there is a structural tendency for the categorial level of righting wrong abstractly to issue in vendetta, this tendency cannot of itself transcend this fate. It would be wrong to interpret Hegel's transition here as a quasi-causal story in which the agents involved in a vendetta are supposed to wake up to the requirements of morality as a result of its structural features. They may or may not. It is not relevant. What is relevant is that it is a requirement of reason that a new category come to life.

It is also a consequence of Hegel's systematic approach that both the claims of the individuals for their rights, and the concern of moral consciousness to do the right thing are presuppositions of any coherent articulation of a legal system of right by the state. This illustrates also a general point about systematic dialectic: that nothing is *lost*, that every 'refuted' position is yet preserved within a more comprehensive form of realization of the concept in question, here that of 'right'.

2. For our first case from *Capital*, let us see how the contradiction between use value and exchange value gives rise to money. According to Marx, this contradiction is present in the commodity as such and expressed already in the simple form of value. Yet if one thinks about such a relation of commodities as constitutive of barter there is a problem, for it is hard to see anything contradictory about the persistence of barter relations. There is a contradiction in the

commodity *only* if it is claimed that it is imbued with a universal, namely value, as a result of its participation in a whole network of capitalist commodity production. Marx's argument in Chapter 1 is that this category, and its contradiction with use value, requires the development of money.

But, again I stress, there is no contradiction whatsoever in supposing that exchange can be carried on without money: barter is a well-attested phenomenon historically and anthropologically. It has no *necessity* to develop into a money system. Yet Marx in *Capital* tries to demonstrate the necessity of money. He predicates this on the fact that 'exchange of commodities implies contradictory and mutu-ally exclusive conditions' (1976, 198). These contradictions arise only because it is *presupposed* in his discussion that the commodity is to be a bearer of value. It is only on this basis that the forms of value Marx considers in his first chapter are said to be 'defective' or 'deficient'. They are deficient in that the presence of value is not adequately expressed in the first three forms considered, but only in the money form. Thus the derivation of money is not based primarily on a 'forwards' argument but rather on a 'backwards' dialectic in which it is assumed that value is to be socially validated and then money is shown to be (at this stage) the most adequate actualization of value through an argument establishing the inadequacies of less developed expressions of commodity relations.

If at the start one imputes value to a single commodity (through an analytical abstraction from the world of exchange relations) one immediately creates a contradiction between use value and value, because value has a purely social reality (Marx, 1976, 138–39). Since in isolation commodities lack 'a form of value distinct from their natural forms' (p. 141) such a commodity can appear only as a partic-ular use value, yet at the same time is required to realize the universal *negation* of use value, for that is how value is socially constituted (p.128). If value *cannot* appear in an isolated commodity, then, since 'essence must *appear*' (Hegel, 1991, § 131), in effect it is not really present in such a case. Thus one can say a 'demand' has arisen for this contradiction to be superseded through the said commodity finding a way of distinguishing itself as a value from itself as a use value, to express this value as *other* than itself therefore. This it does in calling on another commodity to be its equivalent as value. In this simple relation Marx rightly saw the germ of money, which as a special commodity excluded from all others in 'value for itself' and reflects back on them an adequate value form in their price.

It is important to notice that the whole argument is driven *conceptually*: for the concept of value to be meaningful money is required. There is no trace in Marx's presentation of a quasi-causal story about commodity exchangers having as a result of the structure of their situation a tendency to invent money.

If the validating of the value inherent in commodities is only accomplished in the dialectical movement to a higher category, to money, it is also true that the commodity as such retains its contradictory character. The resolution of contradictions does not abolish them, nor discard them, but *grounds* them, gives them 'room to move', as Marx puts it (1976, 198). Furthermore, money itself turns out to embody a contradictory unity of use value and exchange value at a higher level. And so does each further concretization. The key question is this: Is capitalism *finally* able to resolve this contradiction? Or does it remain prey to it however it adapts itself? Will it run out of 'room to move'?

3. The clearest example of the reading of *Capital* as a dialectic informed by the need to reconstitute the given whole is the transition to production which Marx makes in the chapter 'Contradictions in the General Formula of Capital'.

In the previous chapters, he has dealt with simple circulation of commodities and the mediation of this in money. Now it is clear that there is no contradiction involved in the idea of simple circulation at value. There is indeed no contradiction in the idea that clever merchants are generally successful at selling dear and buying cheap. (But notice that it is contingent that an increment in value is gained at the expense of another through luck or judgment or cheating.) Why then does Marx find it *necessary* to turn to production in order to resolve *contradictions*? It arises only from the demand that the concept of capital be actualized. This demand is only supportable on the assumption that the object of the exercise is to explain capitalism as a going concern, trace its potential to reproduce itself together with all its conditions of existence, and identify any insurmountable contradiction. It is presupposed at this point in the argument that capital is defined as self-valorizing value, in which surplus value accrues to capital as a matter of necessity in virtue of its form. Only on this presupposition is Marx entitled to formulate the key contradiction: 'Capital cannot arise from circulation and it is equally impossible for it to arise apart from circulation' (1976, 268). The solution is stated to lie in the purchase of the value-producing agent itself - labor. However, here there is an unexamined precondition, namely that there be a labor market. Yet nothing whatsoever is done by Marx to explain this at the point where it is introduced. This is not because he is unaware that he is making such an assumption; he simply declares the origin of free labor to have no theoretical interest![2] (p. 273). Nothing could show more clearly the nature of Marx's dialectic. He does not derive free labor from the dialectic of circulation as its result. Rather he says the concept of capital demands its prior presence if the dialectic is to proceed. And he proceeds! But this issue is not left hanging forever. This condition of existence of capital which at the outset is taken as a premise (and shown to be historically a contingent result of the developments covered in the last part of *Capital*) is later itself grounded as a result of the capital relation itself (p. 724). We see now why Marx has no interest in deriving the labor market *prior* to the capital relation; it is derived as its *consequence*; capital 'posits' its own preconditions. Nothing could more clearly illustrate that *Capital* is the exposition of the reciprocal conditions inherent in a whole and not a quasi-historical development from primitive conditions to advanced ones.

Marx's development of the capital relation contains no argument of a quasi-causal character purporting to show how capitalism arose, such as the argument that given monetary circulation there will be a structural tendency for some people to start making money of money and then to subordinate the immediate producers to such aims. Rather his dialectic is about the necessity, if valorization is to be secured, of the exploitation of labor. It is a *conceptual* link that is established.

To sum up, what all these cases show is that systematic dialectic, as employed by Hegel and Marx, investigates the conceptual connections between the inner forms of a given whole; a sequence of categorial levels is established in which more developed forms ground earlier ones. This logic does not depend in any way upon the historical developments that first threw up the elementary preconditions of the system, for these are grounded and articulated *within* the logical ordering itself (Marx, 1973, 459–61).

Further research is necessary into the forms of capitalism in order to carry out in a more sustained way the program Marx initiated, evidently under the influence of Hegel's method (Arthur, 2002). It is also necessary to consider exactly how Marx differed from Hegel. On the 'non-metaphysical' view of Hegel, Marx was able to adopt his method wholesale and simply apply it more rigorously and more radically than Hegel. I believe the problem with Hegel lies deeper, for the 'pan-logicism' of his philosophy is an aspect that cannot be ignored; in my view it is this that allowed him to become the ideologist of capital rather than its radical critic. But that would have to be demonstrated on another occasion.

Notes

1. For an attempt to grasp the dialectic of history from the standpoint of its outcome, see Ollman, 1993.
2. Although the chronological origin of free labor has no interest from the point of view of systematic dialectic, which is concerned with the relation of synchronic elements, historically it is of interest, for Marx never tires of pointing out that the origin of capitalism cannot be explained on the basis of free labor as a natural premise. It is, rather, unnatural to separate the worker from the means of production, and this requires a special explanation in terms of an antecedent history. However, this process vanishes in its result and systematically is of no interest, for the system itself reproduces this condition of its existence.

References

Arthur, Christopher J. (ed.) 1996. 'Engels as Interpreter of Marx's Economics'. *Engels Today: A Centenary Appreciation*. London: Macmillan; New York: St. Martin's.

Arthur, Christopher J. 1997. 'Against the Logical-Historical Method: Dialectical Derivation versus Linear Logic'. In Fred Moseley and Martha Campbell, eds, *New Investigations of Marx's Method*. Atlantic Highlands, New Jersey: Humanities Press.

Arthur, Christopher J. 1998. 'The Fluidity of Capital and the Logic of the Concept'. In Christopher J. Arthur and Gert Reuten, eds, *The Circulation of Capital: Essays on Volume Two of Marx's 'Capital'*. London: Macmillan; New York: St. Martins.

Arthur, Christopher J. 2002. *The New Dialectic and Marx's Capital*. Leiden: Brill.

Hartmann, Klaus. 1972. 'Hegel: A Non-Metaphysical View'. In A. MacIntyre, ed., *Hegel*. New York: Doubleday Anchor.

Hegel, G. W. F. 1942. *The Philosophy of Right*, trans. T. M. Knox. Oxford, England: Oxford University Press.

Hegel, G. W. F.. 1969. *The Science of Logic*, trans. A. V. Miller. London: George Allen & Unwin.

Hegel, G. W. F.. 1991. *The Encyclopaedia Logic*, trans. T. Geraets *et al.* Minneapolis, Minneseta: Hacket.

Marx, Karl. 1973. *Grundrisse*, trans. M. Nicolaus. New York: Penguin.

Marx, Karl. 1976. *Capital*, Vol. I, trans. B. Fowkes. New York: Penguin.

Ollman, Bertell. 1993. 'Studying History Backward'. Ch. 8 of *Dialectical Investigation*. New York: Routledge.

Pinkard, Terry. 1985. 'The Logic of Hegel's *Logic*'. In M. Inwood, ed., *Hegel*. Oxford, England: Oxford University Press.

Reuten, Geert, and Michael Williams. 1989. *Value-Form and the State*. New York: Routledge.

Smith, Tony. 1990. *The Logic of Marx's 'Capital'*. Albany, New York: SUNY Press.

17
Marxist Feminist Dialectics for the Twenty-first Century

Nancy Hartsock

This is an effort to argue that from the perspective of feminist theory we need to both excavate and transform Marxist theory to address issues of the present and the future. For me, these issues include most centrally taking analytic account of intersecting axes of domination along the lines of race, gender, and sexuality, as well as class. The central issue I want to address here is that of what Marxist theory, especially the dialectical understanding of the world contained in that theory, can provide in the way of resources for contemporary analysis.

Feminist theory has certainly challenged and rewritten Marxist theory. The period of the 'unhappy marriage' of Marxism and feminism in which the two were one and that one was Marxism has come to a theoretical end (see Hartmann, 1981). Fundamental categories of Marxist theory have been questioned and rejected. First, there is the importance of labor. Feminists have raised questions about how labor is to be understood and have also highlighted the importance of non-waged labor. Second, feminist analysis by its very nature questions the centrality of class as the only foundation for social analysis. Third, and related, feminist theory raises questions about Marxism as a teleological theory of social evolution by noting the importance of issues other than the development of relations of production which center around men's lives, and by noting the continued existence of patriarchal relations in socialist countries. Fourth, feminist theory has in many areas successfully questioned Marxism's claim to be the single theory that can explain all of society, including its history and its future. The questions for me are (1) What Marxism has taught and can teach feminist theorists about political analysis and political practice? And (2) more important, How can we use these tools and insights especially dialectical thinking – to create theories of justice and social change that address the concerns of the present? Or, put differently, How to reoccupy Marxism as feminism?[1]

Here I want to take two fundamental Marxist texts as my guides. The first is the eleventh thesis on Feuerbach: 'The philosophers only interpret the world in various ways, the point is to change it' (Marx and Engels, 1976, 3). The second text is Engels' graveside eulogy for Marx. Engels stated that Marx had 'discovered the special law of motion governing the present day capitalist mode of production and the bourgeois society that this mode of production has created'. But more important for my own purposes is the fact that he continues by stating that 'this was not even half the man.... Marx was before all else a revolutionist' (Engels, 1978). Thus, he stresses the importance of Marx's political legacy, his role as a revolutionary committed to change the world for the benefit of the working class. I see this as a reminder that Marxism is fundamentally about building movements for social change, movements that recognize that injustice and domination are systematic. These movements need both political organizing and theoretical analysis to do the work of supporting the insights as well as the struggles of the many who are oppressed, exploited and marginalized.

What does it mean to reoccupy Marxism as feminism? For me it has come to mean most centrally to take up the methodological and epistemological advice and practices I found there and apply them in new directions. It has come to mean seeing dialectical thinking as applicable to many areas of social life. While I found much of Marx's critique of capitalism and the increasing commodification of more and more areas of social life persuasive, the focus of my concern at that time was to understand the situation of women more specifically.[2] I was coming to believe that feminism was not a set of specific conclusions about the situation of women, but was instead a mode of analysis that could be usefully applied to studying not simply women but society as a whole.

We need an understanding of objectivity that differs from the Enlightenment faith in the neutrality of reason. I would like to suggest that parts of the Marxist tradition represent an important resource for developing such an account, for insisting on the impossibility of neutrality and the necessity of engagement, for recognizing that the social relations in which we live structure (though they do not determine) the ways we understand the world, and for providing tools that can allow us to trace the ways our concepts and categories both structure and express the ways we interact with the world. As Haraway so eloquently puts it, "our" problem is how to have *simultaneously* an account of radical historical contingency of all knowledge claims and knowing subjects, a critical practice of recognizing our own "semiotic technologies" for making meanings, *and* a no-nonsense commitment to faithful accounts of a "real" world...friendly to earthwide projects of finite freedom ...' (1990, 187).

I have a number of problems with Marx's own theories, among them (1) class, understood centrally as a relation among men, is the only division that counts; (2) the analysis is fundamentally masculinist in that workers' wives and their labor are presumed; (3) homosocial birth images mark the analysis in important ways; (4) women come and go in the analysis and are profoundly absent from Marx's account of the extraction of surplus value – the heart of his analysis; (5) he is clearly a nineteenth-century Eurocentric writer who can pay little attention to such contemporary concerns as environmental issues and the rise of service industries.

But given these serious objections, Why should I raise once again the importance of a nineteenth-century European patriarch for late twentieth-century feminist theory? Why Marx? Why now? The fall of the Soviet state and the Berlin Wall have occasioned a global celebration of the market, and of capitalism's successes. Fredric Jameson notes that, for those who do not distinguish clearly between 'Marxism itself as a mode of thought and analysis, socialism as a political and societal aim and vision, and Communism as a historical movement', Marxism can appear to be an embarrassing remnant of the past (1996, 14). And certainly Teresa Ebert is right when she suggests that 'under the pressure of the dominant discourses of Postmodernism, Marxism and historical materialism are becoming lost revolutionary knowledges for the current generation of feminists' (1996, x). Still, even figures such as Derrida argue, regarding *The Communist Manifesto*: 'I know of few texts in the philosophical tradition, perhaps none, whose lesson seems more urgent today' (quoted in Ebert, 1996, x). I would add that in the context of a capitalism which has become truly global, and in which ever more of life is commodified, much of Marx's critique of capitalism remains very apt.[3]

I see Marx as an anti-Enlightenment figure on balance, although it must be recognized that his relationship to the Enlightenment and the whole tradition of Western political thought is that of both the inheriting son and the rebellious son (cf. Benhabib, 1990, 11). Thus, his account of the process of labor itself can be seen in sexual/gendered terms: Marx theorizes the relation of the worker to his own activity as an alien activity not belonging to him: 'activity as suffering, strength as weakness, *begetting as emasculating*...self estrangement' (in Engels,

1978, 76). Marx's account of estranged labor thus uses some of the 'second homosocial birth' images 1 have found in many works in the history of Western political thought. The point of this second birth is to overcome the defects of the first birth – bodies born from women and to replace it with a more durable and intellectual/spiritual one.[4] Thus, for Marx, the worker creates both himself and the world, and herein lies both the core of the problem and the potential solution.

Feminist theory too exists in an ambivalent relation to the Enlightenment. On the one hand, feminist theorists sometimes argue for a 'me too' position to work for women's inclusion in a number of societal institutions (see Ferguson, 1993). On the other hand, women as women have never been the 'subjects' of Enlightenment/liberal theory, so women's insistence on speaking at all troubles those theories (Eisenstein, 1982). (It is certainly my suspicion that this, along with decolonization, and struggles for recognition by oppressed racial and ethnic groups, is one reason why European and North American theorists have lost hold of some of their certainties.)

My reading of Marx is one that some have suggested is itself postmodern. I am greatly indebted to Bertell Ollman's ideas about Marxist dialectics as based on an account of internal relations. I also share David Harvey's very similar understanding of dialectics (Ollman, 1971; Harvey, 1996). Thus, I take from Marx the idea that one must replace the idea that the world is composed of 'things' with that of the importance of 'processes'. In addition, Marx's dialectical method holds that things do not 'exist outside of or prior to the processes, flows, and relations that create, sustain, or undermine them'.[5]

I see my reading of Marx as making several important contributions to my work in feminist theory. First, Marx's dialectical knowledge practices enable an alternative to the Enlightenment account of what is to count as truth or knowledge. Second, Marx's work provides materials for a more nuanced and socially embedded understanding of subjectivity and agency than is available from either contemporary liberal theory or theories influenced by post-structuralism. And third, the understanding of the relation of knowledge and power present in his work provides some criteria for what can count as better, or privileged, knowledges. I will take up each of these points in turn.

In the modernist/Enlightenment version, truth has to do with discovering a pre-existing external something which if it meets some criteria can be labeled as true. Moreover, it must be discovered from nowhere in particular so that truth can retain its pristine qualities. The definition of truth that I rely upon is more complex than this and is heavily indebted to my own reading of Marx. I want to refer to Marx in order to suggest in a shorthand way how my version of standpoint theory approaches the question of truth. In the *Theses on Feuerbach*, he argued against an understanding of 'things' as 'objects', 'especially objects of contemplation', and makes the following statement: 'Man must prove the truth, that is, the reality and power, the this-wordliness of his thinking in practice.' And here we must be brought back to the two texts I took as guides for this discussion: Marxism is about political change and social justice, and these concerns are central to any Marxism-influenced dialectical analysis of social relations.

The Marxian project, then, changes the criteria for what is to count as knowledge: for Marx, to have knowledge includes seeing, tasting, feeling, and thinking. If truth is the reality and power of our ideas in action, then we must treat knowledge and truth in much more historically specific ways and devote attention to the social, historical, and ultimately conventional form of all definitions of truth. (And on this point one can be reminded of Foucault's claim that truth is simply error codified.) We are reminded that the search for knowledge is a *human* activity, structured by human requirements.

But here I become uncomfortable with the language of truth. The search for truth is not at all the way to understand Marx's project. Perhaps a better concept to use is that of certitude: a sense that one has credible knowledge, knowledge that is 'good enough' to act on. The most fundamental point is to understand power relations – in his case, power relations centered on the development of capitalism and the commodification of ever greater areas of human existence. But the point of understanding power relations is to change them. And to this end, Marx's categories move and flow, enacting the fluidity that many postmodernist theorists insist on. To give just a few examples, Capital is described as 'raw materials, instruments of labor, and means of subsistence of all kinds *which are utilized* to produce new raw materials, new instruments of labor, and new means of subsistence', as 'accumulated labor', as 'living labor serving accumulated labor', as 'a bourgeois production relation, a social relation of production', as 'an independent social power' (Engels, 1978, 176, 207, 208). Capital is all these things at various moments and for various analytical purposes. Thus, for example, when Marx wanted to call attention to the specifics of the production process, he was likely to refer to capital as raw materials and instruments of labor. But when he wanted to point to the power of capital to structure society as a whole, he was more likely to refer to capital as an independent social power.

The result is a very complex idea of what constitutes 'truth', which now becomes a difficult term to retain if one is to avoid falling back into Enlightenment categories of analysis. Susan Hekman is right to point to many similarities between Marx's claims about truth and a number of Foucault's positions. She states tellingly that, despite these similarities, Foucault would argue that the discourses of the oppressed are just that, and are not closer to 'reality'. But she also recognizes that these discourses may, however, be closer to 'a definition of a less repressive society' (1997, 10).

Marxist theories (and feminist standpoint theories) also remind us that the categories and criteria for judging truth that come most immediately to mind are likely to be those of the dominant groups. Thus, Marx could argue that everything appears reversed in competition, and that the accumulation of wealth in capitalism is at the same time the accumulation of misery. Yet these categories and criteria are *made* true for all members of society. One can think of many examples such as this –compulsory heterosexuality enforced as a 'truth', not discovered but made real through a variety of practices and sanctions.

My arguments for adopting a feminist standpoint, following Lukács' discussion of the standpoint of the proletariat, recognize the danger of the slogan, 'Ye shall know the truth and the truth shall set you free.' In the context of power relations extant in many parts of the globe, 'knowing the truth' is much more likely to get you jailed or disappeared. Both Marx and Lukács recognized that truth and power are intimately connected: what is to count as truth, methods for obtaining it, criteria for evaluation – all are profoundly influenced by extant power relations.

To turn to the second issue – the nature of subjects and their possibilities of agency – I found in Marx and Marxist theories the kinds of social constructivist theories of the subject that others have encountered only later in post-structuralism. But in contrast to the American tendency (certainly with the help of some European post-structuralists themselves) to interpret these theories in liberal pluralist, and in some cases libertarian terms, terms that rely only on accounts of the micro-processes of power, I found in Marxian thought an insistence on what some have called a 'global' as opposed to 'totalizing' theory (Hennessey, 1993). The focus is on the macro-processes of power, those that, although they may be played out in individual lives, can only be fully understood at the level of society as a whole. To claim that we can understand the totality of social relations from an individual perspective is as futile an effort as the claim that we could see everything from nowhere. But a focus on large-scale social forces highlights different aspects of the subject.

Thus, Marx can be read as providing a theory of the subject as subjected, as does Foucault. That is, one can read the essay on estranged labor, or the theory of surplus value in *Capital* (which I would argue are two versions of the same philosophical argument) as accounts of how men (and for him they are) constitute themselves as subjected, by pouring their lives into objects that belong to others. Yet Marx's theory of subjects/subjection differs from Foucault's in its stress on potentials and possibilities for developing other forms of subjectivity.[6] In addition, the Marxian theory of subjectivity is rightly classified as a 'theoretical antihumanism', an idea developed under this heading by Althusser and passed on by him to Foucault and Derrida. That is, the subjects who matter are not individual subjects who are simply human beings but subjects who are defined by their relation to larger collective subjects, or groups. And these groups must be understood as defined by macro-processes (whether languages, ideologies, or discourses) that structure societies as a whole. At the same time, these groups must not be seen as formed unproblematically by their subjection, that is by existing in a particular social location and therefore coming to (being forced to) see the world in a particular way. My effort to develop the idea of a feminist standpoint, in contrast to 'women's viewpoint', was an effort to appropriate this insight (Hartsock, 1983; 1998). Chela Sandoval's notion of the importance of strategic identity for women of color represents an important advance in understanding this process, as is her development of the notion of oppositional consciousness.[7]

Sandoval argues that U. S. third world feminism can function as a model for oppositional political activity in the United States. She proposes that we view the world as a kind of 'topography', defining points around which 'individuals and groups seeking to transform oppressive powers *constitute themselves* [italics added] as resistant and oppositional subjects' (1991, 4). She holds that once the 'subject positions' of the dominated are 'self-consciously recognized by their inhabitants' they can be 'transformed into more effective sites of resistance' (p. 4). She discusses a 'differential consciousness' which she states operates like the clutch of an automobile allowing the driver to engage gears in a 'system for the transmission of power' (p. 14).

Here, her views parallel to those of Gramsci who suggests that we rethink the nature of identity: 'our capacity to think and act on the world is dependent on other people who are themselves also both subjects and objects of history' (Gramsci, 1971, 346). In addition, one must reform the concept of 'the individual' to see it as a 'series of active relationships, a process in which individuality, though perhaps the most important, is not the only element to be taken into account'. Individuality, then, is to be understood as the 'ensemble of these relations . . . . to create one's personality means to acquire consciousness of them and to modify one's own personality means to modify the ensemble of these relations' (p. 352). Moreover, Gramsci holds that each individual is the synthesis of these relations and also of the history of these relations, a 'precis of the past' (p. 353). The constitution of the subject, then, is the result of a complex interplay of 'individuals' and larger-scale social forces. Groups are not to be understood, as Hekman seems to do, as aggregates of individuals. Moreover, the constitution of the 'collective subject' posited by standpoint theories requires an always contingent and fragile (re)construction/ transformation of these complex subject positions. As Kathi Weeks has put it, 'this project of transforming subject-positions into standpoints involves an active intervention, a conscious and concerted effort to reinterpret and restructure our lives . . . . A standpoint is a project, not an inheritance; it is achieved, not given' (1996, 101).

I shall turn now to my third point, the issue of privileged knowledge. As I have reflected on both these and other discussions of standpoint theories over the years, I have come to believe that it is the intertwining of issues of politics on the one hand with the more traditional philosophical questions concerning truth and knowledge on the other, along with their conflicting criteria for claims of epistemological validity, which have been responsible for much of the controversy. Standpoint theories must be recognized as essentially contested in much the same way that I argued the concept of power is essentially contested: that is, arguments about how to understand power rest on differing epistemologies. Still I prefer to see this as an indication that privileged knowledge claims represent a fertile terrain for feminist debates about power, politics, and epistemology.

Fundamentally, I take Marx to be arguing that the criteria for privileging some knowledges over others are ethical and political as well as purely 'epistemological'. The quotation marks here are to indicate that because of my reading of Marx I see ethical and political concepts as involving epistemological claims on the one hand, and ideas of what is to count as knowledge involving profoundly important political and ethical stakes on the other. Marx makes an important claim: knowledge that takes its starting point from the lives of those who have suffered from exploitation produces better accounts of the world than that of dominant groups. I want to expand this insight/argument and suggest that views from the margins, or views from below (defined in more heterogeneous terms than Marx would have) are both better and more clear-sighted. The criteria Marx proposes can provide important guidelines for contemporary theorists. First he argues that by adopting the standpoint of the working class, or of production, the dynamics of capitalist society can be much more fully understood. That is, not just the supposedly neutral workings of the 'free' market are to be taken into account, but also the ways in which production including the social relations of production creates products, markets, and consumers. Thus, the market becomes one of several social forces to be taken into account. Moreover, such a vantage point aids in the process of developing a utopian vision, a vision that seems particularly difficult to develop and maintain in the last years of the twentieth century with its unrelieved celebration of the market as the solution to all social problems.

Second, Marx argues for the privilege of some knowledges over others on the ground that they offer possibilities for the development of more human-friendly and freedom-friendly projects. Thus, contrary to Foucault's position which stresses the ways the different discourses develop and subject individuals in different ways, Marx stresses the power of groups of people to overcome their subjection and to use their creativity for their own purposes.

There is a third aspect to the claim that some knowledges are 'better' than others, and here I think Chela Sandoval has elaborated the most important point of Marx's analysis: the use of these knowledges for the self-conscious transformation of individuals into resistant, oppositional, and collective subjects. In the current context of a much fuller realization of globalization of markets in both labor and capital, the development of oppositional and collective subjects can only become a much more complicated series of tasks.

But to return more explicitly to the process by which consciousness is changed, or experience reinterpreted in standpoint terms, I think it is worth remembering that the vision of the ruling groups structures the material relations in which all parties are forced to participate and therefore cannot be dismissed as simply false. Given this formulation, I would like to underline once again the extent to which claims that interpretation is involved in an effort to discover truth are problematic. Truth is to a large extent what the dominant groups can make true; history is always written by the winners. Thus the understanding available to the oppressed must be struggled for, and represents an achievement that requires both the systematic analysis and the education that grows from political struggle to change those relations. This point is also the key to the reason I chose the term 'feminist' standpoint, rather than the standpoint of women.

The process of adopting a standpoint or, in other terms, developing an oppositional consciousness is described by Gloria Anzaldua (1987, 87): 'The process is inner...the struggle has always been inner and is played out in outer terrains.' One's location in the social structure does not change, but the understanding of its meaning shifts dramatically. In these terms the work of Michelle Cliff is particularly instructive. She describes the difficulty she had, a light-skinned Jamaican woman with a Ph.D. on the Italian Renaissance, in coming to approach herself as a subject, or in my terms adopting a standpoint. She states, in 'Note on Speechlessness', that she had internalized the 'message of anglocentrism, of white supremacy' (1985, 13). She notes that she began, through participation in the feminist movement, to retrace the African part of herself and to reclaim it. She is clear about the difficulty of the project. She says that, in an earlier book, she wrote as someone who was unable to 'recapture the native language of Jamaica' and so relied on English, but still wrote from a feminist consciousness, a consciousness of colonialism, and a knowledge of self-hatred (p. 16). As she began to write in a way that put her own identity and experience at the center, she notes that her writing style became a kind of shorthand. 'Write quickly before someone catches you. Before you catch yourself' (p. 16). Her writing is informed by and structured by her rage, and marks very clearly the struggle both political and personal – involved in taking up a position from which the dominant order becomes visible with all its distortions.

Michelle Cliff's struggles are illustrative as well of the final charge leveled against standpoint theories – whether my own or Lukács' original argument. These theories are held to describe actually existing working-class views or 'women's perspectives' that are constituted by oppression but are unaware of possible complicity in the oppression of others. As is evident from my discussion of the achieved character of a standpoint, it is constituted by more than oppression. Fredric Jameson has probably put it most clearly when he states that the experience of negative constraint and violence that occurs in the commodification of labor power dialectically produces the positive content of its experience as the self-consciousness of the commodity (1988, 67). Once again, Michelle Cliff's work is instructive. She looks back, to try to locate what happened. 'When did *we* (the light-skinned middle-class Jamaicans) take over from *them* as oppressors?' (1985, 67). Cliff is clearly conscious about her complicity with imperialism and racism. It is a central aspect of her ability to locate herself in a critical context.

In addition, Cliff writes of the 'insanity' and 'unreality' of the 'normal'. She writes of light-skinned middle-class Jamaicans that 'we were colorists and we aspired to oppressor status.... We were convinced of white supremacy. If we failed, our dark part had taken over: an inherited imbalance in which the doom of the creole was sealed.' She steps back to look at what she has written and states that this 'may sound fabulous, or even mythic. It is. It is insane' (1988, 78).

Moreover, I see Cliff, Anzaldua, and others as developing a kind of privileged knowledge that takes nothing of the dominant culture as self-evidently true. The privilege is earned by means of the struggle to overcome what the dominant culture tells us about the world and ourselves, the struggle to construct and live in a political community, and to build with it an accountable epistemological community.

The most important issue for me is the question of how we can use theoretical tools and insights to create theories of justice and social change that address the concerns of the present. Marx, for all of the difficulties with both his theoretical work and the state of actually (non) existing socialism, calls our attention to certain macro-level issues to be addressed. In addition, one can find in the work of theorists such as Gramsci much more useful and complex theorizations of relations between 'individuals' and society as a whole, which open up the possibilities for both new knowledges and new collectivities.

Notes

1. I owe this phrasing to Kathi Weeks.
2. Note that I write here of women with no effort to mark the category. I do so because that is faithful to the project I had at the time I read Marx, and to the projects of many other feminists in the early 1970s.
3. See, for example, Donna Haraway's chapter 'Universal Donors in a Vampire Culture' and her discussion of OncoMouseTM in *Modest_ Witness@Second_Millennium* (New York: Routledge, 1997).
4. Achilles was one of the first to want to be born again in legend and song. He prayed that he would do some great thing before he died and so could live on after his bodily death.
5. Harvey (1996, 49). See also Ollman's statement quoted by Harvey (48):

   'Dialectics restructures our thinking about reality by replacing the common-sense notion of 'thing' as something that *has* a history and *has* external connections to other things, with notions of 'process', which contains its history and possible futures, and 'relation', which contains as a part of what it is its ties with other relations. (Ollman, 1993, 11)

6. Because I want to adapt Marx to the concerns of contemporary feminism, I want to change the ideas about the potential subjectivities of the proletariat and its 'historic mission' and expand on the concept of potential. Bell hooks (1990), rather than arguing for such a mission, has discussed potential subjectivities under the heading of 'yearning' for a different and better world.

7. She made an excellent point in her essay on the development of the category of 'women of color' out of the consciousness-raising sessions at the 1981 National Women's Studies Association meetings; see Sandoval, 1990. Much of what follows comes from Sandoval's article, 'U. S. Third World Feminism' (Sandoval, 1991).

References

Anzaldua, Gloria. 1987. *Borderlands/La Frontera*. San Francisco, California: Aunt Lute Foundation.

Benhabib, Seyla. 1990. 'Epistemologies of Modernism'. In Linda Nicholson, ed., *Feminism/Postmodernism*. New York: Routledge.

Cliff, Michelle. 1985. *The Land of Look Behind*. Ithaca, New York: Firebrand Books.

Cliff, Michelle. 1988. 'Speaking from Silence'. In Rick Simonson and Scott Walker, eds., *Graywolf Annual Five: Multicultural Literacy*. St. Paul, Minnesota: Graywolf Press.

Ebert, Teresa. 1996. *Ludic Feminism and After*. New York: Routledge.

Eisenstein, Zillah. 1982. *The Radical Future of Liberal Feminism*. New York: Longman.

Engels, Friedrich. 1978. 'Speech at the Graveside of Karl Marx'. In Tucker, ed., *The Marx-Engels Reader*. Second edition. New York: Norton, pp. 681–82.

Ferguson, Kathy. 1993. *The Man Question*. Berkeley, California: University of California Press.

Gramsci, Antonio. 1971. *Prison Notebooks*, ed. and trans., Quintin Hoare and Geoffry Nowell. New York: International Publishers.

Harraway, Donna. 1990. 'Situated Knowledges'. In *Simians, Cyborgs, and Women*. New York: Routledge.

Hartmann, Heidi. 1981. 'The Unhappy Marriage of Marxism and Feminism'. In Lydia Sargent, ed., *Women and Revolution: A Discussion of the Unhappy Marriage of Marxism and Feminism*. Boston: South End Press.

Hartsock, Nancy. 1983. 'The Feminist Standpoint: Toward a Specifically Feminist Historical Materialism'. In *Money, Sex, and Power*. New York: Longman.

Hartsock, Nancy. 1998. 'The Feminist Standpoint Revisited'. In *The Feminist Standpoint Revisited and Other Essays*. Boulder, Colorado: Westview Press.

Harvey, David. 1996. *Justice, Nature, and the Geography of Difference*. New York: Blackwell.

Hekman, Susan. 1997. 'Truth and Method: Feminist Standpoint Theory Revisited'. *Signs: Journal of Women in Culture and Society*, 22 (Winter).

Hennessey, Rosemary. 1993. *Materialist Feminism and the Politics of Discourse*. New York: Routledge.

Hooks, Bell. 1990. 'Postmodern Blackness'. Ch. 3 in *Yearning*. Boston: South End Press.

Jameson, Fredric. 1988. 'History and Class Consciousness as an "Unfinished Product" '. *Rethinking Marxism*, 1:1 (Fall).

234 Marxist Feminist Dialectics for the Twenty-first Century

Jameson, Fredric. 1996. 'Actually Existing Marxism'. In Saree Makdisi, Cesare Casarino and Rebecca F. Karl, eds., *Marxism Beyond Marxism.* New York: Routledge.

Marx, Karl, and Frederick Engels. 1976. *Collected Works,* Vol. 5. New York: International Publishers.

Ollman, Bertell. 1971. *Alienation: Marx's Concept of Man in Capitalist Society.* New York: Cambridge University Press.

Ollman, Bertell. 1993. *Dialectical Investigations.* New York: Routledge.

Sandoval, Chela. 1990. 'Feminism and Racism: A Report on the 1981 National Women's Studies Association Conference'. In Gloria Anzaldual, ed., *Making Face, Making Soul? Haciendo Caras.* San Francisco, California: Aunt Lute Foundation.

Sandoval, Chela. 1991. 'U. S. Third World Feminism: The Theory and Method of Opposition Consciousness in the Postmodern World'. *Genders,* No. 10 (Spring).

Weeks, Kathi. 1996. 'Subject for a Feminist Standpoint'. In Saree Makdisi, Cesare Casarino and Rebecca E. Karl, eds., *Marxism Beyond Marxism.* New York: Routledge.

18
Dialectic as Praxis

Joel Kovel

As a theoretical identity dialectic is considered passé by fashionable schools of thought, Marxist and non-Marxist alike (Smith, 1993). Yet few are the commentators upon the human situation who can resist the impulse to employ the term in the most diverse intellectual settings. What is striking about this is that 'dialectic', so used, is frequently assigned a positive value. It is tacitly considered good to be dialectical, or some argument is rejected on grounds of not being dialectical enough, and so forth. We have all seen such usage on countless occasions. It is as if thought retrieves a memory of some primeval dialectical virtue long past the moment when prevailing philosophical opinion would justify this.

At first glance this virtue of dialectic seems easy to explain as a function of being a methodological principle. If dialectic is a way of seeking out the truth in propositions, then it would seem self-evidently good to be dialectical, or to do something dialectically. It is odd, however, to find virtue in something which, so long as it remains a mere methodological principle, cannot have a status greater than the instrumental. It is as if we praised someone for speaking grammatically, or walking upright. To merit the category of virtue, something needs to include an ethical dimension, which in turn implies that it may be chosen with greater or lesser degrees of freedom. If we apply this line of reasoning to dialectic, we are led to greatly expand its meaning over that of a method, or technique.

I would argue that the term, dialectic, refers not simply to a method. It is better to call it, with Ollman, 'a way of thinking that brings into focus the full range of changes and interactions that occur in the world' (1993, 10). But this raises the questions, first, of what the world has to be like in order that dialectic help us to see it better, and second, of what we have to be like in order to think dialectically in the world. And these questions suggest that dialectic is best regarded as a form taken by *praxis*: consciously chosen, transformative activity grounded in and reflective of a particular worldview. Praxis implies a dynamic unity of theory with practice. Dialectic as praxis includes a methodology of thought, but dialectical thought surpasses a simple reflection of reality to the degree that we participate in and transform the real (Marx, 1978a).

This might be better appreciated with a look at the genealogy of the term. The notion of dialectic appears at the dawn of reflective thought on the European continent. (Given the limits of this essay, I will not be able to consider associated developments in China, India, and elsewhere, important as these may be.) As employed in the ancient Ionian/Greek setting, the term arises from the notions of discourse, *dialektike*; and of the art of debate, *dialektos*. In other words, insofar as dialectic is a methodological theme, it was not originally a set of logical rules, but a social relationship from which logical rules were secondarily abstracted. As first employed by the Parmenidean, Zeno, and later expanded by Socrates, Plato, and Aristotle, dialectic contains the sense conveyed by its congener, 'dialog', as a collective pursuit whose means is conversation. Dialectic is distinguished from dialog and other kinds of debate by its ends, the sense of which is conveyed by the 'love of wisdom' that is the literal meaning of 'philosophy'. Wisdom, of course, is much more than validation. It is an appropriation of reality, from the cosmos to life forms to the world of humanity, in proper interrelationship and integrated with the sense of right conduct. Beginning with the Pre-Socratic Ionians, ancient Greek speculative thought was engaged in an endeavor for which the emblem of science could be just as well applied as that of philosophy – a science, needless to add, as far above the segmented domain of contemporary science in theoretical scope and ethical implication as it was below it in technological capacity. In any case, the original sense of dialectic is clearly an instance of praxis.

All humans, and all human groups, are not only capable of philo-sophical thought; they freely produce this as an integral part of their encounter with existential givens (Radin, 1957). To paraphrase Marx, however, they do not produce it as they please, but from their specific historical situation. The worldview of early Greek philosophy was defined by a developing twofold recognition: that nature undergoes continual change and flow; and that society is shaped by the vagaries of a conflicted, power-hungry human creature. Therefore reality was not transparent, and a truth existed behind appearances. Specific social conditions defined both the necessity and the limits of early dialectical thought. As Edward Hussey put it, these included, 'an alphabetic script, a fairly general distribution of wealth, and a sense of belonging to a natural community, upon the welfare of which one's own welfare closely depended' (1972, 9). This can be abstracted as follows: the emergence of dialectical praxis, and speculative thought within that praxis, depended upon a threefold social process: (1) a development within language that permitted its practical and self-reflexive use; (2) production and distribution of social surplus that permitted a division of labor in which relatively autonomous speculation could take place; and (3) the development of mutually recognizing individuals drawn together for this purpose.

For the third characteristic we have to thank the peculiarities of Greek society, in which, to return to Hussey's words, 'for the first time in human history communities of men were regulated by impartial rules which they themselves had deliberately chosen and assented to, and which could be discussed and altered with the consent of the majority' (1972, 9). The value of this arrangement should not be inflated. With its exclusion of women, slaves, and the poor, the Greek *polis* was only a way station on the road to real democracy. But it represented a valid transitional form, a place where self-positing individuals, equipped with the potentials of literacy and a degree of free time, could come together to ponder the nature of things beyond appearances, and pass this along to future generations.

Dialectic posits a social relation grounded in dialog and struggle – and also the internalization of that relationship into rules of logic that can be carried out by individuals and formalized. Dialectic is a faculty arising at a certain stage of historical development, in which a newfound power is affirmed, but also a degree of uncertainty and conflict. Indeed, conflict is its matrix, as well as what it overcomes not with finality, but only to arrive at new levels of contradiction. Dialectic is specific to class society, because this is the site where its basic preconditions – literacy, the leisure of a privileged minority gained through an expropriated surplus, and a problematized individuality in a field of conflict - are produced.

Literate culture comes at a cost when viewed against the backdrop of the sensuous immediacy of the directly transmitted speech experienced by state-free primitives. However, its very departure from the more finely differentiated life-worlds of primary societies introduces a temporalization into thought that is to be decisive in human intellectual history, including the history of dialectic. Once an alphabetized script is employed for philosophizing, then thought becomes objectified and reproducible. It is, so to speak, put on the table where it can be examined and tested. Since this is spread out over time and across generations, and since the philosophical positions thus advanced are to become the province of differing social formations, each necessarily partial, it follows that a literately produced philosophy must become differentiated into 'schools' which fight out their individual interpretations of truth. This process, which roughly speaking first takes shape in the contestations of Pythagoreans, Parmenideans, and Heracliteans, and then among other schools of Greek thought, continues in today's ever more fragmented intellectual field. It is harder to imagine a class-based civilization without intellectual warfare than one without military warfare.

Praxes are not automatic but matters of choice; and what can be chosen can also be not chosen. Dialectic therefore expresses no necessity; it can be no more than an option allowed within class society. But one does not mark a ballot with the word, dialectic, upon it to take this option. The choice follows, rather, from attending, within the manifold of life processes, to forms of becoming, creativity, and contingency, as against those of being, stability, and predictability. In the history of class society, this position coincides with that of the underclass, while the suppression of dialectic has come to express an option for the *status quo*. This may suggest a reason for the eclipse of dialectic in our reactionary time.

To practice dialectic well, an individual has to be open to contradiction and emergence. Dialectic is therefore for those who accept struggle, in the hope that truer knowing and a better world might be the outcome. This choice is made existentially and in a state of risk, as struggle can also make things worse. Though dialectical thinking needs to be objectively testable, there can be no intellectual proof for these essentially pretheoretical options. Nonetheless, the virtue of dialectics adheres to this complex of dialog, openness to conflict, and hopefulness. As a praxis, dialectic implies an ethic as well as a method. We act dialectically as we remain open to contradictions, even to preserve them in a kind of suspension, through a faith that this leads to a deeper knowledge and a freer development. Dialectic is inherently emancipatory: it allows otherness its presence and welcomes difference even as it eschews relativism. It knows that the *Aufhebung* does not happen automatically, but requires that contradictions, which tend to fly apart like the similar poles of a magnet, be held together so that their inner, hidden life can unfold. Dialectic is for those with radical hope, which is suppressed in counter-revolutionary times such as ours.

The nature of dialectic and the dialectic of nature

We talk of *a* dialectic, as the particular line of contradictory development open to something (as, the dialectic of sex, of enlightenment, of money, of an individual life, etc.), and think of history as a kind of fabric woven out of the strands of individual dialectics according to the orientation of the superordinate dialectic of class struggle. But dialectics is also the system of thought woven out of the ontological assumptions inherent in and consistent with dialectical praxis and method. The first thinker who can authentically be called dialectical (though we lack evidence that he used the term), Heraclitus, put it in some of his fragments, composed before the formalization of dialectic into pure method tended to seal off ontological claims: 'The nature of things is in the habit of concealing itself' (Fr. 123); 'war is father of all, and king of all . . .' (Fr. 53); 'conjunctions: wholes and not wholes, the converging the diverging, the consonant the dissonant, from all things one, and from one all things' (Fr. 10: Hussey, 1972, 35, 49, 45).

At its most abstract this can be stated as follows: there is a tendency in reality toward absencing and presencing which devolves into a general 'becomingness' that affects thought as well as the external world. Further, this pattern problematizes all seemingly stable formations. There are a number of implications to be drawn.

First, dialectic is intrinsically critical. Since its central term is becoming, nothing can be seen as merely what it is, or appears to be. This critical function can – and should – be applied to dialectic itself. That is, all practiced dialectics can be no more than approximations to their own potential. Were a dialectic perfect, it could not be dialectic, since it would be outside the domain of becoming and creativity. This principle tells us that individual dialectics admit of (dialectical) study. We can talk of dialectical stasis, fragmentation, splitting, differentiation, flow, and so on; in short, develop a critique of dialectical forms (see Bhaskar, 1993, for an exploration in this vein).

Efforts to read dialectic directly into non-human nature are undialectical. Since a 'dialectic of anything' must include praxis, a dialectic of nature posits that nature directly manifests the relation between theory and practice characteristic of human beings. This would make the human and non-human worlds identical in their most fundamental feature. However, since it is the 'nature' of human beings to differentiate themselves from the rest of nature (as by wearing clothing, preparing food, ritualizing death, etc.), such a proposition denies human being itself, and thereby denies dialectic. A denial of this kind masquerading as dialectical thought may be considered a 'split' dialectic, in the sense developed above. A more fully realized (or 'differentiated') dialectic, by contrast, uses the principle of negation, in which difference is both affirmed and sublated, in the sense first postulated by Heraclitus' fragment 10. The disjunction between humanity and nature extends to the knowing of nature, which can never be fully realized. Even though the project of scientific reflection upon nature has no end, science itself sets the limits of human cognition of nature (as, for example, through discoveries such as quantum indeterminacy and Gödel's Theorem).

Dialectic resists totalization, yet moves in the direction of totality. The 'what is not' that accompanies every existent being links each entity to a more inclusive whole without collapsing the part into the whole, and demands that the perspective of this whole be taken if the reality of any being is to be comprehended (or, in terms of dialectic, approximated). This kind of reasoning resembles what has been called the 'ecocentric position', and has been extensively used to criticize the mechanical paradigms of an ecologically annihilating society. What is missing in most ecological thought of this kind, however, is the rigorous distinction between human and non-human spheres of nature given in dialectical negation.

Within nature, we see interconnectedness and processual flow, but nothing so stark as a consistently unfolding negative. Negation may be regarded as the abstraction of the critical method essential for dialectical practice. It is the reasoning through contradiction, seeking the 'what is not' within the 'what is', and the succession of negations and negations of negations that follow from this. The error of seeking a 'dialectics of nature' consists in seeking to impose upon the subtleties of nature, which dialectic itself shows to be fundamentally unknowable, the spurious formulaic of a procession of logical negations, negations of negations, and so on. What can be used as a laser for logical dissection turns into a chainsaw when projected directly into nature. In this respect projecting a series of negations into the actual physical world amounts to a false positivism; it is, in a word, undialectical.

Dialectic would not split humanity from nature, however, but needs to find ways of differentiating the two. This reasoning raises two questions, although they are really a single question viewed from different ends:

(1) Can more be said as to objective correlates within nature to the principle of negation; that is, can the subtle processes of nature be further abstracted into some 'negation-like' principle without

sinking into the positivism which imposes a logical category onto a physical one?

(2) What can be said about the condition of humanity within nature – 'human nature' that helps account for dialectical logic; that is, what can be said about the mediations between nature, practice, and logic that give rise to a dialectic configured to reality?

In shorthand jargon, we seek a 'metaphysics' and a 'philosophical anthropology', consistent with each other and free from essentialism and social reductionism. About the first project, the search for a metaphysic adequate to account for the emergence of dialectic, which is to say, of conscious human beings prone to negativity, I can have nothing to say here except that some very interesting work is being done toward this goal (see, for example, Gare, 1996, for a comprehensive view; and in a very far-reaching, though inconclusive and highly controversial, contribution from mathematical physics, Penrose, 1990; 1994).

As to the latter consideration, a bit more may be said, though only in a most fragmentary and preliminary way. To understand human nature is to use dialectical methodology to reflect upon the origins of dialectic in a natural creature. For what is specific about human nature is, as noted above, the propensity to break with nature while remaining part of nature. Thus human nature is defined negatively: the human being is the animal who says 'no'. We refuse to accept the difference between the sexes; we refuse to accept separation; we refuse domination; we refuse to accept death. Or, through further negations, we can refuse to refuse, and come to accept all these things as well, in different lines of dialectical development. Negation is as much part of our species identity as flight defines the eagle or colony building the ant. Marx framed it in a foundational passage from the *Manuscripts:* 'Neither nature objectively nor nature subjectively is directly given in a form adequate to the *human* being' (1978b, 116). This indicates the anthropological basis for production, as the species-specific activity which transforms nature into adequate objects.

Marx does not reflect further into the reasons for humanity's restless dissatisfaction. To do so would require enquiry into the nature of the self, that uniquely human formation in which consciousness is detached from immediacy and given space to reflect upon itself as subject. The medium of this reflection is not physical light but the stuff of language (which enters into dialectical praxis when it can be written down). Language is not confined to the accumulating of information or any merely biological schema. It is the actual locus for the coming to be of what is human. We may trace here that twofold motion in language in which the naming of a thing both claims that thing and separates from that thing (Kovel, 1989).

Nature gives rise to distinct beings who interconnect and flow back and forth into one another; this is the primordium of dialectic. Then nature evolves human being, wherein the separateness and unstructuredness of a being (co-evolving with neurological capacity, upright posture, an opposable thumb, etc.) enable representational, subjective, inner space to emerge along with physical, outer space. Negativity is the relation set going by this pairing, as languaged consciousness emerges, to claim and deny reality. Mutually interacting beings with divided subjectivities come together to create society and, at their best, strive for wisdom, using the abstractions from negativity that cohere into dialectic.

Dialectic indicates the whole, but cannot itself be the end. Dialectic is emancipatory insofar as it remains grounded in a refusal that protests the mutilations imposed by class society – a refusal that must, if spun out, extend to the overcoming of class society itself along with all domination that splits human beings from one another, from non-human nature, and from their own nature. At that moment, which today only appears in imaginary form, dialectic will yield, and a new form of radical knowing grounded in a unified subject may make its claim.

References

Bhaskar, Roy. 1993. *Dialectic: The Pulse of Freedom*. London and New York: Verso.

Gare, Arran. 1996. *Nihilism, Incorporated*. Sydney, Australia: Eco-Logical Press.

Hussey, Edward. 1972. *The Pre-Socratics*. New York: Charles Scribner's Sons.

Kovel, Joel. 1989. 'Things and Word'. In *The Radical Spirit*. London: Free Association Books.

Marx, Karl. 1978a (1845). 'Theses on Feuerbach'. In Robert Tucker, ed., *The Marx Engels Reader*. New York: W. W. Norton.

Marx, Karl. 1978b (1844). 'Economic and Philosophical Manuscripts'. In Robert Tucker, ed., *The Marx-Engel Reader*. New York: W. W. Norton.

Ollman, Bertell. 1993. *Dialectical Investigations*. New York and London: Routledge.

Penrose, Roger. 1990. *The Emperor's New Mind*. New York and Oxford: Oxford University Press.

Penrose, Roger. 1994. *Shadow of the Mind*. New York and Oxford: Oxford University Press.

Radin, Paul. 1957. *Primitive Man as Philosopher*. New York: Dover.

Smith, Tony. 1993. *Dialectical Social Theory and Its Critics*. Albany, New York: State University of New York Press.

19

Livant's Cure for Baldness

Bill Livant

Shrink your head to fit the hair you've got left. It's Livant's cure for baldness. And it's free. If you're not bald, this may be funny. If you are, it's probably not. Why? Why not? This example simply highlights what is true of 'fitting' in general. It is never symmetric. It is never equal. The problem of fitting *appears* to be a problem of fitting *two* things into *one*. But two things are never 'fit together'. One thing is always fit to the other. The amount of hair can be adjusted to fit one's head, but the size of one's head can't be altered to accommodate the amount of hair one has left. Fitting is always *asymmetric*, always *unequal*. And when it appears that fitting is equal, you will find that this is a temporary, local moment in that particular fitting process as a whole.

Notice that the bald fellow has a problem; he is trying to turn a bad thing into a good one. He is trying to fix something that is wrong. This is the most concrete way we can grasp the particular character of 'fitting': it is an attempt to *fix* something. Here we encounter the problem of fitting in a form where it is *inherently in motion*. We are not just trying abstractly to 'fit things together'; we are trying to repair a wrong. This brings out very dramatically the *inherently asymmetric* nature of the things being fitted. No matter what area you apply this to, you will see that the *right* and the *wrong* of the two things you *appear* to be trying to 'combine' are never equal. There is always a solvent and a solute, always a main thing and a secondary thing. One is always primarily wrong with respect to the other.

With this in mind, we need to devote more attention to *mis*fitting, to when two things *don't* fit. Here, one thing appears to be 'too big', or 'too fast', or 'too sharp', or 'too slow', or 'too dull' for the other. Now, *formally* you might have said that the latter is 'too small', or 'too slow', or 'too dull' for the former. *Formally*, they appear to be two descriptions

243

of the same identical inequality. But *in practice* they are never the same. They are always different. This is why you *do* have *too little* hair for your head. You *do not* have *too much* head for the amount of hair you have.

We can make the same point if we consider this from the point of view (as we should) of *motion* of your hairless head. Your head is not increasing in size; your hair is diminishing. The problem arises when that motion is turned into its opposite. It is the motion of the whole which, if we take a frozen snapshot, appears fixed as an *equality of inequalities*. It appears that

$$A > B = B < A$$

A good deal of our present mathematics depends on that appearance. But, when we really get to work on a concrete problem, this is never so.

The problem of fitting is important because of its particular practical character. We can study through a microscope what is also true of matters that are far grander and far more theoretical than growing hair. Consider, for example, Darwin's fundamental dynamics of evolution. What is it that powers evolution for him? It is asymmetry, in which we can find both quantitative and qualitative aspects. Regarding the first, there are always *too many* organisms for their habitat. As for the second, there are always some organisms that are *more fit* for their conditions than others. These distinctions constitute the logical core of Darwin's theory of evolution.

The asymmetry that we discover wherever we look leads us to still another conclusion. An inequality always has *two aspects*. They are > and <. Just what is the relation of A > B and B < A? Do they require each other as a condition of each other's existence? Yes, of course. They are in fact a unity. Also, is it the case that one can be transformed into the other? Again, yes. In formal mathematics, this is not just a possibility; it is *absolute*, always and everywhere true. But as soon as we consider it from the point of view of *material practice*, we find that this transformation is *not* absolute. It is *relative*. It happens only under certain conditions, and these conditions do not last. They are temporary and local. > and < are a *unity*. What we have just described is the *identity* of > and <. But in practice, as we found, there is also *struggle*. In fact, one formulation of the inequality will prevail; the other will be defeated. Go back to our bald man again; this is just what happens.

What we have been describing above is, in fact, no less than the *identity* and *struggle of the unity of opposites*, '>' and '<'. This is quite general.

Consider for a moment the social and natural science of the bourgeoisie with which you are familiar. It is not so crude as to say that inequalities do not *exist*. It does not claim that > and < do not exist, that A = B = C = D, and so on. But what we must attend to is the way it treats inequality, the way it treats > and <. The science of the bourgeoisie *reduces the unity of > and < to their identity*. It makes permanent what is really temporary; it makes general what is really local; it makes absolute what is really relative. This is the *analytical liquidation of struggle*, and it pervades virtually all the analyses made within bourgeois science.

To sum up, 'fitting' is always asymmetric, and, therefore, so too is what is taken to be 'combination'. Yet, so long as we view it as combination, its necessary asymmetric character remains to be explained. But, within this view, an adequate explanation is impossible. The alternative is that what we have before us is *not combination at all but division*. But to grasp it as division requires that we understand 'fitting' as really 'fixing', for it is only then that the right and wrong character of each part inside their mutual dependence stands out in sharp relief.

The moral? 'Combination', wherever it is invoked, conceals asymmetry. It therefore conceals the *struggle of opposites*. And it erases the *class struggle*. This is why in the *Communist Manifesto* Marx and Engels did not begin their analysis of capitalist society with the middle class. They knew that to start an analysis with a symmetric notion like the middle class, one wouldn't know what they were in the middle of. To discover what is in the middle, they had to begin with the two ends. They had to begin with and emphasize social asymmetry. Of course, neither Marx nor Engels was ever in much need for Livant's cure for baldness.

20
Dialectics and Wisdom

Ira Gollobin

Wisdom is seldom even mentioned in presentations of dialectical materialism, let alone treated as a constituent part of its subject matter.[1] Yet wisdom is not a mere adornment or contrived appendage to an exposition of dialectical materialism, but an integral component, essential to round out, to complete its wholeness. The rationale for studying it is that the aspects of dialectical materialism are very general constituents of wisdom and that wisdom involves a vital sphere, an integral level of their exemplification. Knowledge of these aspects is invaluable in guiding thought (the intellect and the feelings) to a high level of rationality, to a totality, a fullness of farseeing profound insights characteristic of wisdom. In providing the very general underpinning for a scientific approach to wisdom, philosophy returns to its classic form of genesis as a sense of wonder and love of wisdom, but enriched by the content of thought garnered during the intervening millennia.

Prescientific views

The origins of wisdom long antedate civilization's first philosophers. For Cro-Magnon man, who possessed a range of tools, as well as a lunar calendar, and also humans who lived in earlier epochs, their technology permitted a range of choices with respect to ends and means. However circumscribed this range may have been, choice for them did involve some indicia of wisdom, albeit at primitive levels and in incipient, inchoate form. Preclass society assigned to wisdom a vital place in tribal affairs, conferring on the personifications of wisdom, such as a shaman or sachem, a major role in tribal decisions.

Preclass society's collective, tribal wisdom was replaced by antagonism: the wisdom of the ruled (the oppressed) and the wisdom of the ruler (the oppressor). Attesting to the high esteem in which the mass of people regarded wisdom, rulers in early class society sought to place this attribute beyond the reach of the oppressed. By ascribing wisdom exclusively to divinity, the possession of wisdom by mortals became a dispensation granted or withheld at a deity's caprice. In Sumerian mythology, in which possession or lack of wisdom often made the difference between success or disaster for humans, the god in charge of the abyss (Enki) 'was the god of wisdom' (Kramer, 1959, 94).

In the Book of Job in the Bible, there is the query:

> Where shall wisdom be found and where is the place of understanding? Man does not know the way to it and it is not found in the land of the living. The deep says: Not in me and the sea says: not in me. It is hidden from the eyes of all living and concealed from the birds of the air; only abyss and death say: we have heard a rumor of it with our ears. (Tillich, 1963, 165–6.)

Wisdom is thus hidden in a realm beyond human aspiration, an eternal mystery, a prerogative of deity.[2] 'With God is wisdom and might...he will extend a nation to destroy it, he will enlarge a nation to enslave it....Should not his majesty cause you to shudder?' (Tillich, 1963, 166). For the mass of people there is only obeisance. A biblical maxim concisely sums up the essence of the wisdom that rulers reserve for the oppressed: 'The fear of the Lord is the beginning of Wisdom...' (Proverbs, 7:19). In Greek and Roman mythology, wisdom is associated with great power, arising full-grown as a goddess (Athena, Minerva), the mental offspring of the ruler of the gods (Zeus, Jupiter).

Whether in veiled form as descendants of a deity or in outright ruling-class garb (e.g., in ancient China), rulers in slave society treated wisdom as an attribute to which only they had access. Thus, Confucius 'believed that "the upper class of men" were "those born possessing knowledge" and "the lowest of the people", namely the slaves, were "those who are dull and stupid and do not learn." "The wise upper class" and "the stupid lower class" were born so and could not be changed' (*Peking Review*, 1971,8).

An awareness of this swindle, this denial of basic human capacity and the worth of skilled labor, is reflected in Lao Tzu's comment some 2500 years ago: 'It was when "knowledge" and "wisdom" appeared that the Great Lie began' (Needham, 1956, 109). And Chuang Tzu wrote, 'Do not those who are vulgarly called wise prove to be but collectors for the great thieves? And do not those who are considered sages then prove to be but guardians in the interest of the great thieves? ... Therefore, if an end were put to "sageness" and "wisdom", great robbers would cease to arise. ...' (p. 102). Yet, indicating its initial positive, work-related connotation, the Greek word *sophistes* originally meant 'skilled craftsman' or 'wise man' (Freeman, 1962, 125).

Some intellectuals among the ruling class refused to toady to the dominant mores. For them 'the distinction between science and philosophy did not exist' (Piaget, 1972, 44). Identifying wisdom with objective fundamental truth, Heraclitus wrote that wisdom is 'to understand the purpose which steers all things through all things' and 'to speak the truth and to act according to nature, paying heed thereto'; those 'who love wisdom must be inquirers into very many things indeed' (Freeman, 1962, 27, 32). Aristotle maintained 'that wisdom is a science dealing with first principles' and that 'sophistry', the partly true and partly specious learning dispensed by some itinerant teachers, 'is but apparent wisdom ...' (1963, 221, 65). He affirmed that 'physics too is a kind of wisdom' (p. 67).

In popular mythology, as in the legends of Prometheus and Hercules, and in proverbs, the exploited evinced an unshaken belief in their own version of wise ends (values) and wise means to attain these ends. Confronted by a world infested by monsters, both human and supernatural, that served their oppressors, the people in their wisdom created a hero to symbolize their defiance of material and spiritual bonds. The titan Prometheus was chained to a rock by Zeus for having brought fire to mankind and instruction in the crafts. To Hermes, the messenger of the gods, who brought Zeus' offer of release in return for submission, Prometheus responded,

> In simple words,
> I hate the pack of gods.
> Be sure of this, I would not change my state Of evil
> fortune for your servitude.
> Better to be the servant of this rock
> Than to be faithful boy to Father Zeus.
>
> (Aeschylus, *Prometheus Bound*)

Marx concluded the foreword to his doctoral dissertation on Greek philosophy: 'Prometheus is the most eminent saint and martyr in the philosophical calendar' (Marx, 1975, vol. I, 31).

Folklore constitutes a treasury of the people's deep inner life, their wisdom – the basic, durable residue of age-old collective experience and insight. Much of folklore expresses the masses' invincible aspirations for a better life – the values conducive to their welfare, and the interim principles for survival and eventual success.

A minority of the people turned toward introspection, seeking to escape oppression and scorning or fearing arduous and hazardous resistance. Withdrawal from social involvement, where possible, to a life behind monastery walls was proclaimed the way to wisdom. This transition is evidenced in the origins and history of the term *maya*, meaning wisdom.[3] Its roots are in preclass society in India, and 'the prehistory of this concept reveals a primordial complex of theory and practice, knowledge and action.... The concept of wisdom was originally inconceivable without the concept of activity... in a society in which the contempt for *karma* or action was yet to develop' (Chattopadhyaya, 1959, 648–49). Later, in class society, *maya* came to mean illusion (*avidya*), rationalizing withdrawal from the world and preoccupation with introspection. Wisdom became identified with the sage, envisaged as a person who, through contemplation, and in serene detachment from the travail and strife of class society, seeks and finds basic, eternal truths, and values which he implements in his mode of life.

Buddha's 'Four Noble Truths', declared by his disciples to be the quintessence of wisdom, convert the very real suffering of the enslaved masses in class society into the unreal, eternal suffering of all humanity (Chattopadhyaya, 1959, 502). The Buddhist way of wisdom via ceasing resistance to oppression was basically compatible with the exploiters' way of preserving themselves from assaults by the disaffected, for them a prime aspect of wisdom. Although exploiters regarded with disfavor Buddhism's moral code (which revived aspects of the more humane, egalitarian ethics of preclass society), the mode of social withdrawal– a safety valve – held up by Buddhism served to subdue and mute the masses' opposition to rulers. This weighed heavily in inducing slaveholders to vouchsafe sanctuary and prestige to the minority immured in monastic dissociation from society. Essentially, this wisdom of the few – assuring themselves a moral life based on a simplistic, isolated milieu, as well as safety from death or from enslavement by a master – was hinged on a pessimistic estimation of the prospects for liberation of the many. 'The individualists learned to use their own fear [of life] by trying to induce working people to accept it as sublime wisdom, as penetration into mysteries beyond the reach of reason' (Gorky, n.d., 219).

During the thousands of years of class society, despite period when the masses seemed dormant, they rejected social withdrawal and impotence. Whatever their fantasies, however blind their action and obscure their modes of resistance, a wisdom was present in their struggles, making these struggles links, in defeat as well as in victory, in social development toward a communist society. Underlying the struggle of the exploited – under slavery, feudalism, or early capitalism – there is a course of development of thought about communism, no matter how subterranean, that connects ancient with modern classless society. Whether in the fonn of the slave's fantasy of a regained Eden (a state of nature without oppressive labor) or of 'islands of the Sun' where 'land is by nature common and man by nature free (Siculus)' (Farrington, 1963, 84), or of the 'land of Cokaygne – the serfs dream of a world of peace, leisure and abundance' (Morton, 1952, 171) –throughout the epoch of class society, the aspiration for a world-to-be rid of social antagonism, continued in revolts of slaves, serfs, and wage workers – as well as in utopias – to challenge the imagination and will of the oppressed.

Scientific Views

Almost a thousand years ago, at a time when interest in science barely stirred in Western Europe, the center in Cairo, Egypt, of the efflorescence of science in the Muslim world, was named the House of Wisdom (Dar-el-Hikma). This acknowledged the pivotal relationship of science to wisdom. Joseph Dietzgen, however, maintained that such wisdom is a feature of the infancy of science, in which 'philosophy was at first impelled by the nebulous desire for universal world wisdom' (Dietzgen, 1906, 442), and that with the advent of the special sciences wisdom became an anachronism:

> While humanity had still little knowledge, a man might well be wise. But today it is necessary to specialize, to devote one's self to a special science, because the field of exploration has grown so extended. The philosopher of today is no longer a wise man, but a specialist. (Dietzgen, 1906, 334)

This view that specialization has supplanted wisdom is one-sided and mechanical. Specialization is not a terminus of cognition, but only a stage in advance that helps provide the data for a scientific synthesis, for a scientific level of wisdom, in place of the more elementary, somewhat 'nebulous' prescientific version. Specialization in science may in fact often be coupled with philosophical backwardness: 'It is true that many scientists are not philosophically minded and have hitherto shown much skill and ingenuity but little wisdom' (Born, 1949, 2).

Wisdom denotes a high level of comprehensiveness and profundity of knowledge and of values, much above the ordinary level of insights. It also possesses a considerable degree of concordance with reality, while expressing the highest interest of the individual, group, or class concerned. This enables a choice of ends and the means for their effectuation that would otherwise never come to mind. This extraordinary level of insight arises from a considerable range of knowledge, extending from a broad base of experience (especially regarding critical situations) to very general, scientific social knowledge (historical materialism) and very general, scientific philosophical knowledge (dialectical materialism). Wisdom constitutes a peak of thought, a high level of comprehension of wholeness, a wholeness that integrates the very general with the less general, as well as the intellect with the feelings, in understanding and in action.

Piaget states that dialectical materialism has 'all the features of a rational approach to the whole of reality, the concept of totality being central to Marxism' (Piaget, 1972, 40). Dialectical materialism is scientific philosophy, and, as such, 'a rational approach' to totality, just as chemistry, the science that superseded alchemy and other prescientific variants, is a rational approach to the molecular world.

Dialectical and historical materialism undergo continual deepening. The highest level of wisdom attainable at a particular time and locale is vitally connected with the most profound level of the theory and practice of dialectical and historical materialism realizable under the existing material conditions.

What is wise differs qualitatively from what is unwise. Each involves differences in levels and of degree that range from profound insights to folly. While it is true that a genius stands on the shoulders of giants, it is also true that, fundamentally, genius is centrally an extension of the wisdom of the people. Their creative thought and labor brings into being the basic material conditions that make possible the insights of genius.

There is an inherent societal wisdom, Marx noted, in the problems mankind undertakes to solve:

> Mankind ... inevitably sets itself only such tasks as it is able to solve, since closer examination will always show that the problem itself arises only when the material conditions for its solution are already present or at least in the course of formation (1970, 21)

For humans, values are a central part of reality, of the totality that dialectical materialism helps explore scientifically. Although humans do seek truth for the sake of truth, they above all seek it as a means to improve their lot in life. Values have two interrelated spheres: the relations of humans to each other and their relations to the universe. Both sets of relations develop and are clarified through technology, the sciences, and the arts, in the course of class struggle, the struggle for production, and scientific experiment. Major scientific discoveries impact on each of these spheres of values, discoveries in such spheres as (1) the origin of the universe (of this particular universe and as a stage in a recurrent, only partly similar cycle) and of life (on this planet and in general); and (2) plate tectonics, fusion power, computer 'intelligence', gene engineering, and colonization of other planets. This ceaseless human outreaching to the infinite bounds of basic knowledge and practice is expressed in Ivan Michurin's 'Man must not wait for favors from Nature, he must wrest them from her' (Bernal, 1954, 668), and in Konstantin E. Tsiolkovsky's 'Our planet is the cradle of reason, but one cannot live forever in the cradle' (Vanvarovond and Fadeyev, 1962, 21).

Values are not confined to the realm of ethics, but are present in the sciences as well:

> Thus the world of physics does not consist of isolated atoms or isolated qualities, and the world of ethics does not consist of isolated preferences. The world of physics, like the world of ethics, is a world in which there are real connections, and if we recognize the reality or objectivity of these connections, then we shall have no difficulty in recognizing that ideals are the proper subject matter not only of ethics and mathematics, but also of physical and other theoretic sciences (Cohen, 1956, 172; cf. 78–9, 178, 182–3)

The 'why' and 'how' of values – their generality – are largely susceptible to scientific analysis and synthesis. Coordinated and structured in systems of morality (or moral theories), values are mainly law-governed, and only secondarily a matter of chance. Taken as a whole and in the long run, systems of morality and moral theories are correlated with a society's mode of production, and in class society they exhibit an essential polarization:

> All former moral theories are the product, in the last analysis, of the economic stage which society had reached at that particular epoch. And as society has hitherto moved in class antagonisms, morality was always a class morality; it has either justified the domination and the interests of the ruling class, or, as soon as the oppressed class had

become powerful enough, it has represented the revolt against this domination and the future interests of the oppressed (Engels, n.d., 109)

Knowledge and values are the inseparable outgrowth of the intellect and the emotions – the two basic components of thought. Thought and action involve ends, that is, a choice among values (including ethical and aesthetic norms) and means, such as the knowledge requisite for attaining these ends: 'philosophy certainly includes a position of·synthesis, which relates, however, to the coordination of all human values, and not to the coordination of knowledge alone' (Piaget, 1973, 13). Despite basic differences inherent in philosophies – in nonscientific philosophy as well as in dialectical materialism – there exists a uniformity of aim, the coordination of knowledge and values.

Dialectical materialism rejects absolutist, idealist versions of ethics (such as those that treat ethics as ordained by God) or relativist·versions (whatever a person desires is deemed to be good), as well as an eclecticism that bases ethics on abstract norms, ostensibly dissociated from the needs and aims of social classes, but actually grounded in the needs and aims of a particular class. The subordination of less general values to very general social values, and the preservation or destruction of an exploitive order, involve law-governed processes. Lenin wrote,

> We repudiate all morality that is taken outside of human, class concepts. We say that this is deception, a fraud.... our task is to subordinate everything to the interests of this [class] struggle. And we subordinate our Communist morality to this task. We say: Morality is that which serves to destroy the old exploiting society and to unite all the toilers around the proletariat (1943, Vol. IX, 475, 477)

Again quoting Lenin, ideals must be meshed indissolubly with 'the "narrow" and the earth-bound questions of the everyday life of the given class...' (Ignat'eva, 1962, 33).

Class society places its imprint on wisdom. The musings of the sage (the product of social contact and of considerable solitary contemplation or claimed divine inspiration) and the guile of rulers (in maintaining their oppression of the many) have been acclaimed as wellsprings of wisdom, while the masses' hard-earned experience and insights, gained in labor and class struggle amid a multitude of afflictions, have been denigrated by oppressors as the responses, sometimes docile, sometime violent, of beings little above the level of brutes. On the contrary, Mao claims, as regards the oppressed, 'in a sense the fighters with the most practical experience are the wisest and the most capable' (*Peking Review*, 1971, 15). The monopolization of the term 'wisdom' by exploiters has for centuries been so pervasive that not only for the mass of people in class society is wisdom usually remote, awesome, and elusive, but many Marxists study and even write about dialectical materialism without being aware that there is any significant gap left by their omission of wisdom.

In the last analysis, the masses are the makers of history: 'All wisdom comes from the masses' (Mao, 1977, V, 468); and, according to Lenin, 'the wisdom of tens of millions of creators creates something incomparably higher than the greatest prediction of genius' (Glezerman, 1970, 14). Throughout the ages, the role of the people has been central. Laboring people 'are far better than those lofty, erudite literati [Confucian classicists] at distinguishing between right and wrong' (Lu Hsun, 1960, IV, 241–2). It is absolutely essential for socialist intellectuals to 'feel themselves the same flesh and blood as the most humble, the most backward, and the least aware of our workers and peasants' (Gramsci, 1957, 16). Only in this way can intellectuals root themselves in the wisdom of the people and these two streams of wisdom realize their integrated and continually enlarging potential as the wisdom of the wise.

Admittedly, the average intellectual knows more than the average person in the street, but at issue in wisdom is not only what one knows but also what one does. Plekhanov says,

> The 'consciousness' of a man from the 'intelligentsia' is more highly developed than the consciousness of a man from the 'masses'. *But the 'being' of a man from the masses prescribes to him a far more definite method of action than that which the social position of the intellectual prescribes to the latter.* (Quoted in Lenin, 1961, 529)

Wisdom is not the exclusive prerogative of the longer living. Contrary to Hegel, who declared that 'the owl of Minerva begins its flight only at dusk' (Kaufman, 1960, 124), history continually evidences the talents and profound insights of the young in the sciences, in the arts, and in technology, as well as in philosophy. In its full potential wisdom is truly a collective, ceaseless intermingling of new infusions from the three generations (young, middle-aged, and longer living), an intermingling which in communist society will be pervasive and without systemic social barriers, whether of class, nationality, age or gender.

Such a collectivity of expertise in dialectical and historical materialism is essential for profound, wise foresight and provides the basis of scientific investigation and theory. For Lenin, 'the Marxist *is the first* to foresee the onset of a revolutionary epoch and to begin to arouse the people and ring the alarm bell, while the philistines sleep the slavish sleep of the loyal subject' (Glezerman, 1970, 17).

This foresight has limits. Marx rejected a dogmatic anticipation of the future and the elaboration of ready-made solutions for all future times. Similarly, Lenin disclaimed such superhuman wisdom:

> We do not claim that Marx or the Marxists know the road to socialism in every concrete detail. That would be nonsense. We know the direction of the road, we know what class forces are following the road; but the concrete and practical details will be learned only from the experience of the millions, when they begin to take action. (1943, VI, 388)

The most profound, the most complete, the wisest anticipation necessarily falls short of the actual dimensions of an historical event, especially as regards social revolutions. A flexibility comporting with history's partial predictability is requisite, a wise anticipation coupled with an adequate receptivity to the totality of events. According to Lenin,

> History in general, and the history of revolutions in particular, is always richer in content, many-sided, alive, 'shrewd' than is imagined by the very best of parties and the most conscious vanguards of the most advanced classes. This is understandable, for the very best vanguards express the consciousness, will, passion and fantasy of tens of thousands, while a revolution is carried out at moments of particular elan and tension of all the human capacities, consciousness, will, passion and fantasy of tens of millions, whipped up by the most acute struggle among classes. (Glezerman, 1970, 12)

Such passion is not incompatible with logic. In fact, 'nothing great in the world has been accomplished without passion...' (Lenin, 1961, 308). For full rationality, passion must be combined with logic, with logic in command, especially in the struggle against bourgeois power: 'criticism is no passion of the head, it is the head of passion' (Marx and Engels, 1957, 44).[4] Marxists 'can, and must, combine the most intense passion in the great revolutionary struggle with the coolest and most sober estimation of the mad ravings of the bourgeoisie' (Lenin, 1943, X, 144). In such a struggle, the integration of these levels of feeling (expressed in values) and intellect (expressed in logic) is the acme of rationality. Albert Einstein said of Lenin, a supreme example of this fusion of intellectual acuity and revolutionary fervor: 'Men of his type are the guardians and restorers of the conscience of humanity' (quoted in Meyer, 1955, 5).

Conclusion

Life, freedom, and happiness, as well as truth, justice, and beauty, are basic to value and meaning, and under material conditions that make practicable an abundance for all (as compared to the poverty for all of primitive communal society and to the abundance for the few of class society) they can become real for society as a whole. Freedom means both 'knowledge of necessity' (Engels), providing basic knowledge of nature, society, and thought, and to be impelled by reason toward one's highest interests (Leibniz). When the conditions for mass freedom prevail, the schisms engendered by class society will eventually be healed, opening new vistas for the head, hand, and heart, no longer wrenched apart, to attain a high mass level of wisdom. Freedom and wisdom are each both means and end.

Two diametrically opposed wisdoms presently confront each other, each with its appearances, one of them essential truth disclosing and the other one essential truth belieing. The wisdom of the working class integrates all that is forward-moving – the scientific and the revolutionary – and discards all that is decayed and false. Increasingly, the wisdom of the imperialists encompasses all that is regressive and enslaving – the unscientific and the counterrevolutionary. The epoch of the class-society sage – such as Confucius, the Buddha, and Moses – is nearing its close. Coming into being on a world scale is the epoch of the long-repressed masses, able to contribute more wisely and significantly than ever before to the shaping of their own and society's future, finally ending the antagonistic dichotomy in wisdom, 'the rift between clever hands and the clever mind' (Gorky, n.d., 215), between culture and labor, and between social science-scientific philosophy and the rest of the sciences.

Whole humans joined together can attain ever-higher levels of scientific wisdom. A new and typical human, wielding the working class' 'best weapon, its sharpest tool' (Engels) – dialectical and historical materialism – makes a giant advance toward the profoundly rational, the truly wise, in intelligence and feeling, casting aside the outworn and constrictive, and launching society on a course much more conducive to humanity's well-being:

> when the narrow bourgeois form has been peeled away, what is wealth, if not the universality of needs, capacities, enjoyments, productive powers, etc., of individuals, produced in universal exchange? What, if not the full development of human control over the forces of nature – those of his own nature, as well as those of so-called 'nature'? (Marx, 1965, 84)

In this epoch, for the people, the acme of wisdom in setting social goals, on which all other wisdoms ultimately depend, is with the least cost and in the shortest time to achieve socialism and the transition to a fully communist society.

The wisdom of class society's rulers is waning; the wisdom of the oppressed, incomparably higher, is becoming ascendant. The 1842 prediction of Marx will be fulfilled: 'Our philosophy will become a world philosophy, the world will become a philosophical world.' The comparatively short period of transition from ancient to modern communism – the epoch of class society – is coming to a close. The much longer age of modern classless society is approaching. Hasten the time, and, as Mao adjured, 'Be resolute, fear no sacrifice and surmount every difficulty to win victory!' (1977, 182).

Notes

1. A fuller version of this article's content appears at the concluding chapter of the author's *Dialectical Materialism: Its Laws, Categories, and Practice* (Petras Press, 1986).
2. Cf. Thomas Acquinas, 'Holy teaching should be declared the wisdom highest above all human wisdoms, not indeed in some special department but unconditionally' (1969, 50). In fact, human wisdom is to be extirpated: 'For it is written: "I will destroy the wisdom of the wise".... Has not God made foolish the wisdom of the world?' (Corinthians, 1:19–20).
3. 'The word is derived from the root *man*, to measure, with the suffix *ya* meaning 'by which the objects are given specific shape...' (Chattopadhyaya, 1959, 649).
4. In an opposite vein, Hume declared, 'Reason is, and ought to be, the slave of the passions and can never pretend to any other office than to serve and obey them' (1977, 127).

References

Aquinas, Thomas. 1969. *Summa Theologica*, ed., Thomas Gilby, O. P. New York: Doubleday.

Aristotle. 1963. *Metaphysics*, trans. Richard Hope. Ann Arbor, Michigan: University of Michigan Press.

Bernal, John Desmond. 1954. *Science in History*, 2 Vols. New York: Cameron Associates.

Born, Max. 1949. *Natural Philosophy of Cause and Chance*. Oxford, England: Clarendon Press.

Chattopadhyaya, Debiprasad. 1959. *Lokayata: A Study in Ancient Indian Materialism*. New Delhi, India: People's Publishing House.

Cohen, Morris R. 1956. *A Preface to Logic*. New York: Meridian Books.

Dietzgen, Joseph. 1906. *The Positive Outcome of Philosophy*. Chicago, Illinois: Charles H. Kerr.

Engels, Friedrich. n.d. *Anti-Duhring*. New York: International Publishers.

Farrington, Benjamin. 1963. *Greek Science*. Baltimore, Maryland: Penguin Books.

Freeman, Kathleen. 1962. *Ancilla to the Pre-Socratic Philosophers*. Cambridge, Massachusetts: Harvard University Press.

Glezerman, G. E. 1970. 'Lenin and the Problem of Scientific Prediction'. *Soviet Studies in Philosophy* (Summer).

Gorky, Maxim. n.d. *On Literature*, trans. V. Dobev, Moscow: Foreign Languages Publishing House.

Gramsci, Antonio. 1957. *The Modern Prince*. London: Lawrence & Wishart.

Holy Bible. 1974. London: Penguin.

Hume, David. 1977. *Treatise on Human Nature*. New York: E. P. Dutton.

Ignat'eva, L. F. 1962. 'The Problem of Character in Art and Esthetics'. *Soviet Studies in Philosophy* (Fall).

Kaufman, Walter. 1960. *From Shakespeare to Existentialism*. Garden City, New York: Anchor Books.

Kramer, Samuel Noah. 1959. *History Begins at Summer*. Garden City, New York: Doubleday.

Lenin. V. I. 1943. *Selected Works*, 12 Vols. New York: International Publishers.

Lenin. V. I. 1961. *Philosophical Notebooks*, trans. Clemens Dutt. London: Lawrence & Wishart.

Lu Hsun. 1960. *Selected Works*. 4 Vols. Peking: Foreign Languages Press.

Mao Tsetung. 1977. *Selected Works*. 5 Vols. Peking: Foreign Languages Press.

Marx, Karl. 1965. *Pre-Capitalist Economic Formations*. New York: International Publishers.

Marx, Karl. 1970. *A Contribution to the Critique of Political Economy*. Moscow: Progress Publishers.

Marx, Karl and Frederick Engels. 1957. *On Religion*. Moscow: Foreign Languages Publishing House.

Marx, Karl. 1975. *Collected Works*. New York: International Publishers.

Meyer, Hershel. 1955. 'Albert Einstein and Moral Values'. *Masses and Mainstream* (June)

Morton, A. L. 1952. *The English Utopia*. London: Lawrence & Wishart.

Needham, Joseph. 1956. *Science and Civilization in China*. Vol. 2. Cambridge, England: Cambridge University Press.

Peking Review. 1971. September 17.

Piaget, Jean. 1972. *Insights and Illusions of Philosophy,* trans. Wolfe Mays. New York and Cleveland: World Publishing Co.

Piaget, Jean.1973. *Main Trends in Interdisciplinary Research.* New York: Harper and Row.

Tillich, Paul. 1963. *The Eternal Now.* New York: Charles Scribner's Sons.

Vanvarovond, N. and Y. T. Fadeyev. 1962. 'Philosophical Problems of Aeronautics'. *Soviet Review* (June).

Index